Didier LODIEU

with Thierry Guilbert and Frédéric Deprun

"DYING FOR SAINT-LÔ"

Hedgerow Hell, July 1944

Translated from the French by Alan McKay & Philippe Charbonnier

Colour plates by Nicolas Gohin and Frédéric Deprun

Maps by Antoine Poggioli and Denis Gandilhon

To Elmer Kelton, U.S. Army Veteran
and best author of Wild West novels.

Incident at Saint-Lô

They rode him propped straight and proud and tall
Through St. Lô's gate… He told the lads he led
That they would be the first of St. Lô's fall.
But that was yesterday… and he was dead
Some sniper put a bullet through his head,
And he slumped in a meadow near a wall
And there was nothing to say
Nothing to say, nothing to say at all.

Ride soldier in your dirty, dizzy Jeep,
Grander than Caesar's chariot, O ride
Into the town they took for you to keep,
Dead Captain of their glory and their pride!
Ride through our hearts forever, through our tears,
More splendid than the hero hedged with spears!

Joseph Auslander

CONTENTS

The inhabitants of Saint-Lô hardly had any time to rejoice about the Normandy landings on 6 June 1944: on the same day from eight pm until the following morning at 11 am, wave after wave of bombers flew over the town dropping tons of bombs. Houses collapsed under the violence of the explosions. Mr Jacques Petit, who survived that terrible night, remembers in his memoirs:

"All huddled together, we all thought that our last hour had come and we waited out of breath for that direct hit which would end our anguish. Silence suddenly returned. Had the moment of terror only lasted twenty minutes? More like twenty centuries! Were we really safe and sound? From the road we could make out the spur-like outline of the Enclos, dark against a glowing red backdrop. A large part of the town seemed to be engulfed by the flames. Shocked into silence, we looked at the dancing lights of the fire."

(National Archives/Conseil général de Basse-Normandie)

NOT ENOUGH FOR A DECISION

Allied bombings reduced all the strategic towns in Normandy, such as Caen and Saint-Lô, to heaps of rubble. Shortly afterwards, the inhabitants decided to flee the martyred towns and sought refuge in the countryside. As Mr Petit said, the hours of anguish were enough to bring together neighbours who beforehand hardly knew each other. He continues: "*We left our home at 11. We loaded as much as possible into the pram which we used for our shopping expeditions along the Tessy road (...)*"
(Bundesarchiv)

AT THE END of June 1944, a careful study of the Allies' situation in Normandy reveals that the beachheads were firmly lodged, from Cherbourg down to the mouth of the Orne, only a few miles from Caen.

However the size of the beachheads was far from sufficient. Five times that area should have been captured and the troops which had landed since 6 June were now all bottled up in there, with their backs against the sea. It bode for the start of static warfare, which was the last thing the Americans or the British wanted – this had to be avoided at all costs.

The Supreme Commander, American General Dwight D. Eisenhower wanted to get the troops moving further inland by breaking through the German lines.

General Sir Bernard Montgomery, commanding 21st Army Group, led the two armies that had set foot in Normandy, the 2nd British Army and the 1st US Army. He was faced with a difficult task because the Americans were in a position to launch another army towards

Avranches whereas the British were still held down in front of Caen. At the end of June, American troops out-numbered the British whereas England had already committed three-quarters of its strength to the European campaign; this was not yet the case for the Americans.

At first sight, it seemed as though the LXXXVI. Armee-Korps under Gen. der Inf. von Obstfelder had quite simply immobilised the British divisions since the landings; but it could be said as well that Montgomery had fixed the German divisions in the Caen sector, thereby relieving the U.S. Army in other sectors.

Aware of the reality of the situation, Montgomery tried to break through the German lines by launching several operations using limited means which, with time, would probably bear fruit. He thus wore down the German troops

without however implementing Eisenhower's strategy, which required steady and fast progress.

Generals Eisenhower, Montgomery and Bradley agreed that a breakthrough had to be made along the 1st Army's front with the British 2nd Army drawing most of the German troops round Caen.

On the very day the American offensive started, Montgomery ended the Battle of Caen by improving the position of his troops with a general attack on the town, supported by RAF heavy bombers.

It is worth mentioning that this command decision could in no way create the conditions for the definitive breakthrough along the German front, as Eisenhower recounts in his Memoirs: "…but only establish new defensive positions in order to build up the huge reserves needed to support our troops as soon as we advanced across open ground."

As General Bradley had forecast, the definitive offensive had to be launched from a suitable line of departure near Saint-Lô. The 1st Army's objective was to reach a line running from Marigny to Saint-Lô. Once this was achieved, it would trigger the operation for the definite breakthrough. Its code-name was "Cobra". As of 6 June 1944, because it was the main town of the Manche department, Saint-Lô also became its largest pile of ruins. It suffered a horrendous bombardment, burning like a torch with 90% of its surface area destroyed. Before its destruction, its position in the heart of Normandy made it one of the biggest farming centres in France and now, in the eyes of the American staff, it was also very important and interesting, but for completely different reasons.

Up until now Eisenhower had not been able to get hold of the town

because he did not have enough troops. But on by 2 July 1944, 13 divisions – a million men – had landed with more than 170 000 vehicles of all sorts and supplies were now in sufficient quantities for the possibility of a full-scale operation to be considered.

The 1st Army outdid the Germans in fire power and in men. Along an 80-km front, there were only 12 German divisions grouped together in two army corps: the LXXXIV. A.K. (84th Army Corps) and the II. Fallschirmjäger-Korps (2nd Parachute Corps)

Some of these two army corps divisions had been fighting since 6 June 1944 and had been considerably weakened. Taking the two infantry divisions, 352.I.D. and 91.LL.Div., as examples, they had less than 1,300 men.

On the other hand, the 2.SS-Pz. Div. "Das Reich," which was in the process of moving up from the south of France, reached the rear of the front at full strength, with nearly 20,000 men. At first this armoured division made up the reserve.

The Germans however had the advantage of the terrain. The Vire valley consisted of an ensemble of rocky hills through which flowed the river of the same name. Its pasture land was bordered by the hedgerows with the name of "bocage Saint-Louis." These are three to six feet thick and prevent anyone from seeing through them. When these hedgerows grow on banks which can sometimes be three feet high, they hide paths and can measure up 12 feet high. Sometimes these banks and hedgerows were separated by sunken lanes which the enemy used to set up a gun position.

With these hedgerows, the cattle breeders do not need barbed wire to

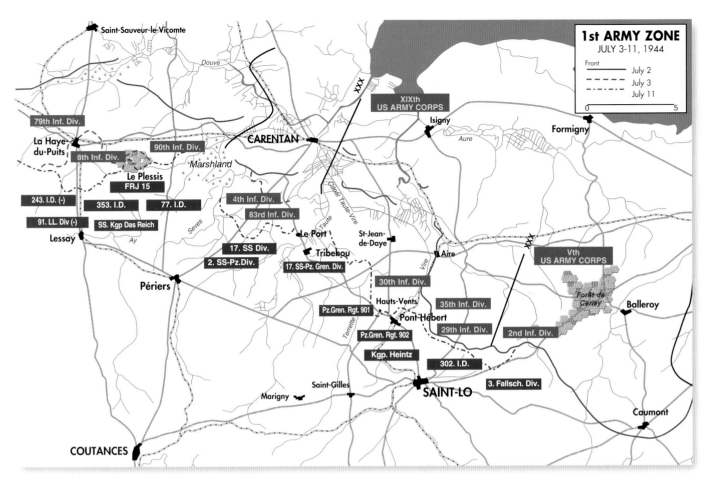

The situation in Normandy before the first phase of the attack against Saint-Lô.

mark the bounds of their land. There is no danger of their animals straying because the hedges are made up of brushwood, bushes, brambles and small trees growing on the bank. Neither man nor beast can get through this obstacle.

These natural defences were used by the Germans who dug their foxholes into the banks running along the side of the roads, lanes or tracks. All of these humid, narrow paths twisted and turned and hid enemy mortar and machine gun positions, invisible in the green hell that the bocage was to become for Allied soldiers. In order to improve their defences, the Germans had flooded the land which was marshy already, before the Americans arrived. These fields were therefore soaked like sponges and the tracks muddy. Rainy weather had settled in since the beginning of June and had transformed the countryside into an absolute mud bath which did nothing to boost the GIs morale.

On the eve of the offensive, the American officers already knew that progress was going to be slow and costly in human lives. They also knew that their artillery would only have a minor part to play due to the lack of visibility. Eisenhower said that in this region artillery was not much use except for long-range harassment. For the lowly infantryman, this was going to be a terrible ordeal. And given the layout of the land, the use of tanks, however risky for the crews, was needed to support the infantry.

If armour support on such terrain appeared to be difficult, air support was even more so. How could the pilot of a bomber flying at an altitude of 9,000 to 12,000 feet identify the nature of a target in an area where there was nothing but thousands of hedgerows?

General and his staff had studied the problem before launching the offensive. The Supreme commander says: *"One of our methods consisted of assigning an air liaison team to one of the tanks in the unit engaged in the attack. Each of these teams had a radio with which it*

could communicate with the aircraft in the air. With this method, mistakes were avoided and aircraft could even be directed over important, very precisely pinpointed targets. A deep study and exchange of techniques was organised between the land and air forces in order to improve coordination."

Before launching XIXth Army Corps' offensive against Saint-Lô, General Omar N. Bradley had to take the town of Coutances with his VIIth Army Corps. As soon as this unit had broken through the lines of the LXXXIV.A.K. along more than 18 miles, it would leave the Cotentin marshes, be able to operate over dry ground and set off in the direction of Avranches, the gateway to Brittany.

While VIIth Corps was progressing through enemy territory, VIIIth Corps would also advance on its left flank.

These two army corps' attack, planned for 3 July, was deemed to eliminate the right wing of LXXXIV.A.K. at the moment when the XIXth US Army Corps was thrown into the battle.

Alas, Bradley's plans did not go accordingly. First, the VIIIth Army Corps committed its three divisions, the 82nd Airborne Division, the 79th and 90th Infantry Divisions. Although the first two had already made an excellent reputation for themselves, Bradley could not vouch for the third unit, which had only just landed.

The offensive was launched with a terrifying artillery barrage at dawn on 3 July; the VIIIth US Army Corps units under General Middleton surprised the Grenadiere of LXXXIV.A.K. who were not expecting an attack on their front. The German commander, Generalleutnant von Choltitz found himself in a very embarrassing situation because the majority of his reserve troops, which up until then had been solidly entrenched on the heights, were heading towards the main line of defence at the time of the American attack.

Von Choltitz contacted the Kdr. of the 7. Armee, SS-Obergruppenführer Hausser to inform him that his troop movements had been ordered by the Führer in person! If he no longer had any reserves on the heights, he would not be able to stop the VIIth US Army Corps. Clear-sighted, Hausser agreed with von Choltitz. The defences in depth had to be maintained and had to be immediately positioned on the group of steep and wooded heights, near La Haye-du-Puits.

Without realising it, General Middleton took advantage of this muddling on the German front by getting his three divisions on the move. The 82nd Airborne and the 79th advanced rapidly towards La Haye-du-Puits during the day; but they paid a very high price: 3,400 men killed, wounded or missing. Likewise, the inexperienced 90th suffered huge losses, about 600 casualties during the morning at the foot of Mont Castre. The terrain gained by this division was derisory.

As for LXXXIV.A.K., it lost between 750 and 1,000 men from 3 to 17 July 1944. Unlike American soldiers who had the advantage of air support when the weather permitted, the Grenadiere had to make do without the Luftwaffe. The commander of the 7. Armee asked Rommel for immediate reinforcements including armoured divisions, without which his infantry divisions would be crushed. But for the time being Generalleutnant von Choltitz would have to make do with the units in his own army corps.

General Bradley was dissatisfied, reproaching the CO of the 90th Infantry Division, General Landrum (the previous CO had been sacked), for not moving far enough inland.

As luck would have it, the following day, the 79th Infantry Division found itself blocked in front of Mont-Gardon in exactly the same circumstances as the 90th Division in front of Mont Castre; the impetus of this unit had been broken by the German defences positioned at La Haye-du-Puits.

Although the VIIIth Army Corps outdid the LXXXIV.A.K. in both men and in materiel, Middleton had to admit that

Generalleutnant von Choltitz

(J. Charita)

Generalleutnant von Choltitz was born on Nov. 9, 1894. He took part in WW1 with the rank of Leutnant.

Choltitz managed to remain in the post-war army as a cavalry squadron commander. On the eve of WW2, he was promoted to Major and Kdr. of III./LL.Inf. Rgt. 16. He captured a major bridge at Rotterdam during the campaign in the Netherlands and took command of this Airborne regiment in 1941.

With the rank of Oberst he took part in the siege of Sebastopol in June 1942.

As a Generalmajor he took command of the 260. I.D. then as a Generalleutnant, he led the XXXXVIII. Panzer-Korps.

At the end of 1942, Choltitz had the XXVII. A.K. then the 11. Pz.Div., the XXXXVIII. Pz.Korps, the LXXXIV. A.K. (as of June 15, 1944), and finally "Gross Paris" from August 7 to August 24, 1944, when he surrendered the city to the French 2d Armoured Division. Choltitz was released from captivity in 1947 and died in 1967. ❐

the Germans were holding onto their positions very firmly, even though these were not elite formations. Moreover, he had to admit that von Choltitz's defences were formidably supported and shrewdly set.

At the end of five days' fighting, the 90th Division finally got hold of Mont Castre, the best observation post in the area. 2,000 of its men had lost their lives for it. It also took the 79th Division five days to take La Haye-au-Puits.

After all this blood letting, the 90th and 79th had to be got back up to strength. Unfortunately for General Middleton, he had to do without the 82nd Airborne which had been called away on another operation. It was replaced by the 83rd Infantry Division which moved over from the VIIth Corps on 1 July.

Bradley realised that breaking through the LXXXIV.A.K.'s lines of defence was turning out to be more than difficult.

On 7 July he launched VIIth Army Corps under General Collins (the victor of Cherbourg). His objective was to reach Pérores.

Collins had at his disposal the 4th Infantry Division, which had landed at Utah Beach on 6 June 1944; the 9th Infantry Division which had campaigned in the Cotentin under him; and the 83rd Infantry Division which was going to receive its baptism of fire.

Across a distance of only two miles, the 83rd Division moved through a marshy area covered with hedgerows. Its objective was to reach Sainteny. This division lost 300 men for weak results - a disaster for Collins who nevertheless persevered in ordering General Robert C. Macon to attack. Bravely, the GIs continued fighting on terrain which was more advantageous to the Germans, losing a further 750 men and gaining barely a mile.

Once again, the American command deplored the new divisions' lack of experience. General Collins therefore sent his 4th Infantry Division, convinced it would reach Pérores. It took three days of both heavy and costly fighting to advance barely one and a half miles.

General Collins had to face the facts: it was not the divisions' experience which was being questioned, but their ability to surmount the obstacles they encountered. It was the hedgerows, marshes, narrow and muddy lanes, used to perfection by the enemy which made the GIs' progress so slow and laboured.

Right.
This shot taken from the heights of Saint-Lô shows the vast panorama the German observers had. Every move by the GIs of XIXth US Army Corps was spotted and subjected to an artillery barrage. Note also the proliferation of hedgerows and the sloping escarpments offering excellent defensive positions for the soldiers of LXXXIV. A.K. and II. Fallschirmjäger-Korps.
(National Archives)

Below.
La Haye-du-Puits suffered terribly from the fighting and bombing before being liberated by the 82nd Airborne Division on 8 July 1944. Taking the two heights situated near the town, Mont Castre and Montgardon, cost the lives of about 4,000 GIs.
(National Archives)

HEDGEROW FIGHTING WES

6 July 1944

ON 7 July 1944, the XIXth Army Corps under Major-General S. Corlett in turn started to take part in the Battle of the Hedgerows. Its objective was to establish a line extending between Saint-Gilles, Saint-Lô and Bérigny which Bradley would use for his breakout.

Above.
Colonel A.V. Ednie of the 119th US Infantry talking to Captain Vodra C. Philipps, Operations Officer of the 743rd Tank Battalion. Coordination between infantry and armour turned out to be essential. The tanks' first objective in the XIXth US Army Corps plan was to capture the crossroads at Saint-Jean-de-Daye. On 14 July, Colonel Ednie transferred to the 29th Division and was replaced by Colonel M. Sutherland. The insignia of the 30th Division, "Old Hickory," can clearly be seen on the sleeve of the man in the foreground, on the right.
(National Archives)

Corlett's zone of operations extended over 6 miles between the rivers Taute and Vire and his plan consisted of launching the 30th Infantry Division towards the north-west of Saint-Lô, rather than making a frontal attack on the town.

Reconnaissance missions for the 30th US Infantry Division

This detour would enable the 30th Division to occupy the heights situated to the east of the town, in particular Hill 192 which overlooked the region.

As soon as the 30th reached the Saint-Lô - Périers road, the 29th and the 35th US Infantry Divisions would attack Saint-Lô directly. Moreover, Major-General Corlett brought invaluable support to the VIIth Army Corps by flanking its left wing with his 30th Infantry Division.

But before launching such an offensive, essential reconnaissance missions had to be made to the west of the Vire. Several elements had been infiltrated in the first days of July. General Hobbs' Staff had to know the identity of the enemy units, their strength, their positions and their armament.

Privates First Class Bertrand J. Mandeville and Hans Richert were designated to carry out one such mission. Both of them belonged to K Company in the 3rd Bn of the 119th Infantry Regiment.

Taking advantage of the heavy rain, the two soldiers

set off into the night in the direction of the river. In order to distract the Germans' attention, the divisional artillery opened fire on the enemy lines.

The two men progressed by leaps and bounds. They ran, threw themselves to the ground and huddled down to avoid being spotted. They were simple GIs, gnawed by fear. They carried only two rations each (one K and one D) and an M1 carbine, much lighter than the Garand rifle, with two magazine, one already loaded and the other as reserve. This was not a lot of ammunition because they were not there to fight but to observe and bring back important information so that the division could cross the river.

Suddenly a burst of machine gun fire, punctuated by tracer bullets, whistled over their heads. The GIs threw themselves to the ground. The Germans had spotted them and they risked getting captured. They crawled as fast as they could, bruising their elbows and knees, puffing and blowing like forge bellows, moving around the enemy position. The machine gun fell silent whereas the friendly artillery kept up its firing at regular intervals.

A little later they were faced the same situation and once again they got away from the angry bursts of a machine gun. Now they had broken through deep into the German lines. Dawn was beginning to break. They decided to hide and to observe, noting the enemy positions and weapons.

OF THE VIRE

It was only during the night of 4 July that they set off back to their company. The 117th Infantry history wrote of them: *"They brought back a wealth of detailed information which turned out to be invaluable for our artillery, in particular concerning our crossing the River Vire."*

The anecdotes about these intelligence gathering patrols are many. Here is what happened to Lieutenant George L. McClanahan from the same unit.

Setting off with four men, McClanahan crossed the Vire Canal silently, without being spotted by the Grenadiere from Kampfgruppe Heintz. The officer had chosen the full moon to carry out his mission. His group was already well within enemy territory when they ran into a German patrol. The scouts held their breath while McClanahan led them on their way towards the enemy. When they reached a lane, the five Americans branched off suddenly. The German patrol continued on its way without batting an eyelid at these soldiers whom they took for some of their own. A bit later, the five GIs found themselves a few yards from a group of chatting Germans. Once more, McClanahan's group froze in the high grass until the Grenadiere peacefully left...

After finding out a lot of useful information about Kampfgruppe Heintz, the five men returned to their lines. They were almost in sight of the canal which they had forded several hours earlier, when a burst from a 'Burp gun' rent the silence. They bent double. "Scram!" shouted McClanahan. They ran even faster when grenades started exploding all around them. This time they had been spotted and the Grenadiere gave them everything they had. When they were out of reach of small arms,

they were potted at with mortars. The 81-mm shells burst violently but by some miracle, none of the men was hit. McClanahan ordered them to the ground because the shooting was getting more accurate. They carried on, crawling this time. Suddenly they recognised the characteristic noise of a Browning machine gun. There was also shots from American Garands. "They're ours!" yelled one of the scouts. Under covering fire from the GIs on the east bank of the Vire, McClanahan's patrol returned to its lines safely.

Thanks to these scouts' courageous action, the intelligence was now in a position to draw up a complete report on Kampfgruppe Heintz's system of defence, which the army corps was going to strike in the first hours of the offensive.

This Kampfgruppe was commanded by Oberst Heintz, Kdr. of Gren.-Rgt. 984. This tactical group stemmed from 275. Infanterie-Division. It was made up of I. and II./Gren.-Rgt. 984 armed respectively with 42 machine guns (43 for II.Btl.) and eight 81-mm mortars, a section of infantry guns from the Inf.-Geschütz Kp., a Panzerjäger platoon, Pi.-Btl.275 (less one company), Panzerjäger-Kompanie 275, Füsilier-Bataillon 275, a medical company, Nachrichten-Abteilung (2 Funktruppe and 2 Fernsprechtruppe) and III./Art. Rgt. 275.

Kampfgruppe Heintz was attached to the 17./SS-Pz. Gren. Div., and had suffered heavy casualties. It had subsequently been positioned along the west bank of the River Vire and along the Vire-Taute Canal. Its strong points were at Saint-Fromond and Saint-Jean-de-Daye.

Above.
Corporals Willis D. McFadden and Mack J. Ellen are cooking some chicken in their bivouac behind the lines. Most of African-American soldiers were committed in the support services, apart from some black engineer and artillery units. The U.S. Army was segregated at the time and very few senior white officers put - unfairly - some stock in the Black soldiers' fighting ability.
(Dite/Usis)

Following page.
The Grenadiere from Kampfgruppe Heintz were solidly entrenched when the XIXth US Army Corps launched its offensive. When this unit arrived on 12 June 1944 to reinforce 352.I.D., it had a strength of 4,100, including officers.
(BA 101 I.582/2120/29)

LAUNCHING THE OFFENSIVE

First the GIs from the 30th Infantry Division had to cross the River Vire then they had to cross a canal with its two bridges which had been destroyed by the Germans.

Finally Major-General Corlett decided to launch two staggered attacks, one later than the other. The first was to start at dawn with the 120th Infantry Regiment crossing the river in inflatable assault boat. It would then head west.

XIXth US Army Corps shoulder insignia

The second attack with the 117th Infantry would take place in the afternoon. The soldiers would cross the canal then rush south, in order to establish a solid bridgehead for the following operations. These two infantry regiments from the 30th Division would join up at Saint-Jean-de Daye, a village situated where two roads vital to the XIXth Army Corps operations crossed.

In order to secure the left flank of the 30th Division, the 29th Infantry Division of XIXth Army Corps would stay on the eastern bank of the Vire. Positioned only two miles from Saint-Lô, its main mission was to fix the fearsome paratroopers of II./Fallschirmjäger-Korps.

The 35th Infantry Division which was moving up, was about to join up with the 29th Division for a later attack. Finally, the 3rd Armored Division was held in reserve near Isigny.

The night of 6-7 July was short for Lieutenant-Colonel Arthur H. Fuller and his men of the 2/117th Infantry. They had been designated to spearhead the attack.

Stunned by exhaustion and numbed by the cold and the freezing rain which fell intermittently in the area, they advanced in long columns towards the bank of the Vire. Thick mist shrouded the countryside. Lt.-Col. Fuller looked anxiously at his watch: *"Its 03.28"*, he murmured to one of his company commanders, *"another two minutes and the Krauts[1] are going to get a bellyful!"*

In other words, the nine artillery battalions from XIXth Artillery Corps opened fire on the German gun emplacements, those that the Americans had located and those they supposed existed. An awesome deluge of fire thus descended upon the enemy.

Major-General Corlett was pleased. Up until now, the 1st Army's vehicles had been under fire from the German artillery which located and shelled the supply convoys as they made their way down from Cherbourg or Bayeux. Today at last the roles were reversed.

E and F Companies carried on advancing carefully towards the river Vire whilst G Company deployed to cover them while they crossed. The worried GIs paddled through the mist, clutching their Garands tightly. Their orders were to reach a hedge located about 400 yards from the river.

Suddenly they saw two silhouettes appearing out of the fog. *"Don't shoot! They're ours"*, shouted several NCOs.

They were guides from the 105th Engineer Combat Battalion. They told the GIs that 18 assault boats were waiting for them. Both companies had ten minutes to get over to the other side because Oberst Heintz's Grenadiere could appear at any time.

The GIs followed the guides, took the boats and set off clumsily down to the bank. Their gear and weapons got in the way. Fortunately the engineers were there to help them.

Suddenly the characteristic staccato of a MG 42 machine gun echoed across the water. They had been spotted. Even worse, these bursts of machine gun fire would alert other German troops located in the sector. Crossing the river in

1. Kraut, from Sauerkraut, a derogatory term for German soldiers.

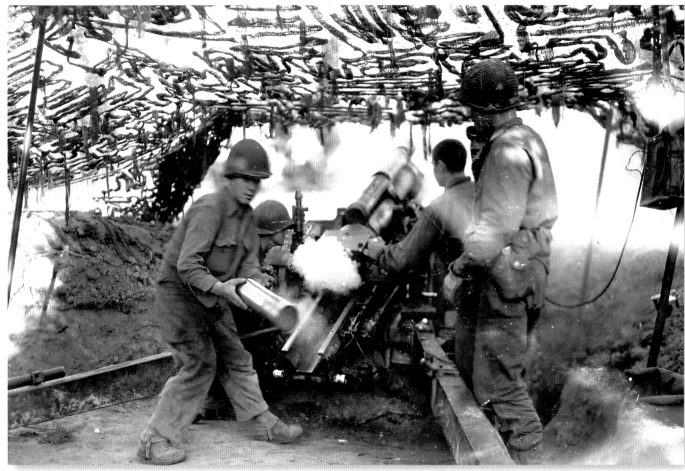

the planned spot was too risky now and another site had to be found where they could embark in safety.

An officer appeared from nowhere and came up to the two company commanders. *"You'll have to cross further north, near the Saint-Fromond bridge. We didn't know there was a machine gun nest just here. Goddammit, now we're running late. Get a move on!"*

Alerted by the machine guns which had opened fire on the GIs, the German artillery started firing but not very accurately

Their arm muscles aching with the weight of the boats, the GIs left the bank and headed in the direction indicated. The attack was off to a bad start. Nevertheless, the soldiers in one of the leading companies reached their destination without any casualties which was a miracle in itself.

They then leapt down the steep river bank, trying to slow down as they reached the bottom. Luckily the engineers slowed them down, and then helped them to get into the boats with all their equipment.

When the 12-man complement was aboard, the helmsman edged the boat away a few yards. Once all the boats were full, the helmsmen were ordered to advance in line abreast. All the barrels of the machine guns and rifles were pointing towards the opposite bank still shrouded in mist. The GIs realised that the boat engines were not

going to be powerful enough because they had overloaded the boats. They therefore had to paddle as well. Once the soldiers had landed with all their heavy gear, the Engineer helmsmen went back to the other side to pick up the second company and take it across. It was about time these crossings ended because the German artillery was getting more and more accurate.

By 04.30, E and F companies of the 117th Infantry had landed on the west bank of the Vire. Fortunately the slope on this side was not very steep. They now had to get away from the river as fast as possible because the Germans were beginning to react. The GIs' objectives – taking the sector east of Airel and the Saint-Fromond Bridge – had to be reached before the enemy was reinforced.

Although protected by a very effective artillery barrage which fell 400 yards in front of them, the GIs from E and F companies still had difficulty moving forward. Set up on Hill 45 and overlooking the flat terrain over which the GIs were advancing, the Grenadiere benefited from superbly located and dug-in positions, which had been established several weeks earlier.

Breaking through the first line of defence and taking Hill 45, the GIs from the two assault companies headed for the Airel - Les Champs-de-Losques road without encountering serious opposition. They then separated after half a mile.

Preceded by two vanguards and protected by two machine guns on their flanks, E Company fanned out to the north of the road and F Company positioned itself to the south.

Surprisingly, it was not the Germans who held the GIs up but the hedges. This led to a problem with the artillery which had plotted its shots to match the infantry's progress. In the end the company commanders preferred to do without artillery support; they only had G Company to back them up.

It did not waste any time. Landing shortly after E and F, it headed straight for the Saint-Fromond Bridge, its primary objective. Here it fought hard against the Germans who were protecting the bridge. Once it had taken the bridge, G company headed southwest to position itself on the left wing of F company.

The F company GIs had just crossed the road when they came under heavy fire. They hardly had time to see where the shooting was coming from. They only thought of getting under cover but there was only one refuge: the hedges on the far side of a completely exposed field. They ran for their lives, praying to God to get them out of this predicament.

In the panic, one platoon got lost. It had advanced too far into enemy territory. Another which had got through a hedge with thousands of scratches to show for it fell upon the Grenadiere escaping from the GIs who had just chased out of their positions. The Americans were outnumbered by the Germans two to one. They were about to give in when they saw another platoon coming to their rescue. They were saved.

The rest of F company did not have such luck. The soldiers were cut down by machine gun fire when they were not under cover.

Alongside his men, Colonel Fuller screamed: *"Hit the dirt, all of you or you'll all be for it!"* Getting his breath back, the dynamic officer asked: *"Are there four sons of a gun here who are ready to follow me to get rid of that f... machine gun?"*

Four voices replied immediately above the racket of the gunfire. Their comrades were cool-headed again and started firing at the German positions.

Furtive shadows came up close to the Colonel who was determined not to let things stand: *"Look, we'll rush round on the right and get round the back of the Krauts while the others stay here and keep them busy."*

The volunteers nodded in agreement. They hooked grenades onto their belts, slammed a clip into their Garands. One of them, a sergeant, was chewing gum nervously and making sure his Thompson SMG worked properly.

"The rest of you, fire!" the Colonel shouted to the GIs who remained in the position. Then he started crawling in the tall grass across the marshy field, soaking the knees and elbows of his uniform.

Huddling in their position in the embankment under a hedge, the team of Heer machine gunners was busy looking after their Spandau. The gunner was constantly squeezing the trigger while his No 2 was feeding the long belts of

7.62-mm bullets which were sucked into the breech. Further back a Grenadiere was ready to bring forward a case of ammunition. The gun commander had placed his binoculars on the ground and held his sub-machine gun tightly. He was watching the zone where the GIs were entrenched. He did not spot the colonel and his four volunteers until one of his Grenadiere fell with a bullet straight through his head. He turned in the direction where the shot had come from and saw five Americans advancing towards them with guns raised. He threw down his sub-machine gun and ordered his men to move clear of the machine gun.

Thanks to Colonel Fuller's action, the GIs in F Company were able to get up without fear of being hit. Their officer's voice reassured them. They could advance safely now. The German machine gun had been silenced. Shortly afterwards they came across soldiers from G company; this comforted them because they now knew that reinforcements were on the way. For this action, Colonel Fuller was awarded the Distinguished Service Cross.

As for E company, the situation was much better since it had not suffered casualties. Its CO was relieved to see two sections from H company join his rear. When he looked at his watch, the hands read 08.30. He knew that the 2nd Bn of the 117th Infantry had accomplished the first phase of the attack.

However, it was not just one battalion which was supposed to be on the west bank of the river but the whole 30th Division! That was the engineers' task: they were working all out to repair the Saint-Fromond Bridge which was vital for the division's move across. They had been at it for four hours now and twice, German shells had damaged it again. *"The successful outcome of the operation depends on this bridge,"* remarked an officer.

Cursing him, an engineer said to his friend: *"If he's so much cleverer than us, he can come and do it himself!"*

To which the other replied: *"Perhaps he doesn't know that 20 of our men have already copped it this morning."*

The bridge had been hit so many times that the engineers were now getting discouraged. On top of that, it had become the target for the Oberst Heintz's Grenadiere who used not only artillery but also snipers.

Another Engineer unit, the 247th Engineer Combat Battalion was called up. Its CO realised the danger and only a dozen men worked with two Brockway heavy bridging trucks. In order to save time, they used reinforced wire netting to cover the holes rather than fill them in. An hour later, the brave engineers had fulfilled their mission. The bridge was ready and shortly afterwards, a large number of trucks pulling supply trailers or guns, crossed the Saint-Fromond Bridge under fire from German artillery. Further north a new bridge was built.

These two bridges were not enough: a third one had to be built, rapidly. Before starting his men off on this new mission, the engineer battalion staff studied the terrain in order

This machine gunner is pointing his -1919A4, calibre .30 Browning machine owards a field that the infantry will have to cross. This weapon was issued to all infantry battalions. It could fire 400 to 500 rounds/minute. It was fed by a canvas or metal belt with 250 rounds.
(National Archives)

to build the bridge in a sector where there were no German defences. In the end, one of the 247th Engineer Combat Battalion companies managed to set up this bridge, a floating one this time, before midday.

These three bridges enabled the other two 117th Infantry battalions to get across immediately and join up with the 2nd without delay. The 1st Bn positioned itself on the left wing and the 3rd on its right wing between the Airel – Les Camps des Loques road and the east of Saint-Jean-de-Daye. One of the companies of the 3rd Bn set itself up on Hill 30, the highest point in the sector.

In turn, the 2nd Bn of the 119th Infantry set itself up between Saint-Fromond-Eglise and the left wing of the 1st Bn of the 117th Infantry.

With the bridgehead now in place, the GIs from the 30th Infantry Division had to advance in perfect coordination backed up by the Shermans from the 743rd Tank Battalion which had been attached to them. The objective was to get hold of the crossroads situated to the south of Saint-Jean-de Daye.

Oberst Heintz was surprised to find such a large force of Americans on his Kampfgruppe's front. He believed he was protected by the river and the canal. His Grenadiere attempted to stop Hobbs' GIs but the Germans were ignorant of the breaches that had been made in their own lines and often found themselves isolated. An attack was launched to dislodge the GIs of the 3rd Bn of 117th Infantry set up on Hill 30 (to the west of la Ruette) but this was very quickly dispersed. The Germans fell back. The GIs were ordered to rush to Saint-Jean-de-Daye by going round the hamlet from the east and fanning out, facing south, a mission which they carried out successfully.

There was now a very strong risk of Kampfgruppe Heintz, positioned to the south of the Vire-Taute canal, being overcome from the rear by the 117th Infantry Regiment which had reached the important Saint-Jean-de-Daye crossroads. If the regiment continued advancing west, Oberst Heintz would not be in a position to oppose the 120th Infantry Regiment under Colonel Birks located to the north of the canal, half a mile away.

After lunch, Colonel Birks told his officers that the regiment's 1st and the 3rd Bns were going to cross over while the 2nd would be held back in reserve.

Birks placed his 3rd Bn on the right wing of his front and the 1st on the left. According to the G-2 (intelligence staff officer), enemy forces were reduced to less than a battalion, i.e. half the strength of the Americans facing them. If the 2nd Bn was also counted, they were only a third of the strength.

The Germans however had the advantage of the terrain. Established now in the zone for the best part of two weeks, the Grenadiere had had the time to build up solid defences and to dig in on the heights. Not only did they have the canal as a rampart but also the vast expanse of marshland which would not fail to hinder the Americans in their attack.

There were only two ways forward for Birks' men. The first was situated in the attack zone of the 3rd Bn and ended up on a narrow spit of land which extended to Graignes. The second passage, assigned to the 1st Bn was restricted to two narrow corridors which flanked the Pont-Hébert - Carentan road.

Of course, if Colonel Birks had spotted these two passages, then Oberst Heintz had too. That was why his Grenadiere had reinforced their defences at these strategic points and mined their approaches as well as the banks of the canal.

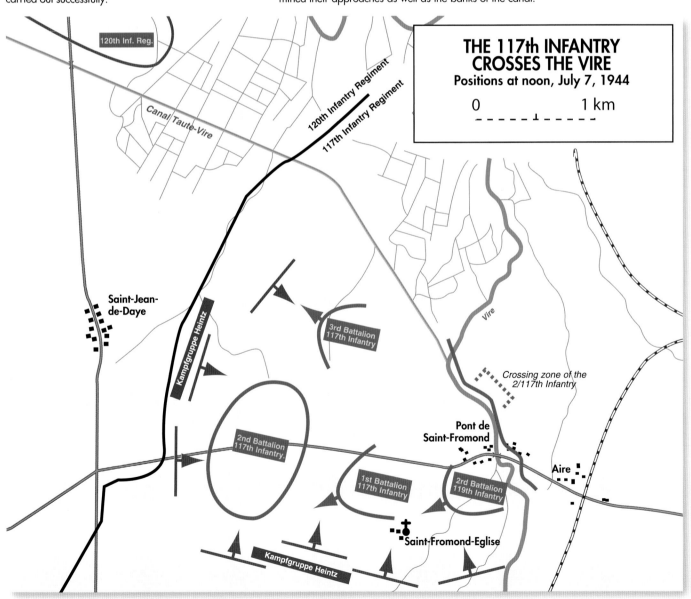

THE 117th INFANTRY CROSSES THE VIRE
Positions at noon, July 7, 1944

0   1 km

120th Inf. Reg.

Canal Taute-Vire

120th Infantry Regiment

117th Infantry Regiment

Saint-Jean-de-Daye

Kampfgruppe Heintz

3rd Battalion 117th Infantry

Vire

Crossing zone of the 2/117th Infantry

2nd Battalion 117th Infantry

Pont de Saint-Fromond

1st Battalion 117th Infantry

2nd Battalion 119th Infantry

Aire

Saint-Fromond-Eglise

Kampfgruppe Heintz

Strangely enough, the 3rd Bn advanced without encountering any strong opposition. It was subjected to machine gun and 81-mm mortar fire but the German resistance was quickly reduced to nothing. GIs elsewhere reported likewise: German troops falling back in isolated groups towards Graignes. The battalion commander was beginning to wonder whether or not his men were not being drawn into a trap further on. He reported this to the Regimental HQ who encouraged him to carry on moving forward; they told him that the 1st Bn was hanging on firmly to the ground that the Grenadiere were defending with such stubbornness.

The American artillery however did not spare the Landsers. The GIs from the 1st Bn were only able to advance when the artillery barrage started, pulverising the machine gun nests. By looking at the enemy corpses, Birks' men realised that they were fighting infantrymen who only had a few heavy weapons. Their anti-tank guns, 75-mm Pak 40s mainly, were limited to about fifteen and their artillery comprised only twelve 105-mm cannon.

No matter how heavy the artillery barrage was, it did not mean that all German resistance was eliminated. Once the curtain of explosions moved on, further away to the south, German soldiers entrenched in the small strongpoints opened up again. Many GIs fell never to get up again. Others were wounded, begging for help when they still had the breath to do so.

Above.
One of the Shermans from the 743rd Tank Battalion supporting the 117th Infantry, which is moving through Saint-Fromond in ruins. Two companies from this battalion were attached to the regiment for the XIXth US Army Corps offensive. One of them supported the 2nd Bn and the other the 3rd.
(National Archives)

In the end though, the Gren.-Rgt. 984 Grenadiere were forced to give way. Some were captured; others managed to escape towards Pont-Hébert. This time their front was disorganised, not only by the action of the two infantry battalions from the 120th Infantry Regiment who had gained a foothold to the south of the canal, but also by the intervention of the 117th Infantry which had harassed the rear of the enemy forces holding the canal under their fire.

The second phase of the operation had been carried out. Colonel Birks of the 120th Infantry and Colonel Kelly of the 117th were ordered to press on. A tank company was even called up to support the GIs, but crossing the canal turned out to be too difficult for the Shermans. The infantry would have to do without them.

Meanwhile, the 2nd Bn of the 117th Infantry had gathered on some heights to the southwest of Saint-Fromond. From this position taken at 12.50, the GIs under Lieutenant-Colonel Fuller secured the eastern flank for their regiment.

As the 1st Bn of the 120th Infantry Regiment came into sight of Saint-Jean-de-Daye, it was subjected to heavy gunfire from elements of Kampfgruppe Heintz, which had been ordered to hold the village whatever the cost.

This resistance worried the CO of the American unit because it meant a bloody assault for his men. One of his companies, which only had one officer left, was ordered to

Previous page, top.
At about 7 am on 7 July, three platoons of C/743rd Tank Battalion were engaged alongside the GIs from the 1st and 3rd Bns of the 120th US Infantry, together with the men from C company of the 105th Engineer Battalion. Together they forced the crossing of the Vire and the Taute on the Saint-Jean-de-Daye road.
(National Archives/Conseil général de Basse-Normandie)

Above.
These soldiers probably belonging to Gren.-Rgt.984 were gunned down by GIs from the 117th or from the 120th Infantry. They belonged to a machine gun section - witness the ammo belt still hanging from the neck of the man in the centre and the spare barrel carrier lying on the ground, next to a mess tin. These three Grenadiere have already been searched, judging by the papers lying all around the bodies. Even the gas masks containers have been emptied of their contents.
(National Archives)

invest the village. In order to encourage his soldiers, Colonel Birks himself joined the fray and was even among the first to enter Saint-Jean-de-Daye. Shortly afterwards, he asked Lt. Col. Hugh I. Mainord (1st Bn) to continue to the south. The main thing was to get hold of as much terrain as possible.

Sergeant Jonathan G. Mullinex from A Company, 1st Bn, 120th Infantry, was ordered to lead the march with his squad. In the anguished silence troubled only by the sound of rain, the NCO felt that disaster was just around the corner. With soaked uniforms, his men gathered in a circle around him while he explained what their mission was.

For an hour Mullinex's men advanced gripping their weapons tightly. Nothing happened. Just when they started to be less watchful, a German machine gun opened up. It was set up right in front of them and they had no time to drop to the ground before two of them were torn apart by a burst.

The deadly firing continued, spraying the squad which was now under cover. Sergeant Mullinex popped his head above the undergrowth and managed to spot where the machine gun that killed two of his men was located. Furiously, he fixed a rifle grenade to the Garand he snatched from one of his men, then pointed the barrel towards the sky and guessed the angle so as to hit the target.

The grenade whistled off and up and exploded not very far from the Germans. The gunner and his No 2 continued firing. Irritated by his shot being too short, Mullinex fixed another grenade to his rifle then left his shelter so that he could aim better. He just had time to fire before a swarm of bullets whistled around him. Now without cover, he was wounded in the nose and foot, and fell to the ground twisting in agony. He covered his face with both hands as though wanting to stop the abundant flow of blood.

Forcing back the pain, he took heart again, quite determined to finish with the enemy position. Blood continued to stream from his face and he felt his energy leaving him, but he was still intent on avenging his two men. A wave of hatred swept through his mind. He dragged himself across the ground to get hold of his rifle and another grenade. Another burst cut up his back. He struggled not to pass out. Gathering his last strength, he got up slowly, leaning on his knees. His foot wound made him suffer atrociously. Bullets were

flying all around him. Concentrating all his attention on the machine gun nest, he fired one grenade then another. His movements were mechanical. The two explosions echoed further away. Then suddenly there was silence. His mind fading into a deep mist, he barely heard the voices of his men running towards him. One of them was shouting: *"The Sarge's got rid of the machine gun. All the Krauts are dead."*

Sergeant Mullinex's action enabled his company to reach its objective.

The Germans did not wait there without doing anything, particularly the artillery which had deployed its batteries near Le Dézert. There were three Gruppen with 105-mm cannon and a heavy Gruppe with 150-mm cannon in position there. The battery commanders vied with each other, shooting at the crossings over the Vire-Taute canal.

Generalleutnant von Choltitz had been quite firm in his orders. *"The six American battalions which have crossed the river must be cut off from their rear. On no account must they be resupplied and all their communications must be cut."*

With its formidable firepower, the XIXth Army Corps artillery tried to submerge the German artillery batteries. In vain. Major-General Corlett's HQ called in the Air Force to find out exactly where these artillery pieces were located, but the bad weather did not help very much. He did not get any more information.

Because the Americans could not silence the enemy artillery, the reinforcements started building up at the rear of the 117th and 120th Infantry Regiments and there were traffic jams. When he learnt that the streams of vehicles were getting longer by the hour, Major-General Corlett asked for further reinforcements to be halted for the time being.

Meanwhile the 113th Cavalry Group under Colonel William S. Biddle had positioned itself at the junction of XIXth and VIIth Army Corps whilst remaining in General Hobbs' zone of operations. This enabled the zone between the canal and the rear of the 120th Infantry Regiment's front to be cleared.

At the end of the evening, one of its elements crossed the canal and headed towards Le Mesnil-Vénéron but it was stopped by strong opposition to the east of La Goucherie. Forty or so German soldiers, set up in excellent positions and supported by some Paks, tied down Troop A of the 113th

Cavalry Group for the night. Some of the enemy was captured and searched.

According to their *Soldbuch* (pay book) the Troop A GIs learnt that they belonged to Inf.-Btl. 639, led by Waffen-SS belonging to II./SS-Pz. Gren. Rgt.38 from 17. SS-Pz. Gren. Div. *"Götz von Berlichingen."*

This Panzergrenadiere battalion had arrived in the Pont-Hébert sector during the night of 5-6 July, ordered there by the 7. Armee in anticipation of the American offensive.

They had just arrived when their CO, SS-Sturmbannführer Nieschlag, received a counter-order. They had to return to the area where his division was committed and now under threat from VIIth Army Corps. The situation was alarming and the breach had to be filled between Les Champs de Loques and La Varde. His battalion fulfilled its mission but Nieschlag was furious. His unit had suffered casualties just to make a pointless return trip.

During the morning, he gathered his companies and launched an attack. Although their advance was slowed down by the marshes, they managed to push the GIs back.

On the following day, 7 July, SS-Sturmbannführer Nieschlag pushed his Waffen-SS forwards, on either side of the Le Port - Le Mesnil-Véneron road, trying to join up with elements of Inf.-Btl. 639 positioned between La Goucherie and Le Mesnil-Véneron. Having got to within a mile of his objective, Nieschlag sent out a group of scouts from the second platoon of 5. Kp. under SS-Unterscharführer Drifftmann. But the scouts from Troop A of the 113th Cavalry were resolutely waiting for them. Several Waffen-SS fell to their bullets. Sensing however that this was going to be a strong attack, Troop A contacted the 3rd Bn of the 120th Infantry to warn them to be on the alert.

Seeing that SS-Unterscharführer Drifftmann and his men had not come back, SS-Sturmbannführer Nieschlag launched his Waffen-SS into the attack. Caught in the fire from Troop A and the 3rd Bn of the 120th Infantry, they lost a third of their strength in less than fifteen minutes. 5./SS-Pz Gren.-Rgt. 38 lost 28 men and 6./SS-Pz Gren.-Rgt. 38 lost its CO, Obersturmführer Tramontana.

As soon as the news broke, the G-2 got in touch with General Hobbs' command post who informed him of this Waffen-SS battalion's presence. Fortunately it was the only incursion that 17. SS-Pz. Gren. Div. *"Götz von Berlichingen"* ever made into the XIXth US Army Corps operational zone.

To be more on the safe side, Troop A's CO got in touch with the 3/120th Infantry positioned on his left. As for the rest of the 113th Cavalry Group, it had to wait for the next day before joining Troop A.

Towards 17.00, the German forces were getting more threatening. Up until now operations had gone quite smoothly but this time the GIs' luck ran out. The Germans had pulled themselves together and their positions had been reinforced some hours earlier. This situation worried the CO of the 117th Infantry which was the furthest forward of the 30th Infantry Division units.

This detail had not escaped Oberst Heintz's Grenadiere's watchful attention; they started to tighten the noose around this particular unit. The GIs came under a very violent bombardment which terrorised the less experienced troops. There were heavy casualties and their officers had considerable trouble getting their men to advance. Mortar shells went whistling through the air with a sinister screeching, before hitting the ground and exploding near them. The machine gun bursts which kept them with their noses in the dirt took all their courage away.

C·14
GL 14 T
GW 7.5'
HT 8
NM 32428
14T 10 CWT

191237-5

Above.

Once the bridgehead was established, the 30th Infantry Division located to the east of the Vire had to reinforce it. General Hobbs harassed his junior officers unendingly with this, fearing that the Germans would react strongly. The barrel of a 90-mm anti-tank gun can be seen hidden under a camouflage net. A GMC transporting GIs is hurrying towards the bridge while others are coming back the other way empty. This scene takes place at Haut des Landes – Saint-Fromond.
(National Archives: Conseil Général de Basse-Normandie)

Only the G Company infantry managed to carry on across the marshy, putrid fields. Their company commander could be proud of his men. Unfortunately his progress caused a gap in the line because the other companies remained where they were. Now G Company was isolated in the middle of the German lines.

To help G Company get itself out of these dire straits, the 3rd Bn of the 117th Infantry on Hill 30 was ordered to send elements to rescue the isolated company.

Engaged in Kampfgruppe Heintz's zone of operations, G Company's GIs responded furiously to the Grenadiere who were very cleverly concealed in the undergrowth. Most of the time, the GIs fired blindly. With the reinforcements from the 3rd Bn not appearing and with his soldiers close to panicking, the CO of G Company started to fear he would lose his unit. He gave his

The 30th US Infantry Division patch

men the order to fall back on the initial positions without disengaging. When he got in touch with the regiment later, he was ordered to set up to the south of Saint-Jean-de-Daye.

Coordinating the units in the bocage was still a complex matter. Moving forward in a zone covered with hedges, where machine gun nests lay in wait all the time, was enough to discourage even the boldest GIs.

Thus the 2nd Bn of the 119th Infantry, positioned on the left wing of the 2nd Bn of the 117th Infantry, lost all contact with its neighbour when it entered the field of fire of an 88-mm Flak. This battalion was engaged to the south but was no longer capable of attacking Saint-Fromond-Eglise as ordered. One of its companies, placed on the right wing of the battalion, tried to get rid of the Flak gun, but in vain.

A breach started to form between the two American bat-

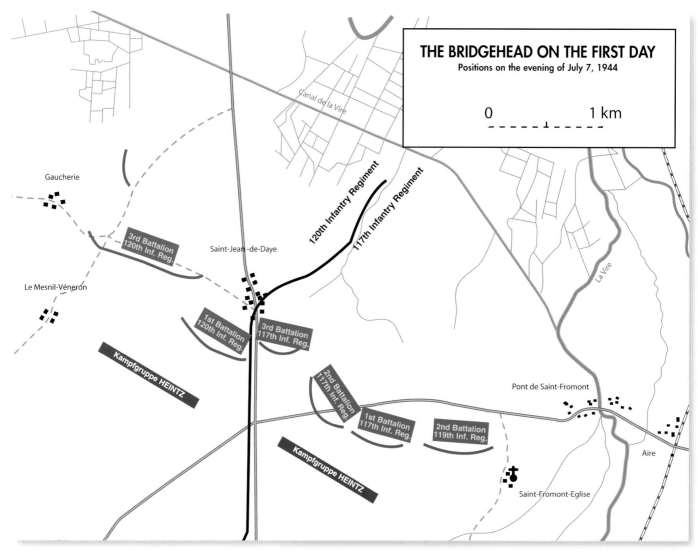

Canal de la Vire

Gaucherie

120th Infantry Regiment

117th Infantry Regiment

Saint-Jean-de-Daye

3rd Battalion 120th Inf. Reg.

Le Mesnil-Véneron

La Vire

1st Battalion 120th Inf. Reg.

3rd Battalion 117th Inf. Reg.

Kampfgruppe HEINTZ

2nd Battalion 117th Inf. Reg.

Pont de Saint-Fromont

1st Battalion 117th Inf. Reg.

2nd Battalion 119th Inf. Reg.

Aire

Kampfgruppe HEINTZ

Saint-Fromont-Eglise

Right.
This Jeep belonging to an infantry battalion is moving forward with great difficulty along a muddy lane lined with high hedges. Quite in spite of themselves, the combatants had to get used to these features which caused so many casualties. The four-wheel drive vehicle is equipped with a wire cutting device at the front. This was originally intended to cut telephone wires which had fallen down across the road but it also saved passengers' lives when the Germans stretched wires across the roads and tracks.
(National Archives)

Left.
The first casualties of the 119th Infantry are laid out on stretchers by medics. Two bags containing first aid supplies are lying on the ground. The soldier who is looking at the camera has been tagged with and evacuation card hanging from his neck. This card gives the exact state and nature of his wounds, information which will be useful for the hospital staff.
(National Archives)

talions. If the Germans reached the Airel - Le Dézert road, they would be in a position to come up behind the 2/117th Infantry which was thus isolated and take it in the rear.

Major-General Corlett was warned of this threat which put the whole front in jeopardy. Moreover he was worried by the fact that the 1st Bn had not yet reached the zone. "The 1st Bn has been slowed down in its advance by the terrain and by enemy harassing fire. It won't be long before it reaches its objective" somebody said to reassure him.

Thinking for a moment, Major-General Corlett said to his subordinates: "You could say, I suppose, considering all the different situations they have been through, that the GIs in the 30th Infantry Division are learning on the job. The survivors of this battle of the Hedgerows will be war-hardened, experienced soldiers!"

As for General Hobbs of the 30th Division, he was also wondering, looking at the large situation big map pinned to the wall at his CP. He was rather satisfied by the fact that the first two phases of setting up the bridgehead had been accomplished. He did realise however that several of his battalions had had to fight particularly hard during the afternoon and that coordination between them had not always been as it should have been. Getting the all regiments to advance together in such a difficult environment was practically

This GI is carrying a water-cooled M1917 A1 Browning heavy machine gun. This was operated by the infantry battalion's fourth (heavy weapons) company. He has draped a 250-round belt on his shoulders. Photographed shortly after landing, he is wearing a lifejacket around his waist. Also noteworthy are the regulation individual weapon for a machine gunner, the .45 caliber pistol, and the assault gas mask in its black neoprene bag under the left arm.
(National Archives)

impossible. He could only get them to advance battalion by battalion.

He suddenly thought of a solution. He spoke to Bradley who added some suggestions. General Hobbs opted for local actions supported by armour. These were much more likely to lead to decisive breakthroughs in the German front. These would destabilise the enemy, cause disruption and catch them in their own trap.

General Bradley even thought that these small scale breakthroughs would rapidly lead the tank units onto the heights situated to the southwest of Saint-Lô, which were the final objective of XIXth Army Corps.

The plan was ambitious but it was feasible. The armoured support was provided by the 3rd Armored Division which until then had been placed in reserve. Its CO, Major-General Leroy H. Watson, was waiting for just this moment. He received a telephone call.

"It's for tonight. You're going to cross the Vire at midnight and then at dawn, you will position your tanks near the Saint-Jean-de-Daye crossroads. Then you'll cut up all those Krauts!"

General Watson was delighted to go into action. But he did not yet know that the roads were clear and that there was still relatively little coordination between the infantry battalions.

One of them, the 2/117th Infantry was still fighting and the 1st Bn, which was supposed to relieve it on its left wing, had not yet arrived. As for the 3rd Bn, it was still in the Hill 30 sector, near Saint-Jean-de-Daye, a hill which had still not been taken.

Major-General Corlett had to organise himself and get his divisions back into order. If he did not, there was the risk of the attack planned for the following day going awry. Colonel Kelly performed miracles to get in touch with his battalion commanders since radio contact was bad and often inexistent. He sent runners to his units to give them the army corps orders. Everything had to be done to get in touch with the neighbouring units again before attempting any operation to grab terrain from Kampfgruppe Heintz.

The battalions managed to set up a coherent front-line during the night and each of their COs was ordered to reorganise his companies prior to the attack planned for the following morning.

General Hobbs could congratulate himself on the day's achievements. A bridgehead had been obtained by his men crossed the Vire then the canal. The following day at dawn, they would attack to the south with the support of the tanks from the 3rd Armored Division.

For the first day of the offensive, his army corps had lost 281 men, of which 44 in the 2nd Bn of the 117th Infantry Regiment. This was a very heavy toll which could have been reduced if the Air Force had been able to operate under more favourable weather conditions.

THE 3rd ARMORED DIVISION
REINFORCES THE 30th INFANTRY DIVISION

Two GIs in a Weasel guarding a column of German POWs mostly belonging to Kampfgruppe Heintz. They were captured near Saint-Jean de-Daye. It is surprising to see a soldier from the Sturm-Artillerie with his particular uniform. Did he belong to the Pz.Jg.Abt.352 or to the Nebelwerfer Lehr-Regiment 101 in which some personnel wore this uniform?
(National Archives)

Before the attack planned for dawn was launched, the 83rd Reconnaissance (Recce) Battalion was given the task of exploring the terrain between the Saint-Jean-de-Daye crossroads and Bordigny.

It was about 3 am when scouts from D Company ran into heavy opposition from the enemy to the north of Bordigny at the far left tip of the bridgehead.

The GIs discovered that powerful defences were set up in this sector which the 2nd Bn of the 119th Infantry, even though it was positioned nearby, had not run into until then. Had the scouts found one of LXXXIV.A.K.'s strategic defence points in its line?

This was most likely because the counter-attack the Americans had to face up to was strong. The soldiers withdrew quickly to Saint-Fromond-Eglise, held by the

2nd Bn of the 120th Infantry. Their mission was to reconnoiter the terrain and not fight. A shower of mortar shells followed them as they withdrew.

The few hours which the 83rd Recce had been given to reconnoiter in hostile territory – and what's more at night – were simply not sufficient. There was the risk that the 3rd Armored would pay heavily for this during its attack.

Major-General Corlett was very worried. The plans of attack which he had just received from his subordinates seemed to be unworkable. The axis along which the

Above.
The Saint-Jean-de-Daye crossroads was an essential objective and was the most important crossroads for the XIXth US Army Corps. Here it has just been taken by GIs from the 1st Bn of the 120th Infantry on 8 July 1944. They were immediately joined by the tanks from 3rd Armored Division.
(National Archives/Conseil général de Basse-Normandie)

Previous page, inset.
The 3rd Armored Division shoulder patch.

Right.
General Leroy Watson, the 3rd Armored Division commanding general.
(National Archives)

Top right.
This artillery piece, found near Saint-Jean de-Daye, is a 152 mm calibre gun. Its precise designation was 15.2 cm K 433/1 (r); it was of Soviet origin. It most certainly belonged to 3./Artillerie-Abteilung 456 or 457; both were equipped with this type of gun. They were engaged in the Cotentin peninsula on 6 June then sent south in order to avoid being encircled. On 22 June 1944, they supported 353.I.D and 17. SS-Pz.Gren. Div. The presence of one of these guns in Kampfgruppe Heintz's sector shows that it was there to support the Grenadiere facing the 30th Infantry Division.
(National Archives. via Fred Deprun)

3rd Armored Division was intending to advance, across terrain captured by his division, was not yet adequately protected by his own troops. Moreover the plan was for the infantry battalions to attack at the same time as general Watson's armoured division. This was an un wise decision as the two divisions would most certainly get in each other's way. It was however too late now to change things.

Harassed by German artillery fire, the three Task Forces in Combat Command B got into line for the beginning of the attack. Combat Command A remained in reserve for the time being.

To the consternation of Major-General Watson, the infantry had not cleared the main lines of advance and the important crossroads located to the south of Saint-Jean de-Daye which his tanks had to use, meaning that his armour was going to be taking heavy risks. So, in the end, he modified the plans using the minor roads. Half way along his Task Forces left the road linking Saint-Fromond to the crossroads south of Saint-Jean de-Daye and headed diagonally southwards. They passed through zones occupied by the infantry to the east of the Saint-Jean-de-Daye – Pont-Hébert road. When it was in sight of Saint-Fromond-Eglise, Task Force X came up against strong resistance. The other two Task Forces were slowed down, and even stopped in places, by 30th Infantry Division units deploying.

At 6.42, the Shermans started for the German front. Lost in the bocage, the tank crews were on edge. What they feared most was getting stuck in the marshes and being shot at by Panzerfausten.

The first Task Force to come under fire from the ene my was Task Force X. It had reached the Saint-Fromond-Eglise road when the Germans counter-attacked in its direction.

This enemy force comprised I. and II./Gren.-Rgt. 984, Pi.-Btl. Angers, the scouts from Füs.-Btl.275 supported by the Panzer IVs of 6./SS-Pz.Rgt.2 under SS-Obersturm-führer Karl-Heinz Boska (I./SS-Pz Gren.Rgt. "Deutsch-land") and 13./"Deutschland". These were fearsome troops but they were understrength and underequipped.

As for Pi.-Btl. Angers, it had been reduced to compa ny strength from the 433 sappers engaged in the fighting a few days after the Allied landings. This battal-ion, initially attached to 352.I.D., had lost its Kdr., Haupt-mann Scheffold, at the beginning of the fighting (he was still listed as missing) and the unit was now led by Leutnant Winterstein, the former CO of 4./Fallschirm.-Aufklärungs-Abteilung 12, who had become an instruc-tor with Pi.-Btl. Angers.

A platoon of E Company, 2nd Bn of the 119th Infantry which had set up its positions near the church at Saint-Fromond, found itself in the line of the enemy attack. The soldiers were worried because Colonel Alfred V. Ednie's HQ was just nearby.

In the midst of the howling engines and the deafening explosions, the American platoon stood up to the ene my with all the energy of despair. Two Grenadiere were killed by a burst from a BAR (Browning Automatic Rifle) and several others were hit. The Panzers advanced. One of them sprayed the American positions with the co-axi-al machine gun.

Suddenly the platoon commander, Lieutenant Beatrice, collapsed without a sound. His steel helmet rolled over to a GI who was holding his thigh with both hands, trying to stem the flow of blood which was spurting from it.

Other GIs were wounded. They felt as though they had failed but the instinct to survive pushed them to fight on.

A tank duel followed. Four Panzer IVs were destroyed for one Sherman. One of the Panzers lost its turret to a direct hit by an armour-piercing shell.

The scouts from Kampfgruppe Heintz withdrew, close-ly covered by a Pz.IV. As they crossed the bridge which had been damaged by countless impacts, the tank sud-denly ground to a halt. The crew had no time to scuttle it and left it intact for the Americans to take.

Across the whole of 30th Division's front, the Shermans went through one field after another, each inevitably sur-rounded by hedges which they sprayed copiously with their machine guns to flush out any enemy soldiers lying in ambush.

For the tank crews, the most terrifying moment was when the tank had to get over those high banks, when it lifted itself up into the air, exposing its underbelly - the perfect target for the Panzerfauste. The only protection the tanks had was the infantry which most of the time was alongside to escort them.

Advancing like this took time, all the more so as it was crucial to move carefully. Major-General Watson was aware of all these difficulties, but he would not stand for his armoured units getting behind schedule.

6./SS-Panzer Regiment 2

Far left.
portrait of Obertsturmführer Karl Heinz Boska commanding 6./SS-Pz.Rgt.2. His Pz. IVs supported the scouts from Kampfgruppe Heintz during the counter-attack against Saint-Fromond. Here he can be seen with the rank of SS-Hauptsturmführer and wearing the Knight's Cross awarded on 16 December 1944. He was first a scout in the reconnaissance battalion of the *"Das Reich"* Division in 1940, and then he became a platoon commander when the division received its tanks at the end of 1942. He became ordnance officer in II./SS-Pz.Rgt.2 then CO of 6./SS-Pz.Rgt.2 at the beginning of December 1943. He ended up as Kdr. of II./SS-Pz.Rgt.2 in April 1945.

Left.
Johann Thaler was awarded the Knight's Cross on 14 August 1943, following Operation Citadel. When he was attacked by several T-34s, he succeeded in destroying three of them but his tank was brought to a standstill by a direct hit. Under fire Thaler repaired the machine then tried to get back to his lines. In order to do this he and his crew had to destroy another three T-34s. He was killed in Austria in April 1945. *(BA)*

6./SS-Pz.Rgt.2 crews getting ready to set off.
This tank company lost four of its Pz.IVs against
one Sherman on 8 July 1944.
(BA 101 1721/387/4)

Suddenly, in the 2/119th sector, some Shermans came under heavy fire. There were still Germans in the area the 83rd Recce Bn reckoned had been cleared.

The crews responded with their 75-mm shells which whistled through the fresh, moist morning air exploding behind the curtains of greenery. The bullets from the Brownings cut through the leaves and branches. There was screaming and moaning everywhere.

The armoured infantry which got to the spot as quickly as possible heard voices which seemed friendly. *"Stop shooting, they're ours,"* could be heard from all sides.

Warned by radio, the tank crews therefore stopped firing. Their CO was furious. *"Why wasn't I told the infantry was here?"*

The reason was quite simple: the 3rd Bn of the 119th Infantry, which had arrived during the night, had relieved the 2nd Bn of the same regiment which had itself been placed on the left wing of the XIXth Army Corps without Major-General Watson's HQ being informed… This set up could have turned into a disaster.

On the XIXth Army Corps' right wing, the situation was not really any better. Held up half a mile to the west of La Goucherie by a battalion of Osttruppen (Soviet prisoners inducted in the German army), Troop A from the 113th Cavalry Squadron had dug in on its positions and then spent the night waiting for the order to attack. Meanwhile, it learnt that some Waffen-SS were present on the left wing of VIIth Army Corps. It is quite likely that these Waffen-SS had been brought up into the sector because of the Osttruppen's lack of fight and morale.

Troop A, joined by Troop C from the 113th Cavalry Squadron and the 125th Cavalry Squadron, could at last attack Ost.-Btl.639 and get hold of La Goucherie. Shortly afterwards, the 125th Cavalry along with part of Troop C from the 113th Cavalry headed south to take Le Mesnil-Véneron.

The 230th Field Artillery Battalion bombarded the German positions for ten minutes; then Troop A and part of Troop C attacked the village with a simple pincer movement. The German defences were still lively in spite of the artillery barrage but, nonetheless, at 7.30, the 'Eastern volunteers' surrendered.

Encouraged by the capture of La Goucherie, the 125th Cavalry Squadron pushed on south. It was soon stopped in its tracks by impenetrable German positions. It withdrew to the village it had taken just half-an-hour earlier. The CO of the 125th Cavalry Squadron then got in touch with the CO of 113th Cavalry Group to draw up a new plan of attack to the south. Troop A from the 125th Squadron would lead the attack on from La Goucherie.

At 9.00, Troop A set off southwards but the undergrowth greatly slowed down its vehicles and it was soon under fire from the Germans who continued harassing it. The GIs were not in a position to dislodge the enemy, who were firmly dug in. Any endeavour here against the Germans was bound to fail. The Troop A's GIs were able to extricate themselves only with the help of a few elements from the 113th Cavalry Group.

This time, the resistance was nothing like that put up by the Osttruppen. The Waffen-SS in SS-Pz.Gren. Rgt.38 were battle-hardened and ruthless fighters. The Cavalry Groups had their work cut out fighting them.

Above.
The original Signal Corps caption states: "These soldiers from Tiflis in Georgia are shown with some Americans belonging to an armored unit. They have just surrendered after deserting from the German army. The first Osttruppen who surrendered claimed that there were 29 of them commanded by two German officers. When the Americans advanced, three were killed by the Germans. After that incident the Georgians killed their officers and deserted. Six of the 29, starving and delighted to be in the hands of the Americans showed them where their comrades were hiding."
Judging from a report by the 113th Cavalry Squadron, Ost. Btl. 639, which held the La Goucherie sector was thought not to be very reliable and that was why the Waffen-SS from SS-Pz.Gren.Rgt.38 had been brought in to bolster them.
(National Archives)

At 11 am, the 113th Cavalry Squadron handed La Goucherie over to Troop A of the 125th Cavalry in order to effect a turning movement from the west to the south. This was brought to a standstill by the Panzergrenadiere from II./SS-Pz. Gren. Rgt.38.

Suddenly bright flashes spat out from the undergrowth, aimed at the American vehicles. For a moment the Americans were stunned then they got their reflexes back. A series of explosions fell around their vehicles making the ground under them shudder.

The terrain was so impracticable because of the sodden earth that the GIs were forced to jump down from the armoured cars. Moreover the Germans, cleverly hidden by the embankments, or even hidden in the trees, were in the position to decimate the unit rapidly had the Americans not melted away into the countryside.

For Lt.-Col. Allen D. Hulse, the Germans had definitely planned this manoeuvre. Now his men were having to fight as infantry. They had to hide, listen and catch the slightest noise which would give potential enemy positions away. After the racket of gunfire, silence took over again. The GIs rose, pointing their guns forward, their guts knotted with fear. Some of them leapt forward, the others held back ready to support the others with their fire.

Death stalked behind every bush, scrub, tree, hedge and embankment. A single, well-placed machine gun nest could wipe out a whole group of soldiers crossing a lane or a field. Following an in-depth study of the operations in the 113th Cavalry Group's sector, General

Hobbs of the 30th Infantry Division asked Colonel Biddle to take over the protection of the XIXth Army Corps' right flank. A solid line of defence had to be set up between La Goucherie and Le Mesnil-Véneron. Two forward positions made up of 12-man groups, supported by tanks were positioned beyond the line in order to prevent any attacks.

Nonetheless, for the 113th Cavalry Squadron, this layout turned out to be inadequate. A breach appeared where its right flank joined the 2nd Bn of the 117th Infantry. To prevent the enemy trying anything on, the 3rd Bn of the 120th Infantry which had just taken the heights near Le Dézert, was ordered to consolidate the front with the tanks from the 743rd Tank Battalion. Moreover, it had to liaise with the 113th Cavalry. This was a lot to ask of an infantry battalion which had already suffered heavy casualties since Saint-Jean-de-Daye was captured; but General Hobbs had no otherw choice since the 3rd Bn of the 120th Infantry was right next to the 113th Cavalry.

The battalion's advance and particularly the capture of the heights embarrassed Generalleutnant von Choltitz… The Americans now held a position which gave them an excellent view over the Vire Valley on the outskirts of Saint-Lô. He had to drive them back.

The worn out GIs from the 3rd Bn of the 120th Infantry had to face 300 Panzergrenadiere and three tanks coming from Le Dézert. They did not yet know that they were facing a Kampfgruppe from the SS-Pz. Div. "Das Reich",

Below.
The situation was critical for the soldiers using this road. They had just been ambushed a few moments earlier but the German machine gunner was shot. His body is lying behind the machine gun ammunition cases. One of the Americans has most likely been hit as there is an American helmet lying on the ground near the hedge on the left. Two GIs are ready to open fire with their Garands whilst another pair is running along the left-hand hedge with a bazooka.
(National Archives)

comprising the I./SS-Rgt. "Deutschland" under SS-Sturmbannführer Schuster, the 14. (SS-Hauptsturmführer
Filber) and 16./"D" (SS-Obersturmführer Macher)
and the SS-Pz. Pi. Btl. "Das Reich" under SS-Hauptsturmführer Brosow.

SS-Obersturmbannführer Wisliceny, the Kdr. of the SS-
Rgt "Deutschland", was in command of this tactical group.
This very brave officer had been awarded the Knight's
Cross in July 1943 after the Battle of Kursk. He was a
National-Socialist from the early days when, in 1933, he
joined the SS-Stabswache Berlin, later to become the
Leibstandarte Adolf Hitler. He was then transferred to the
SS-Division "Das Reich" in which he remained for the
duration of the war. He was always at the head of his
men in all the fighting; he was a very experienced
officer and a formidable adversary for the GIs of the
30th Infantry Division.

SS-Hauptsturmführer Brosow, commanding the SS-Pz.
Pi. Btl.2, was cast in exactly the same mould. He too was
awarded the Knight's Cross in November 1943 after
countering a Soviet breakthrough. He had gathered the
remnants of his company - only forty or so men - and
thrown himself, and them, at the enemy in a furious hand
to hand battle. His action quite simply saved the whole
division from a terrible fate.

During the afternoon of 7 July 1944, SS-Obersturmbannführer Wisliceny received the LXXXIV.A.K.'s
marching orders: to relieve Kampfgruppe Heintz situated on the right wing of 17.SS-Pz. Gren. Div. to which
it was attached. "The Grenadiere of 275.I.D. have suffered terrible casualties and the Americans of the XIXth
US Army Corps risk taking Saint-Lô so we have to intervene to halt them in their drive," SS-Obersturmbannführer Wisliceny announced to his HQ staff and to the
commanders of the Stabs-Kompanie, and 14. Kp. and
16. Kp. With nightfall, the units set off in their allotted
directions. Wisliceny and his staff passed through Saint-
Martin d'Aubigny - Remigny sur Luzon then arrived in
Le Dézert. They set up their command post in a cluster
of houses near Le Haut-du-Duc.

Soon they were joined by SS-Hauptsturmführer Brosow
and by the Kdr. of II./Gren.Rgt.984. The latter, one of
Oberst Heintz's junior officers should theoretically have
been able to give him accurate information about the situation, but the SS leader was swiftly disappointed. Kampfgruppe Heintz's headquarters were no longer in contact
with its units which were now fighting alone. The Kdr. of
II./Gren. Rgt.984 had to admit that there was no longer
any front line as such and that the Americans had completely disrupted everything since Saint-Fromond had fall-
en into their hands.

Studying the maps, SS-Obersturmbannführer Wisliceny quickly grasped the village's importance, and especially the bridge there. He decided that he would attack
it with his Kampfgruppe.

The CO of the 3rd Bn of the 120th Infantry called for
immediate artillery support as soon as the Waffen-SS
group, intent on breaking swiftly through, was sighted.
Two minutes later, he contacted the CO of the 743rd Tank
Bn. whose tanks had to take up positions from which they
could drive the Germans back.

Although seriously taken to task, the American tank
crews got close to the heights which were targeted by
three Pz.IVs from 6./SS-Pz.Rgt.2. None of them was hit.

The infantry soon opened fire and managed to drive
back the attackers, aided by the Shermans' continuous
firing. The counter-attack's impetus was broken, but morale
in the ranks of the battalion was low. The unit's losses for
the day were the heaviest in the 30th Division and it was
relieved by the 2nd Bn of the 120th Infantry Regiment.

This battalion had not fought since the bridgehead to
the west of the Vire had been established; it arrived during the night and positioned itself at the head of the 30th
division's order of attack, planned for the following day.

Meanwhile, the "Das Reich's" engineer battalion, com-

Right.
Two of the four destroyed Pz.IVs from 6./SS-Pz.Rgt. 2. The insignia – the combat rune - of 2.SS-Panzerdivision "Das Reich" is easily recognisable. This shot was taken on 9 July 1944. A tank from Task Force X is going past them.
(National Archives/Conseil général de Basse-Normandie)

Below from left to right.
This Pz.IV from 6./SS-Pz.Rgt. 2 is being removed by a Ward LaFrance heavy wrecker. It has received a direct hit to the front, no doubt a 75-mm shell, which penetrated right between the driver's and the radio operator's positions.
(National Archives)

This Pz.IV has been hit in on the rear left axle, invisible on this shot and has most probably been pushed aside by a bulldozer to open up the road. The GIs from the 2nd Bn of the 119th Infantry are watching the ditch carefully where German soldiers could be hiding.
(National Archives)

Three GIs are trying on the black jackets taken from crews of SS-Pz.Rgt.2. The "Das Reich" cuff band can just be made out on the soldier on the left.
(National Archives)

manded by the energetic SS-Hauptsturmführer Brosow had reached its objective. Its Kdr. established its CP fifty or so yards from Wisliceny's, in a hamlet built on Hill 22. His assignment was to make contact with Kampfgruppe Heintz. His sappers ran into Grenadiere in small groups unfortunately more intent on saving their skins than their positions.

In order to simplify liaison between the armour and the infantry, General Hobbs asked for the 3rd Armored Division to be attached directly to the 30th US Infantry division and no longer to the army corps, hoping that the two units would thus be able to cooperate more effectively and thereby save a lot of precious time.

Task Force X played a vital role in continuing the offensive. Its objective was to reach the Pont-Hébert road by passing through the 1st Bn of the 117th Infantry and the 2nd Bn of the 119th Infantry. Moving the tanks through this sector took a long time but went off without a hitch, thanks to the infantry which had cleared the minor roads and the lanes.

After passing through the 30th division's front line Task Force X tanks headed for La Bernarderie.

They did not progress very far. 88-mm Flak guns took them to task between La Borderie and La Bernarderie. Several tanks were hit and the crews noticed that machine gun positions were located along the road, hidden in the hedgerows.

Task Force X had just run into Oberstleutnant von Ausess' Kampfgruppe coming from Pont-Hébert. This officer, the Kdr. of the Schnell-Brigade 30, had been ordered by Generalleutnant Kraiss at the beginning of the afternoon to form a tactical group to help Oberst Heintz and

Left.
Two medics are tending to wounded GI's hand. They are wearing the red cross Geneva convention brassard, on the arm or tucked under the helmet net. Note the wounded man's helmet, camouflaged with hessian strips, most certainly taken from the larger nets for artillery and vehicles.
(National Archives/Conseil général de Basse-Normandie)

Right.
This Sherman is advancing carefully through the bocage. The crew have popped their heads out of their hatches to look at the lie of the land and try to locate where a Panzerfaust team might be waiting in ambush. The tanks' progress towards Pont-Hébert was extremely slow taking because of the hedges and Flak guns, firing in a flat trajectory.
(National Archives/Conseil général de Basse-Normandie)

his Grenadiere in the Saint-Fromond sector. Caught unprepared, he could only bring up his brigade's 2.Kp. which was in the 352.I.D. reserve in the La Croix sector.

His available strength for this operation was limited to 300 men but his brigade was reinforced by two batteries from III./Art.Rgt. 266 and one 88-mm battery from Fallschirmjäger Flak-Abt. 2.

Luckily, Fallschirm.Aufklärungs-Abteilung 12 (without its 1. Kp.), one of the best-equipped and entirely motorised organic units of the army corps, under Generalleutnant Meindl, was with Oberstleutnant von Ausess for this mission.

In the middle of the afternoon, Kampfgruppe von Ausess set up a defensive line between Cavigny – Le Dézert – Le Mesnil-Angot which slowed the 30th division down. Its positions protected the rear of SS-Kampfgruppe Wisliceny and Kampfgruppe Heintz. The right wing of the von Ausess elements was protected by his brigade and the left wing by the paratroopers.

Under the circumstances, for the American tank crews, pressing on was simply suicidal. The Task Force X CO asked his men to withdraw; the capture of la Bernaderie was put off to the following day. The night was used to repair the tanks.

Task force X's progress was disappointing; the same could not be said of the 119th Infantry Regiment which had managed to drive a one-mile deep wedge in the German lines. This regiment's 3rd Bn even got as far as Cavigny, hoping to find Task Force X's tanks on its right flank but they had been driven back as seen above.

A breach had nevertheless been made between Kampfgruppe von Ausess and Pi.-Btl. 275. Hauptmann Göttsche, Kdr. of Fallschirm.Aufkl.-Abt. 12., launched his companies into the attack supported by the MG company (the 3rd, with 47 machine guns and two 81-mm mortars) and the heavy company (the 4th under Leutnant Winterstein with 15 machine guns, four 20-mm Flak guns, nine 75-mm Paks and two infantry cannon). All his men's efforts were in vain. They did manage however to establish a line of defence during the night one and a half or two miles to the northwest of Le Dézert.

The main progress of the day that the XIXth US Army Corps made was not just the extension of the bridgehead over more than half a mile, but the capture, once and for all, of the crossroads situated to the south of Saint-Jean-de-Daye, by the 1st Bn of the 120th infantry Regiment. This was the most important communications centre in the zone assigned to the XIXth US Army Corps. The losses suffered by the 120th Infantry however had to be taken into consideration, in particular those of the 2nd Bn which had had a lot of trouble holding out against the three counter-attacks of the day. During one of these attacks, SS-Sturmbannführer Schuster, Kdr. of I./ "D", was killed.

The casualties on both sides were very heavy. The CO of the 1st Bn, Lt.-Col. Hugh I. Mainord was wounded as were several company commanders. Two of them were battalion veterans. The six Shermans which opened the way for the 120th Infantry were

FALLSCHIRM.AUFKLARUNGS-ABTEILUNG 12

In March 1944, its strength was less than one thousand men. They came mainly from Fallschirmjägerregiment 9 under Major Stephani. Hauptmann Göttsche took command of this new unit which was trained at Moret near Paris.

Ex-Oberjäger Paul remembers this period: "To our great dismay, Leutnant Winterstein who was in command of the heavy company had to leave for Anzio-Nettuno at the request of General Student.

"Before leaving us he put me up for Oberjäger on condition that I went to the Oberjäger Training School or that I went on a training course for sharpshooters.

"I chose the second possibility. So off I went to the land combat school at Le Courtin, near Paris. After advanced instruction in sharp-shooting, I became an Oberjäger then started training sharpshooters in Fallschirm.Auklärungs-Abteilung 12. We received new weapons fitted with sights. We trained at night and during the day and the terrain in Champagne was ideal for our training with its hedges, trees and hills.

"It was during this period that we were ordered to Brittany where it was possible that the Allies might land. We left immediately for this region. We had to break off our training to help with coastal defences.

"We had resumed our sharp-shooting training when our former Company Commander, Leutnant Winterstein, turned up. He was on his way back from the Ministry of Armaments in Berlin and was there to teach us all about the new weapons for sappers, in particular a new mine which could be placed underwater. He had ten days to train us. Time flew by. Among other things we learnt how to work a flamethrower. Finally Leutnant Winterstein told us that he had been appointed instructor at the school for sappers at Angers. Hauptmann Raabe became our Company Commander (the 4./Fallschirm.Auklärungs-Abteilung 12.)

"On 6 June we learnt that the Allies had landed in Normandy. Our battalion and the 3.Fallschirmjägerdivision were ordered to leave immediately for the Saint-Lô area.

"All the roads were under fire from enemy aircraft which attacked our columns, even medical ones. We could move about by day only if it rained; otherwise we had to move by night. Our battalion reached Saint-Lô on 9 June, shortly before the 3. Fallschirmjägerdivision."

The parachute reconnaissance battalion was assigned to the II.Fallschirmjäger-Korps, itself attached to LXXXIV.A.K. under General Marcks. It was positioned alongside 352.I.D. then sent to the west of the Vire to break the XIXth US Army Corps' offensive on 8 July 1944. On 12 July, it was attached to Kampfgruppe Scholze. It strength was limited to eight officers, 56 NCOs and 235 men. On 14 or 15 July, the battalion joined II.Fallschirmjäger-Korps to the east of the Vire. ❏

Fallschirm.Aufklärungs-Abteilung 12

This parachute reconnaissance battalion was created at the beginning of January 1944. An independent unit attached to II. Fallschirmjäger-Korps, it was led by Hauptmann Gotsche. The company HQ had six Italian armoured cars and three B4 Italian tanks.

It comprised five companies:

● **1. Kp.:** equipped with Panzerspähwagen (armoured reconnaissance vehicles)
● **2. Kp.** equipped with SPW (half-tracks, with 47 machine guns and two 81-mm mortars
● **3. Kp.:** like the 2.Kp.
● **4. Kp.:** the Schwere Kompanie (heavy company) equipped with 15 machine guns, four 20-mm Flak guns, nine 75-mm Paks and two infantry cannon.
● **5. Kp.:** Versorgungskompanie (Supply Company)

Above.
One of the very few pictures showing the FG 42 automatic rifle in Normandy. This paratrooper could be from Fallschirmjäger-Aufklärungs-Abteilung 12, as we know that the Sturmtrupps of 1, 2 and 3. Kp had this type of weapon. A Sturmtrupp of one NCO and ten other ranks was armed with a light MG, 2 FG42 and another with a telescopic sight, a flamethrower, a Püppchen anti-tank weapon, 80 S-mines, 100 type 28 explosive charges (to blow holes for mines), and several heavier explosive charges.
(BA 101I/720/344/11)

Below.
These Fallschirmjäger are getting ready for a recce mission with a Type 82 Kübelwagen. With its 50 mph top speed, this four-wheel vehicle was perfect for the job. The driver and passenger both have the regular steel helmet.

Above.
The two look-outs perched at the back are watching for fighter-bombers. From their equipment, these are telephone signalmen.
(BA 101I/585/2182/27&31a)

all destroyed, four of them by SS-Kgp. Wisliceny and the other two by Hauptmann Göttsche's scouts from Fallschirm. Aufkl. Abt. 12.

On this particular point, the following is to be found in the official history of the 120th Infantry: *"The news that several German tanks (Author's note: there were never more than 22 Panzer IVs.) had destroyed our leading tanks spread like wildfire to the rear. Young inexperienced recruits transporting ammunition abandoned their vehicles believing that the enemy had broken through. In no time soldiers panicked and the road became all clogged up.*

The 1st and 2nd Bns who needed ammunition desperately could not be supplied because of the traffic jam.

Lt.-Col. Peter O. Ward, the Regimental Executive Officer with a group of soldiers from HQ Company very cleverly left for the St. Jean-de-Daye crossroads where they managed to contain the panic and stem the withdrawal.

After a while the situation stabilised and the two battalions engaged were re-supplied with ammunition first. At the end of the day, the German counter-attack had been pushed back and the positions partly retaken..."

It is worth mentioning that more than half the 2nd Bn's casualties occurred when the soldiers left the safety of their positions. When the platoons remained in their positions they came out of the fighting better, even if they ran into German tanks which later outflanked them. With the coming of evening, Lt.-Col. Eads G. Hardaway relieved Lt.-Col. Bradford who had to be evacuated to hospital.

To the south of the crossroads, on the Saint-Jean-de-Daye - Pont-Hébert road, the 3rd Bn of the 117th Infantry had advanced courageously along to Les Osmonds. Its advanced position seemed to defy the LXXXIV.A.K. under Generalleutnant von Choltitz whose units were no longer able to communicate with each other. Major-General Corlett considered the positions of his Army Corps units to be satisfactory, all the more so since they had prevented SS-Kgp. Wisliceny from joining up with Kampfgruppe Heintz. However the news that he received was alarming. German troop movements were converging on his lines of defence.

Bradley and Montgomery found the fact that elements

Right, continued from page 39
Heavily covered with freshly cut foliage, the light car looks like a thick bush. It was only 5 ft 2 in wide and this enabled it to thread its way easily along the lanes of the bocage in the Saint-Lô area.
(BA 101 I/585/2182/30a)

Bottom.
Once again, this D7 bulldozer opens the way for the infantry vehicles waiting in the background. As soon as the GIs captured more terrain, these engineer vehicles came up to clear roads and fill shell craters.
(National Archives)

Opposite page.
For these soldiers who had left home and homeland, getting a letter was a very special moment. Risking their lives far from the tenderness of their loved ones, they came to France to fight and enable France to regain its pride once more. Let's hope that the French will be able to hold onto what the GIs won back for them.
(National Archives/Conseil général de Basse-Normandie)

of the Panzer-Lehr Division were leaving the Caumont sector irrational but they could not overlook the possibility of their being engaged in a counter-attack to get rid of the XIXth Army Group's bridgehead to the west of the Vire, which seemed perfectly justified. To the west, 2.SS-Pz.Div., the "Das Reich", seemed to be leaving the VIIth Army Corps front to reform near Le Hommet d'Arthenay. Was it going to join up with Kampfgruppe Wisliceny already engaged against XIXth US Army Corps?

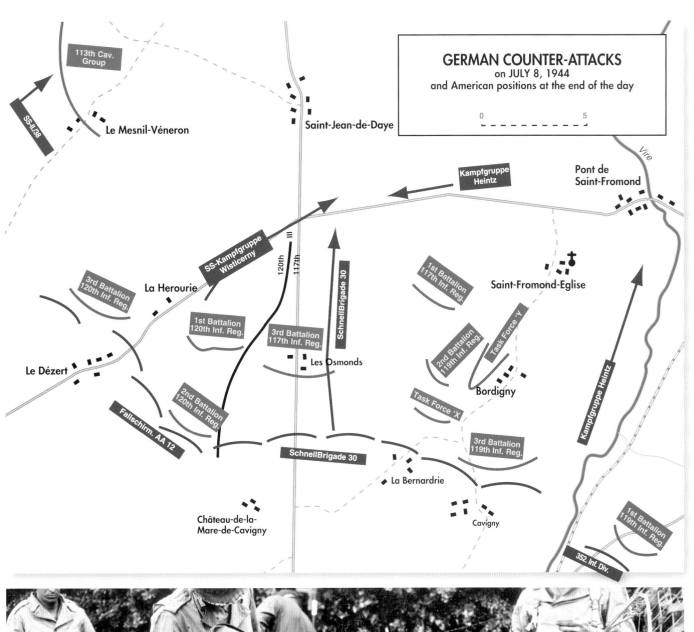

GERMAN COUNTER-ATTACKS
on JULY 8, 1944
and American positions at the end of the day

0   5

113th Cav. Group

SS-11/38

Le Mesnil-Véneron

Saint-Jean-de-Daye

Vire

Kampfgruppe Heintz

Pont de Saint-Fromond

SS-Kampfgruppe Wisticerny

120th

117th

3rd Battalion 120th Inf. Reg.

La Herourie

1st Battalion 120th Inf. Reg.

3rd Battalion 117th Inf. Reg.

SchnellBrigade 30

1st Battalion 117th Inf. Reg.

Saint-Fromond-Eglise

Task Force 'Y'

Le Dézert

Les Osmonds

2nd Battalion 119th Inf. Reg.

Kampfgruppe Heintz

2nd Battalion 120th Inf. Reg.

Task Force 'X'

Bordigny

Fallschirm. AA 12

SchnellBrigade 30

3rd Battalion 119th Inf. Reg.

La Bernardrie

Château-de-la-Mare-de-Cavigny

Cavigny

1st Battalion 119th Inf. Reg.

352. Inf. Div.

When the church bells began ringing and did not stop, the few villagers who had remained in their houses came out intrigued. With bated breath, they left their homes and looked up and down the empty street, then furtively at the town hall where they sighted the first liberators; at the same time a reconnaissance plane flew over. Suddenly a flag, star spangled, appeared at a window. *"So there were a few stars missing from our flag, so what! It was the intention that counted,"* Jacques Petit remembers. *"People felt like crying a bit."*
(National Archives/ Conseil général de Basse-Normandie)

9 JULY 1944

Right.
Heavily laden, these GIs from the 9th US Inf. Div. are rushing to rescue their comrades in the XIXth US Army Corps. The divisional shoulder patch is visible on the medic at right.
(National Archives/ Conseil général de Basse-Normandie)

Left.
Major-General Eddy and his officers are studying the lines of advance for the 9th Division. This unit played a vital role in the success of the XIXth Corps offensive by positioning itself on the left wing of the 30th Division. It faced the toughest adversaries from LXXXIV AK: SS-Kampfgruppe Wisliceny.
(National Archives)

MORE FIGHTING FOR THE "VARSITY"

Above.
The 9th US Infantry Div. shoulder patch

THE RIGHT WING of the XIXth US Army Corps had to be secured. SS-Kampfgruppe Wisliceny was liable to reappear at any moment and the columns of the Panzer-Lehr heading towards the XIXth Army Corps front led the Americans to believe a strong counterattack could be expected.

Reinforcements were needed and Major-General Corlett turned to the VIIth Army Corps which detached its 9th Infantry Division positioned in the Cotentin peninsula. Its CO, Major-General Manton S. Eddy was ordered to position his units rapidly to the north of the Vire-Taute canal and wait for Corlett's instructions. It was still too early to assign any particular objectives.

While waiting for the division to move up, the 113th Cavalry Group reinforced by Combat Command A of the 3rd Armored Division ensured that the XIXth Corps west

flank was secured by remaining on the defensive from the west of La Goucherie up to the southwest of Le Mesnil-Véneron.

The rainy weather considerably slowed down its units' movements. The soldiers were exhausted. They needed sleep and dry uniforms. They had been fighting in the bocage now for two nights and two days. The couple of hours' sleep they managed to snatch here and there were just not enough. It was difficult to sleep in the muddy foxholes with the likelihood – quite frequent - of enemy raids

MAJOR GENERAL EDDY (1892-1962)

Manton Sprague Eddy enlisted in 1916 and fought with the 4th Division in France. In 1941 he was the commander of the 114th Infantry before taking the 9th Infantry Division in 1942. He led this Regular army unit in combat in Tunisia, then Sicily and France. He was entrusted with the XIIth Corps of Patton's 3rd Army in August 1944 and later distinguished himself again by strongly holding the southern shoulder of the Bulge. General Eddy was shipped back to the States in April 1945 on medical grounds and held several major functions after the war. Among his decorations are the Distinguished Service Cross (for Cherbourg), the Distinguished Service Medal, Silver Star, Legion of Merit, Air Medal and Purple Heart; the Order of the Bath, French Légion d'honneur and Croix de guerre, and many Allied decorations. General Eddy died in April 1962, and rests at Arlington National Cemetery. *(National Archives)*

at any moment. The Germans were quite at ease fighting at night.

At 2 am, the GIs were ready to take up the fight again on their company commanders'instructions. Corlett decided to use all possible means to reach the ridge of Les Haut-Vents (Hill 91) situated on the Pont-Hébert – Le Hommet d'Arthenay axis.

The GIs in the 119th US Infantry watched the Combat Command B tanks passing. After leaving La Bernarderie, they headed straight for Les Hauts-Vents, which had been strongly fortified by the Germans. Hill 91 was an excellent observation post for the enemy and Major-General Corlett preferred to attack it under cover of darkness for the surprise to be more effective.

Placed in the centre of the XIXth Army Corps front, Combat Command B of the 3rd Armored Division deployed its Shermans then launched itself forward. The infantry ensured it was protected on its flanks.

Except for the 3rd Bn which remained on the heights situated near Le Dézert, the other two battalions of the 120th Infantry Regiment attacked in the direction of Les Champs de Losque, positioning themselves to the west of the Saint-Jean-de-Daye crossroads. The 743rd Tank Battalion, which had landed at Omaha Beach on 6 June 1944, was attached to the 120th.

The 117th Infantry Regiment had to make CCB's advance easier by securing the Pont-Hébert road which it followed parallel on the west side. The tank busters from the 823rd Tank Destroyer Bn were ready to intervene in case the German armour counter-attacked.

On the left wing of CCB, the 2nd and 3rd Bns of the 119th Infantry had been given a very important mission: capture Pont-Hébert situated to the east of Les Hauts-Vents. If the GIs reached their objective, the road to Saint-Lô would be wide open.

Launching the attack turned out to be difficult because of the mud which clogged up the smaller lanes. Vehicles

Above.
Asphalt-covered roads were a rare thing in the operational zone covered by XIXth US Army Corps. When they were encountered, troop movement could be faster. The GIs were delighted to be able to travel by tank and not to have to walk across the muddy ground. The heavy rains had made some of the lanes completely impassable. Moving on wheels - as shown on this shot - was only possible when the terrain had been cleared by the infantry. If this had not been done, it meant certain death.
(National Archives)

from the 119th Infantry Regiment, which should normally have let the tanks from CCB through, had been brought to a standstill. The tank crews had to wait until these vehicles were towed out, wasting precious time. Bulldozers were called up to drive gaps through the hedges. Once a path had been traced out, the armour followed them then crossed the fields until they were back on the road again. Colonel Ednie of the 119th Infantry was ordered to hold his men back because the armour, which had priority, had to pass through first.

Forewarned by the growling engines, the Germans guessed that an attack was imminent. As a precaution, they contacted their artillery which fired blindly at the XIXth Army Corps lines.

With the first light of dawn, Major-General Corlett knew that the enemy were on their guard and that his corps would probably suffer heavy casualties.

However one of the CCB Task Forces, Task Force Y, managed to advance despite the heavy opposition it encountered from the outset of the attack. It branched off down a sunken lane hidden by all the greenery and its tanks advanced with relative ease.

The German infantry, lacking men and reserves, were in no condition to fight. The GIs following the tanks systematically cleaned out all the resistance points. But suddenly the tank crews' attention was drawn to the right where infantry movements had been spotted. The 75-mm barrels swivelled towards this new threat then spat their shells. Unaware that there were any Shermans present on the Pont-Hébert road, the GIs from the 1st Bn of the 117th Infantry naturally thought that they were the target of some Panzers so they dropped to the spongy ground or hid behind an embankment waiting for the deluge to sweep over them.

Furious, the battalion commander, Lt.-Col. Robert E. Frankland got in touch by radio with CCB which immediately stopped the shelling. The CO of the 117th Infantry,

Colonel Kelly had to clarify the situation on his front. As a precaution, he asked Lt.-Col. McDowell to withdraw his 3rd Bn which he thought to be too far forward in relation to the other two battalions in the regiment, particularly the 1st which had been stopped by the enemy's delaying action. Task Force Z soon joined it on its flank.

Since morning, the 3rd Bn of 119th Infantry had had other worries. First of all, L Company had suffered losses from an enemy machine gun position. Fortunately this had been dealt with by Sergeant John R. Church who succeeded in setting up his mortar less than 150 yards from the enemy MG, and the gunners were all killed.

Encouraged by the results of his shooting, he took another team of machine gunners to task and put them out of action too. Cavigny was taken. S/Sergeant Heinz K. Schwartz captured ten Germans all by himself.

The 30th US Infantry Division opposing SS-Pi. Btl. 2 "Das Reich"

The Germans' stubborn resistance meant that the 3rd Bn of the 119th Infantry used up more ammunition than originally planned for and after supplies had been held up for several hours, its CO, Lieutenant-Colonel Courtney P. Brown had to sort this out by himself. The GMC trucks could not use the roads because they were under enemy fire so there was only one solution: send small groups of men to fetch the ammunition together with water, rations and first-aid supplies. There was another serious problem however: how to evacuate the ever-increasing number of wounded.

In the 120th Infantry Regiment's zone, the 743rd Tank Battalion and B Company from the 2nd Bn attacked first. The rest of the 2nd Bn moved up behind them. Their objective was to reach Hill 32, to the south of Le Dézert

But all the XIXth Army Corps movements were sighted by the German artillery observers perched on the heights,

Above, left.
At the slightest suspicious movement in the hedges or banks, the Shermans spearheading the attack began shooting off their 75–mm guns or raking them with their machine guns. Other tanks were waiting, further back. Here we can see an infantryman on the right of the photo waiting for the signal to move forward. Note the number of foxholes dug in the bank, covered with wood boards. It is quite likely that they belonged to the Germans who, after firing at the tanks, had slipped away through a furrow to the other side, allowing them to get away from the tanks.
(National Archives)

Above.
A team of medics is trying to evacuate an infantry officer over a hedge. The operation is difficult and is really an ordeal for the wounded man. Nobody was safe from a burst of machine gun fire in such a situation, even though the stretcher bearers all show Red Crosses on their helmets and a neutrality flag has been attached to the jeep's bumper.
(National Archives)

MORTARS
IN THE BOCAGE

The Germans had a heavy mortar which was similar to the Americans,' both in weight and calibre. This 8 cm Granatwerfer 34 had a team of three. The firing drill was always the same and this photo report is a perfect demonstration. The observer watches the GIs through his 6 x 30 binoculars. He then transmits the map coordinates to the crew by means of a field telephone, here a captured American EE-8 in its leather carrier.
(BA 101 I/582/2106/26)

Left.
Mortars in bocage country were particularly deadly so they were constantly used by both sides. These two GIs have just fired an 81-mm M1 mortar. Its long, almost 2500-yard range was useless in hedgerow country. On the other hand it was ideal for breaking German attacks at short range: 300 yards minimum. Consisting of three parts: tube, bipod and base plate, it weighed 136 lb. Its rate of fire was 18 rounds a minute. According to an American veteran, when the Fallschirmjäger counter-attacked, the mortar's rate of fire could climb to 30 rounds per minute.
(National Archives)

Opposite page.
According to the coordinates received by phone, one of the crew sets the Granatwerfer with the Richtaufsatz 35 optical sight. Then the loader slides a shell into the barrel whereas the paratrooper at right grasps one of the bipod legs to keep the firing accurate. When the mortar was fired, the crews always lowered their heads to avoid the gas and powder residues. According to the manual, mortar observers were to be found in a field behind the forward machine gun nests, the mortars themselves were sited in dried-up streams or depressions in the terrain.
(BA 101 I/582/2106/32)

Above.
After a few weeks in 'hedgerow hell,' the Fallschirmjäger scarcely had the time to shave. They really looked like pirates. Hygiene conditions were very hard to put up with. The Panzerschütze could remain three whole days, buttoned up inside their Panzers; the Grenadiere and the Fallschirmjäger could stay the same length of time in their foxholes… To relieve themselves there was only one solution: use an empty shell case or a mess tin.
(BA101 I/582.2106/35)

Right
These Waffen-SS huddling near a farm gate seem to be waiting for an approaching tank. In a moment, the soldier on the right is going to stand up, shoulder his Panzerfaust weapon and aim it at the target. His comrade is going to cover him with his 98 K rifle. There are only two possible outcomes: either the hollow charge will take out the tank or both these brave soldiers will die, side by side on the road, their chests torn apart by a burst from the co-axial machine gun.
(DR)

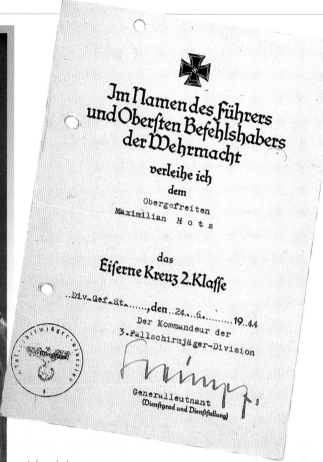

Left and above.
Obergefreiter Hotz of 3./Fallsch. Aufkl. Abt.12 was awarded the Iron Cross 2d Class for his valour in Normandy on June 24, 1944. He was wounded on 9 July and evacuated to Rennes, then Paris and Strasbourg. The award diploma is signed in ink by Generalleutnant Schimpf, commanding the 3. FJD.
(Jean-Yves Nasse collection)

Below.
Gefreiter Wilhelm Grode. *(Tanguy Le Sant collection)*

This mess tin lid was dug out near Le Dézert in Normandy. The soldier, Wilhelm Grode, had etched his name on it. Grode was killed on July 8, 1944 near where the lid was found. Later on, T. Le Sant tracked down the soldier's brother, who provided the following details. W. Grode was a Gefreiter when he fell. He was born in Hindenburg (Silesia) on July 20, 1924. He belonged to 2./Fallschirm-Aufklärungs-Abt. 12, his identity disk bore the markings *624-Flpl. Kdo.A. 9/VII*. Grode was first interred at Ruffey, near Saint-Lô, and later transferred to Orglandes (Manche department).
(Tanguy Le Sant collection)

Colonel Birks was surprised to find out that Fallschirm-Aufklärungs-Abteilung 12 had set up a line of defence to the north-east of Le Dézert, which was used as the base for SS-Kampfgruppe Wisliceny's counter-attack.

Towards 11 am, the GIs from 120th Infantry heard engines growling. *"The Panzers are coming right at us!"* could be heard from the 2nd Bn lines. In fact it was only motorised infantry, for the moment.

For an hour and a half, the 2/120th Infantry fought against soldiers who were like devils unleashed. They were mainly sappers from the Engineer battalion of the "Das Reich" armoured division (SS-Pi. Btl.2), war-hardened veterans of the Russian front accustomed to close-quarter combat. However, despite their lack of experience the GIs managed to hold on to their positions.

At 13.00 the Waffen-SS withdrew. The Kdr. of SS-Pi. Btl.2, SS-Hauptsturmführer Brosow immediately got in touch with the CO of 14./ "D", SS-Hauptsturmführer Hilber. The support of this company was essential for launching another onslaught. Unfortunately, his soldiers had left all their equipment at the rear and therefore had to fight as mere infantrymen.

SS-Oberscharführer Balfanz (3./SS-Pz. Pi. Btl. 2) which operated near Le Hommet, drove off several counter-attacks. Although he had lost all contact with the battalion, Balfanz elected to stick to his guns. During the next few days he distinguished himself several times, particularly near the Chateau d'Esglandes, where he repulsed the Americans yet again with barely a handful of Pioniere. His bravery was rewarded with the German Cross in gold.

Colonel Birks' men barely had time to congratulate themselves and gobble down a few spoonfuls of rations when, at 14.30, Brosow's Waffen-SS appeared, quite intent on retaking the terrain abandoned by their third company. Their unit turned out to be particularly powerful with its 150-mm Hummel self propelled guns and its five SdKfz 251 half-tracks.

All hell was let loose on the right wing of the 2nd Bn of the 120th Infantry. Shermans from the 743rd Tank Bn tried to force their way through the bocage to rush the German half-tracks. Suddenly there were explosions all around them. The Panzer IVs of SS-Unterstrumführer Boska were attacking in order to try to stop them.

According to the 3rd Armored Division intelligence, fifty or so tanks had been on their way to the 30th Infantry Division's front during the morning. The American crews were now caught in a trap. They could neither advance nor retreat. The 743rd Tank Bn's after-action report declares: *"The battalion found itself dangerously isolated after the first attack by enemy armor. B Company of the 743rd was lured away by two Panzers used as decoys.*

The Shermans drove down a narrow lane which ended at a crossroads then reached a spot about 200 yards from a farm situated near the road. Hidden behind the farm's buildings were the Panzers from 6./SS-Pz. Rgt. 2 which opened fire then slipped away along a smaller road."

Caught broadsides on, the Sherman crews were taken completely by surprise. Very quickly Brosow's sappers and the soldiers from Hilber's Flak Company set upon them. In 15 minutes B Company was wiped out and the tank crews had to abandon their tanks.

During the day, B Company lost 12 tanks of which three had to be abandoned. Left with no armoured support, the 2nd Bn of the 120th Infantry was outflanked by the sappers from SS-Obersturmführer Macher's 16/ "D". This Waffen-SS officer was keen to take part in the bloody hand to hand fighting and fought alongside his men.

Above.
Briefing for the following day's fighting for K Company, 120th Infantry. On the left, facing the camera: Staff Sergeant John Adams; on the right, kneeling: Pfc. James R. Googe (killed in action); kneeling in the centre, speaking: Captain Marvin M. Smith (wounded during the counter-attack on 11 July 1944); Staff Sergeant Frank Wylie, leaning on his knee and looking at Captain Smith.
(Photo: John Adams)

Above right.
An 88-mm shell has hit the front of this M16 belonging to the 486th AAA Bn. The crew posing for the camera in front of their machine had a close shave...
(3rd Armored Division Association)

in particular on Les Hauts Vents.

Although the attack had started early, it was slowed down by supply problems and vehicle congestion. This waste of time allowed Generalleutnant von Choltitz and his staff to concert and then call up the necessary reinforcements. He did not hesitate to take troops away from various sectors so as to concentrate all his effort on the XIXth Army Corps.

The German armour's advance was spotted to the south of Saint-Lô but the only thing that General Hobbs could do was warn his officers of the danger. Anti-tank guns were sent hastily to back up the infantry and a large number of bazookas was distributed. The artillery was alerted and the tension mounted hour by hour. One thing was certain: the Germans were going to launch one or several counter-attacks.

The fiercest resistance was in the sector of the 2nd Bn of the 120th Infantry Regiment. For two hours the Doughboys were held up by groups of Grenadiere attacking from the west and the east. They responded with all their weapons, supported by the tanks from the 743rd Tank Bn, but their opponents did not yield an inch of ground.

The Grenadiere from Kampfgruppe Heintz of 275. I.D. were crushed by the XIXth US Army Corps forces to which the "Spearhead" was attached for a few days. The Germans it came across on the way were not merely young Heer recruits who were content to honour their pledge as soldiers; they also included the paratroopers and the soldiers from SS-Kampfgruppe Wisliceny, who turned out to be fearsome adversaries. As a general rule, the GIs of the 3rd Armored Division respected their foe. But after 15 August this turned into fierce hatred when they discovered the body of the 708th Tank Destroyer Battalion's CO, who had been captured by a Waffen-SS patrol, riddled with bullets.
(National Archives)

The American battalion's CO, Lieutenant-Colonel William S. Bradford, was killed and whole groups of GIs lost their grip. They fell back 400 yards to the rear.

Supported by their artillery, the sappers under SS-Obersturmführer Macher had now reached the 1/120th Infantry positions. The latter was beginning to suffer heavy casualties.

Fortunately the GIs could count on the 18 battalions of corps artillery which shelled the sector to prevent Fallschirm.-Aufklärungs-Abteilung 12 from taking part.

Oberjäger Paul, a veteran sharpshooter in 4./Fallschirm.-Aufklärungs-Abteilung 12, recalls: *"Day after day, there were more and more enemy tanks. We had set up a line of defence which enabled us to hold off the Americans. We Scharfschützen (sharpshooters) played an important role. We had to get rid of the artillery observers and then slip away.*

If we didn't, when our infantry attacked according to a plan drawn up by the forward CPs, the enemy artillery and mortars wiped out our counter-attacks. When our heavy guns let off one or two salvoes, they drew in enemy fighter-bombers or artillery. During one of these barrages, our ammunition trucks were hit and everything went up."

In spite of the fact that his forces were not up to strength,

SS-Obersturmführer Macher re-established the front line in his sector. In order to avoid any nasty surprises, he asked one platoon to mine their position's approaches.

During the evening, his Pioniere drove back three attacks, one after the other. Although the last was led by Shermans, the Waffen-SS still managed to hold their line of defence. SS-Unterscharführer Fahl distinguished himself by destroying a Sherman with a Teller mine! Several elements of I/ "D" tried to attack the 3rd Bn of the 117th Infantry which was positioned on the left of the 2nd Bn of the 120th Infantry. But for want of heavy support, they were compelled to turn back.

Encouraged by Kampfgruppe Wisliceny's successes, SS-Obersturmführer Boska sent two platoons of Pz. IVs from his company northwards along the Saint-Lô road.

These Panzers first surprised the GIs in the 1st Bn of the 117th Infantry who tended to give way to panic. But their officers soon had things under control again.

The battalion's CO, Lieutenant-Colonel Robert E. Frankland, got in touch with divisional headquarters who hurried some M-10s from the 823rd Tank Destroyer Bn to him. Fifteen minutes later, the GIs had resumed their positions and the Panzers from 6.Kp. were chased off by the shots from the TDs.

The GIs were now relieved. The Waffen-SS had gone and the tank destroyers were there to back them up. All was well. Steadfast, they waited for the next tank attack and knowing the fate that was in store for the enemy they were almost satisfied to see more tanks rolling up along the road, their barrels pointing towards them.

The tank destroyers crews immediately jumped into action. In less than a minute, the Dogfaces heard them shoot off their 75-mm shells at the reckless Panzers.

When the two leading tanks were ablaze, the GIs noticed with surprise and then horror that the tanks were American. They belonged to I Company from Task Force Y, 33rd Armored Regiment. They had approached the road from the east. It must be remembered that after

SS-Obersturmführer Heinz Macher
Joining the Waffen-SS in the Dresden 2. Kp. Pionier-bataillon in April 1939, he took part in the Dutch and French Campaigns then went to officer cadet school. In October 1942, he was appointed CO of 16./SS-Pz. Gren. Rgt. "Deutschland" which he led in Normandy. He was decorated with the Knight's Cross in April 1943, during the Battle of Kharkov, followed by the German Cross in gold in August 1944, rewarding his leadership under fire between 9 and 17 July 1944. At the beginning of August 1944, he was in command of II./SS-Pz. Gren. Rgt. "Deutschland" with the rank of Hauptsturmführer. He was wounded during the fighting for Bourg-Saint-Léonard in the Falaise Pocket and was evacuated. He returned to active duty in the Heeresgruppe Weichsel and for the defence of Küstrin.
(J. Charita collection)

leaving La Borderie, they had crossed some fields without much visibility. By chance they had taken a sunken lane hardly defended by the Germans, then headed north, convinced they were heading for their own lines. It was a tragedy, just like many others that took place during the fighting in the bocage. Worried and confused by the environment which reduced their visibility, soldiers did not always know where friendly troops were. They often fired at the slightest noise without even seeing the enemy.

The lack of coordination between the units in this warren of country lanes was frequently responsible for this sort of tragedy. Each platoon's exact movements and position were not always known by the company commanders. When one of them scattered in front of the enemy, there was not always time to inform the command echelon.

But a new artillery barrage, an hour-long, reversed the situation. The Germans suffered heavy losses and this took the pressure off. As a result, the 1st Bn of the 120th Infantry regained confidence and defended its positions more firmly. They drove the Waffen-SS back then rejoined their comrades from the 2nd Bn.

This time, the 120th US Infantry had set up an impenetrable defensive wall and the Pont-Hébert – Saint-Jean-de-Daye road was completely clear of any enemy. Unfortunately it had suffered heavy casualties partly due to the 230th Field Artillery's inaccurate shooting caused by the lack of visibility. In one hour it had fired off 3 000 shells.

The 3rd Bn of the 120th Infantry Regiment, still entrenched on the heights near Le Dézert was powerless and had not been able to intervene. It had to weather the German artillery barrage without being able to help the regiment's other two battalions. They spent the day waiting in their foxholes for the enemy attack which never came and were pleasantly surprised to see the first elements of the 9th Infantry Division arriving at dusk. At 18.30, SS-Kampfgruppe Wisliceny was forced to fall back or risk being wiped out. SS-Obersturmführer Boska left

behind five Pz. IVs from his 6.Kp. on the battlefield. The German counter-attack to the west of the Saint-Lô road had completely failed.

As for Major-General Corlett, he regretted that his infantry battalions had not advanced further. He asked General Bohm to reach Les Hauts Vents, the day's final objective, before nightfall.

The plan was as follows: Task Force Y was to head for Pont-Hébert using the road where two of its tanks had been destroyed. Task Force Z would try to protect its right flank by advancing along the main roads and the lanes. As for Task Force X, it would take Les Hauts Vents with the infantry.

Bertrand Close and Task Force Y

A young historian and valued colleague, Alexis Boban has got hold of the precious eye-witness account from Bertrand Close, one of Sergeant Lafayette Pool's crew. *"In the Mood"*, his tank, was part of I Company of the 3rd Bn of the 32nd Armored Regiment (Task force Y). Whilst Michael Wittmann is considered to be the greatest armour ace of WWII with 138 tanks and 132 anti-tank guns destroyed in three years'campaigning, Sergeant Pool is mentioned in the official history of the 3rd Armored Division as the Number One Tanker of WWII with 258 enemy vehicles (off all types) destroyed between 27 June and 15 September 1944.

Veteran Close recalls: *"Our company received some more tanks; we had lost 12 between 29 and 30 June 1944. My tank commander was sergeant Lafayette Pool. Our tank was the only one in the company with a 76-mm gun.*

At dawn we took a winding lane then passed through some hedges which had been cleared earlier and moved off across the grazing land beyond. Our tanks progressed one after the other, shooting at all the hedges we came across with our machine guns and main gun. We could see no German soldiers anywhere. We were not very happy because we had found out after our first battle that

S/Sgt Lafayette Pool.

An infantry division's GI in Normandy. His steel helmet is covered with a net intertwined with hessian strips, as learned from British soldiers. His uniform is the standard issue to all troops: a cotton field jacket with wool shirt and trousers. At this time, but not for long, the American soldier was still shod with shoes and leggings. His combat gear comprises a rifle belt, supporting the first aid packet pouch. More rounds for the M1 Garand rifle are carried in disposable bandoleers across the chest. The light gas mask bag is slung under the left arm, and mostly holds personal belongings and rations.
(Reconstruction, photo Militaria Magazine)

the enemy hid when our tanks went past then destroyed them once we had our backs turned.

We advanced slowly across a field. The gunner of one tank opened fire on the roof of a tall building a few hundred yards away. The shell exploded exactly where an observer had been positioned.

When we reached the edge of the field we came up against a hedgerow which we had to get through. Suddenly without any warning, the leading Sherman burst into flames, shot at by an anti-tank weapon.

The crew succeeded in bailing out and joined the four or five infantrymen who had been following their tank. To cover them, I opened fire with the machine gun in the direction of the hedge from which the shot had come. The tank crew and the GIs ran to get under cover behind our tank.

One of the crew was not under cover and, in front of our tank, guided the tank driver by hand to help him turn the machine around.

Then we waited behind a hedge. Soon some P-47s appeared and strafed the area where the anti-tank gun was supposed to be. The planes – there were three or four of them – made several passes at less than three hundred feet above our heads. It was the closest air support that I ever saw in the whole war. They must have done a good job for I saw black smoke rising from behind the hedge.

We returned to the fields which we had left and crossed through three more without encountering any opposition. We took a met-alled road which led to Pont-Hébert. As the leading tank, we took the high street of a village. There were three-storey houses on either side of the street.

Armored Infantry ran along both sides of the street, covering each other as they moved forward door by door. German snipers or tanks could be lying in ambush anywhere. We were sitting ducks and fearing anti-tank fire we opened fire on a doubtful building. We reached the end of the street. We didn't come across any civilians or any Germans. The place was deserted. Finally we reached a street where there was a little stone bridge over a narrow stream. We did not cross it. It was then that I saw a signpost marked Pont-Hébert (…)"

Task Force X – 3rd US Armored Division

The Task force X tanks rushed off to their objective as fast as possible. Their CO, Lieutenant-Colonel Samuel L. Hogan, had ordered the crews to take the heights at Les Hauts Vents before nightfall. There was not much time left. The hill was in sight when they were formally ordered not to take it. General Bohm was furious. His tanks were on the point of brushing aside the German resistance which was beginning to give way, and now they had to set up defensive positions until the following day!

In fact Task Force X no longer had infantry support. It had not been able to keep up and now its flanks were completely unprotected meaning the unit risked being destroyed if the Germans attacked. Hogan's tank crews settled down a mile from the heights they vowed they would take at dawn.

At the Task Force X command post, there was a certain amount of anxiety: seven tanks from I Company were still unaccounted for. None of the crews answered the radio signals, which was hardly surprising in those rugged landscapes. They had probably got lost. Lieutenant-Colonel Hogan had to wait several hours before there was any information. Radio contact was established. The tanks were on the heights that the Task Force had to take! *"We're on Hill 91 and our planes think we're Germans,"* a tank commander was shouting to anybody who would listen. *"Get back here,"* Hogan ordered. *"Impossible, the Germans would spot us. It's best for us to stay here until dawn and wait for the Task Force,"* was the reply from a young petrified sergeant. *"Okay"*, Lieutenant-Colonel Hogan agreed in spite of himself, rather doubtful as to whether the seven tanks were really on those heights anyway. Many tank commanders had trouble finding their position on their maps, especially with all the subsequent counter-orders which often confused matters.

Near Belle Lande, Task Force Z fought hard during the night. The 3rd Bn of the 33rd Armored Regiment lost almost all its tank commanders. But there were also some triumphs: in the first fifteen minutes of the confrontation, a tank crew commanded by Sergeant Dean Balderson knocked out three Pz. IVs.

This incident is mentioned in *Spearhead in the West* (the 3rd Armored Division's History): *"Sergeant Dean Balderson had got out of his tank at dawn when his machine gunner, Corporal "Swede" Anderson, suddenly spotted the enemy. Four German tanks were positioned on the road, their guns pointing the opposite way, waiting for a company of the 33rd Armored Regiment to appear.*

Anderson's first shot, an HE shell, hit the tank on the turret. All hell was let loose. The enemy tank blew up in a huge flame and a lot of black smoke.

The other Panzers, alerted by the explosion, got moving straight away. Excited, Anderson asked for an armor-piercing shell, but his loader, Pfc. Bill Wilson, slammed in another HE shell. Another direct hit like the first and the second Panzer exploded. Wilson used an AP shell for the third and the gunner sent it into the third tank."

This time the American tank crews were fortunate. The Germans remained where they were.

TASK FORCE X AT LES

UNDER THE POURING RAIN, the Shermans got into position. The crews had barely slept and all during the night they had heard the rain drumming on the armour of their tanks. Most of them had remained inside their machines.

The Task Force X columns dashed towards Les Hauts Vents. The tankers were worried because they could only use a very narrow track allowing a single vehicle to pass at a time. It was a real nightmare. When a Sherman broke down, the whole column ground to a halt and the men had to wait for the recovery vehicles to come up. Progress was very slow and rather demoralising.

Here and there one could hear shooting and the tank commanders popped back down inside their turrets. Enemy snipers often hit their targets then vanished into thin air. 12.7 mm machine guns copiously sprayed SS-Kgp Wisliceny's Waffen-SS's supposed positions.

Suddenly at dawn there was a thunderclap. A Sherman had just been hit. A PaK had just fired. The leading crews wanted to shoot back but they got in each other's way. Only two tanks were in a position to react but by the time the 75–mm guns were aimed, the German anti-tank gun had already vanished. The Americans therefore fired blindly. They would never know whether or not they had hit their target.

"Deploy on either side of the road," they heard over the radio.

Suddenly SS-I/"D" went into action, with explosions coming from the rear of the column. Task Force X was being beset from all sides. Snipers from 16./"D" took out three tank commanders standing in their turrets and the situation got worse because the Shermans were getting within range of concentrated fire from 88-mm Flak guns.

Then the artillery took over, its 10.5-cm guns firing from the heights. Lieutenant-Colonel Hogan was furious. If he'd had his way the day before, the hill would have been taken and lives would have been saved. The Waffen-SS had obviously been reinforced during the night under cover of darkness.

"Task Force X is in a bad situation. It's impossible for us to advance on our objective," Hogan cursed.

General Bohn, commanding Combat Command B asked another Task Force, which was not far away, to attack Hill 91 but the Z tanks had their work cut out disengaging the 119th Infantry near La Belle Lande. More-

Above.
When the recce patrols had secured the area (two of their light vehicles can be made out in the shade of the trees) and when the terrain allowed, the tank crews carried infantrymen with them. This photo, however taken after the battle, clearly illustrates how Americans troops advanced during the battle for Saint-Lô
(National Archives)

Left.
Crammed with prisoners, this GMC from the 83rd Armored Reconnaissance Bn of the 3rd Armored Division is hurrying to the rear. This unit was the first to capture a German town, Roetgen, on 12 September 1944.
(National Archives)

HAUTS VENTS

In this rare action shot, Americans are firing back with a 3-inch (90 mm) antitank gun, which was operated by some towed Tank Destroyer battalions. This piece was more than often as effective as the M-10 Gun Motor Carriage. The gun has not been camouflaged and must have commenced firing as soon as it was unhitched from its tractor.
(National Archives)

Left and far left.
Colonel Roysden, commanding Combat Command B and the 33rd Armored Regiment.
This portrait of Roysden was taken after the three days' intense fighting on Hill 91, Les Hauts Vents, on 10 July 1944. The following day he managed to drive back several German counter-attacks with his considerably weakened Task Force. His armour left the heights early in the afternoon of 16 July 1944.
(3rd US Armored Division Association)

over, all that infantry regiment's units were still being moved up, once again held up by all the traffic congestion in the rear.

For some unknown reason, General Bohn was replaced by Colonel Dorrance S. Roysden. It could be that the decision was taken at a meeting between General Hobbs, General Watson, Colonel Ednie and Roysden himself. The purpose of the meeting was to clarify the situation and to redefine the units' missions. The result was, once again, that taking Les Hauts Vents was the day's priority.

The 30th Infantry Division at Belle Lande

Task Force Z, who was to take Hill 91, would be supported by the 3rd Bn of the 119th Infantry. They would attack La Belle Lande then Pont-Hébert, and head for and reach la Futelaie, taking the German defences set up on Les Hauts Vents from the rear.

As for the 3rd Bn of the 120th Infantry, relieved by the 9th Infantry Division which had just reached the XIXth Army Corps operational zone, they had to get hold of Le Rocher, situated to the west of Les Hauts Vents. The 1st Bn of the 120th Infantry was waiting, ready to support them, as were the Combat Command B tanks.

Oberjäger Paul (Fallschirm. Aufklärungs-Abt.12) found himself right in the path of the 3/120th Infantry. He recalls what happened: *"First of all, the Americans thought that our battalion no longer existed after all the intensive artillery barrages and fighter-bomber attacks we'd been through. They were surprised to see us spring up out of our foxholes at a distance of 20 or 30 yards firing with our individual weapons and machine guns. I survived more than one such situation, where our casualties increased at a terrifying rate. Our line of defence was getting thinner and thinner."*

Right.
This 76-mm gun Sherman equipped with a hedge cutter belonged to the 32nd US Armored Regiment. This armoured unit's motto was "Victory or Death." Commanded by Colonel Boudinot, the 32nd was engaged for the first time in Normandy at Villers-Fossard on 29 June 1944. Its reconnaissance company and 2nd Bn were awarded the Distinguished Unit Citation.
(National Archives)

GIs are scattering from this house which is now the target of German artillery. One of the shells has hit the roof of an isolated building which has caught fire.
(National Archives)

The Signal Corps original caption indicates that these two men have just shot a sniper, although this is more than likely a staged shot. An SCR-536 handie-talkie can be seen at the shoulder of the pistol-toting NCO. Three German grenadiere lie dead in the orchard. On of them had donned his camouflaged tent section, and a non-regulation net covers his steel helmet. This was probably cut from a larger net for artillery gun pits.
(National Archives)

The plan was more than bold, it was almost suicidal: the 3rd Bn of the 120th Infantry had to break through the German lines then move on, far to the south of the Saint-Lô – Le Hommet d'Arthenay road.

When the 3rd Bn of the 119th Infantry was ready to launch the attack, the 1st Bn took over its former positions. Their objective was to support the 3rd Bn by taking La Bessinière.

As for the regiment's 2nd Bn, it remained to the west of the Pont-Hébert/Saint-Jean-de-Daye road. Its mission was to take La Belle Lande then Pont-Hébert. The GIs had

barely started forward when they ran into a solidly entrenched enemy and had to give up La Belle Lande for the time being. There was fierce shooting from both sides. Four Panzer IVs from 6./SS-Pz Rgt. 2. went for the Americans.

Colonel Ednie from the 119th Infantry Regiment thought that elements from 2.SS-Pz. Div. "Das Reich" were facing his regiment. The fighting lasted until the end of the afternoon but no terrain was gained by either side.

At 19.50, Major-General Corlett assigned two platoons from E Company of the 32nd Armored Regiment (a unit in Task Force Y) to Ednie, to support his infantry which had been ordered to invest La Belle Lande where four Pz. IVs were thought to be positioned. The tank destroyers from Task Force Y were to place themselves on the height overlooking the Pont-Hébert road. Corlett's decision was firm and brooked no argument.

Under a heavily clouded, grey sky, the air was cool. The GIs in 2nd Bn of the 119th Infantry were reassured by the presence of E Company's tanks. They finally advanced towards la Belle Lande. They spotted the tank destroyers further away, advancing towards a low hill. They were sure that La Belle Lande would fall and that Pont Hébert would be in their hands before the end of the day.

Suddenly there was a dry clacking sound from the direction of the hill the TDs were heading for. One of them started

In its other configuration, the Browning Cal. 50 (12.7 mm) M2 machine gun was used as an anti-aircraft weapon. It was the heaviest automatic weapon used by American infantry units. It had a rate of fire of 450 rpm. It could be semi-automatic or fully automatic, reloading by recoil. The ammunition box placed near the machine gun contains a 105-round metal ammunition belt. This exceptional weapon is still in service with a number of countries.
(National Archives)

burning, its outline making it a perfect target; the other tanks dispersed like a flight of sparrows. Using his episcope the gunner in one of the Shermans of E Company swivelled onto a German vehicle which was hurrying at full speed towards La Belle Lande. A well-placed shot and it became a flaming wreck. But that had only been a harmless lorry. The three Panzer IVs dug in up to the turret near the village were quite another kettle of fish...

With an angry rumbling of engines punctuated by the deafening explosions, shells started falling all over the Panzers. The sodden earth was thrown up in sprays of mud.

Fear overcame the GIs. At one time or another they would have become the prey of the tanks but for the support of the artillery. G company leading the advance met with slight opposition within sight of Belle Lande which it dealt with easily. Its CO, Lieutenant Krause then sent a

patrol towards the village which came back shortly afterwards reporting that everything looked quiet.

Krause sent his men forward. They took over the empty streets, but suddenly ran headlong into crossfire from machine guns. One GI was killed and others wounded, including the company commander. Near him one of the GIs screamed horribly, rolling over to stare at the sky, his throat torn open.

Trembling, the officer snatched the microphone that the radio operator handed to him. *"Fall back, everybody. We're going to get this place blown to hell!"*

Although weakened by his wound, Lieutenant Krause gave short and precise orders. Ten minutes later all the GIs had assembled at the northern end of the town. Further orders had them establish defensive positions. In a sorry state, Lieutenant Krause asked Lieutenant Earl to

help him eliminate the German tanks.

Out of breath, the GIs dug holes in the embankment, setting up positions along the paths. Soon they could be heard shouting: *"Watch out, the Krauts are coming!"*

Few soldiers could see their opponents. The others could only hear them and try to guess where they were.

The three Pz. IVs from Bolka Company who were leading the attack were barely able to see any better. They let their intuition guide them. When they reached the spot where the G Company soldiers were waiting, they opened fire point blank into the hedgerows, which they also sprayed with their machine guns.

The monstrous racket of the explosions in the middle of splintering branches and leaves, clods of earth and flying stones terrified the GIs. All they could do was do what the Germans were doing: fire blindly.

Suddenly Lieutenant Krause spotted the outline of a Pz. IV. He called the crew of an antitank gun, who could hear the sound of his voice but could not make out what he was saying because of the din. Krause pointed to the tank. Hardly had the gun been aimed that the Panzer disappeared after firing a burst with its machine gun - and Lieutenant Krause was wounded for the second time that day.

For T/Sgt. Guy M. Robinson, the situation was different. A large number of Grenadiere were heading towards his platoon. They were not under cover and had not yet spotted the Americans. *"Don't fire at them until you can see the whites of their eyes!"* he ordered.

The GIs held their breath while the enemy got nearer and nearer. They had fixed bayonets. The firing lasted barely a minute, several Grenadiere were lying on the ground, lifeless or twisting in agony. The others rushed at the Americans, yelling to bolster their courage.

The GIs were paralysed by the idea of the hand-to-hand fighting which was going to follow. Their faces expressed a nameless terror when Robinson got hit by a bullet. One of the NCO's close friends, Private William Seldom, wanted to avenge him. He warned the men that he was taking command of the platoon and then screamed: *"I'll kill the first one who pulls back. Now get rid of all these Krauts for me!"*

The German counter-attack was broken but Belle Lande had still not been taken.

Scouts from the 119th Infantry informed Colonel Ednie's HQ that German forces situated to the east of the Vire had opened fire on their unit.

Although in the 3rd Bn of the 120th Infantry sector the situation was less tense, it had nonetheless not been able to reach Les Haut Vents from the west. They were halted at Le Rocher where German resistance was particularly fierce.

Meanwhile, the 9th Infantry Division had deployed in an arc between Graignes – the east of Le Hommet wood – Le Dézert. On its left flank was the 2nd Bn of the 120th Infantry and on its right flank the 83rd Infantry Division which was part of VIIth Army Corps.

The 9th Infantry Division vs. SS-Kampfgruppe Wilisceny

The troopers of 113th Cavalry Group which had been in the La Goucherie sector for two days had tied down SS-Pz. Gren. Rgt. 38. Finally the 60th Infantry of the 9th Division joined them. These two units got to know each other fighting together, side by side.

The 60th Infantry managed to clear the Graignes Peninsula without too much difficulty. On their way to Tribehou however, they ran into strong opposition which halted them for the day.

The 47th Infantry Regiment was ordered to proceed towards Le Hommet wood and was placed on the left wing of the 60th Infantry and the 113th Cavalry. But what the GIs did not know was that they were going to run into strong opposition from the Waffen-SS under SS-Obersturmführer Macher. However it was only the 4th platoon of the 16./"D", twenty or so sappers in all but quite determined to hold their ground no matter what happened.

This platoon comprised sMG Gruppe Naujocks and the Granatwerfergruppe under SS-Unterscharführer Hanke. To get rid of this dangerous lynchpin, the American commander first used artillery, which did not do Macher's sappers much harm. Then the armour was called in to support the 47th Infantry, ordered to clear the sector. Fate was waiting for them…

Very skilfully placed and concealed from the Americans, the 81-mm mortars under Unterscharführer Hanke caught the Sherman crews by surprise. One of the tanks received several direct hits in a row and in a few seconds

A GI grabs a little sleep while another remains on the alert. Rations have been issued as can be seen from the boxes at right, one of which reads: 'US Army Field Rations Type C.' The C ration was the regular staple for men in the field, comprising mostly meat and vegetable canned preparations, plus biscuits, powdered coffee and sugar. The other box is for K-rations, a sort of lighter, easily carried combat ration, meant to be eaten cold.
(National Archives)

was a fiery furnace. The crew was burnt alive in the hull.

As soon as the sMG Gruppe opened fire, there was panic among the ranks of the 47th Infantry. Then there were the small groups of Waffen-SS screaming *"O, Deutschland hoch in Ehren!"* (lit. "Germany, high in Honour"), who threw themselves against the GIs in fierce and bloody hand to hand fighting. The assault continued inexorably. On the right wing of the heavy platoon of the 16./ "D", the Pioniere of 4./SS-Pz. Pi. Btl.2 had to give way. Refusing defeat, SS-Sturmführer Schmelzer gathered his men then launched them into a fierce counterattack. Confronted with such demons, the GIs in turn fell back. Well versed in this type of fighting, the Waffen-SS suffered fewer casualties than the Americans.

Ten or so Shermans were brought up to try and get the better of 16./"D". Informed by SS-Obersturmführer Macher that an attack against his company was imminent, SS-Obersturmbannführer Wisliceny told him he'd be coming over and to be ready for him. The Kdr of the SS-Kampfgruppe was intent on showing the young Pioniere that bravery was not the privilege of just the other ranks but of their officers too.

At around 17.00, Wisliceny and his young soldiers took some American tanks to task in a sunken lane. Stick grenades flew through the air before falling on their targets and the hollow charges of the Panzerfausts gave off a strident scream as they left the tube. Two Shermans were hit and evacuated by their crews with lightning speed. The other tanks reversed carefully still firing blindly into the hedgerows.

Suddenly a jet of flames shooting out of one of the embankments just missed one of the Shermans. This was Unterscharführer Dornleden using his flamethrower. The result was terrifying. A duel took place between the sapper and the tank crew which lasted for a few terrifying minutes for the two adversaries.

The Sherman and seven others managed to get away without casualties or damage. They regrouped and then returned to the attack a few hundred yards from the sunken lane where they had just lost two of their number. This time they ran into the first and the second platoons of

Macher's company. The American crews had to face the dangerous flamethrowers once again.

Another tank disappeared in a sheet of flames and two Pioniere were killed by the co-axial machine gun just as one of them was introducing the ignition round into his Flammenwerfer. The weapon could not be fired without this bullet being struck.

It was only at 8.20 pm that the GIs from the 9th Infantry Division and the leftovers of the armoured company finally withdrew once and for all, back to their departure line.

Shortly afterwards, the medics in Macher's company started looking after the wounded as quickly as possible with the limited means at their disposal. The Waffen-SS had to look after themselves. Suddenly there was a shot and SS-Unterscharführer Wegener crumpled up. This *Sanitäter*'s (medic) death shocked the Pioniere but this sort of incident was far from exceptional during the Battle of Saint-Lô, on both sides.

Finally, the 3rd Bn of the 39th got into position on either side of the road leading to Le Dézert. Its geographical location was set back from the XIXth US Army Corps' front line and there was almost a gap between the 9th and the 30th Infantry Divisions.

In Major-General Corlett's command post

When at the end of the day, Major-General Corlett looked at his front line, he discovered that his units had achieved a real leap forward but that their progress had been halted, or almost, by increasing German resistance. La Belle Lande, Les Hauts Vents, Pont Hébert, Le Bois du Hommet and Tribehou were still in the hands of the LXXXIV.A.K.

"Tomorrow is going to be another difficult day," General Hobbs of the 30th Infantry Division announced, *"the Panzer-Lehr tanks are going to rush us."*

"It's not just the Panzers, it's also the Panzergrenadiere", answered his chief-of-staff. The CO of the Panzer-Lehr, Generalleutnant Fritz Bayerlein, said the following about his division after the war, *"It was the best armoured division in the German army."* Committed in the Villers-Bocage area, it was relieved by the 276.I.D. before being transferred to Saint-Lô on 7 July 1944. Its task was to drive back the XIXth Army Corps. Taking advantage of the bad weather which prevented any Allied air activity, the Panzer-Lehr reached the south of the Saint-Lô road using two different routes. But it was only during the night of 10-11 July 1944 that most of the organic units were really in place. Generalleutnant Bayerlein was then ordered to counter-attack at dawn.

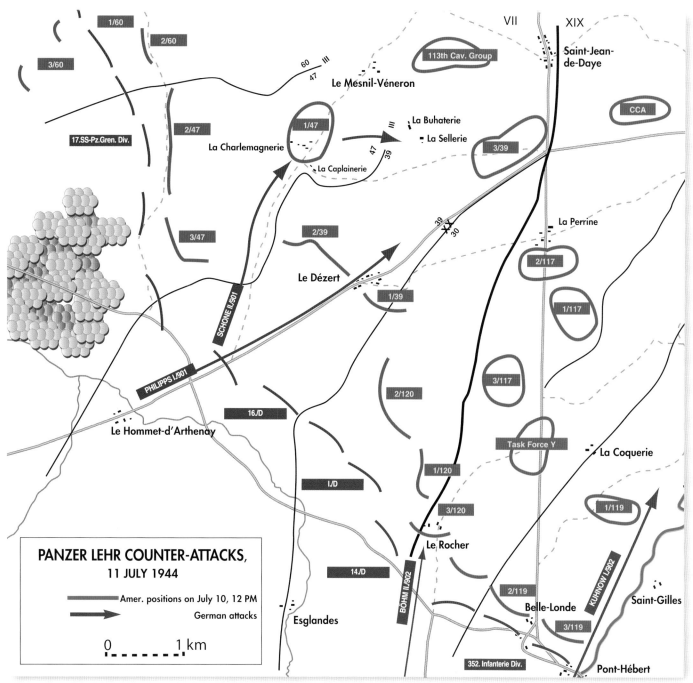

PANZER LEHR COUNTER-ATTACKS,
11 JULY 1944

——— Amer. positions on July 10, 12 PM

——▶ German attacks

0 —————— 1 km

July 11, 1944

These Panthers belong to the
I./Pz.Rgt.6. Detached from
3.Pz.Div, this battalion
comprised 89 tanks and was
attached to the Panzer-Lehr at
the beginning of June 1944,
entering the line on 10 June
(the date of this shot). Its tanks
are gathering here at
Mondaye, in front of the farm
at Les Pallières. Their biggest
engagements were at Lingèvres
(where six Panthers were lost),
the 11 July 1944 counter-attack
and Operation Cobra. Its
remnants were incorporated
into Kampfgruppe von Hauser
on 5 August. Four days later
this group was attached to
LXXXIV. A.K. in Mayenne and
where it fought the XVth US
Corps. Only ten or so Panthers
managed to get across
the Seine.
(ECPAD France)

THE PANZER-LEHR COUNTER-ATTACKS

TO ELIMINATE the American
bridgehead lodged between the Vire
and the Taute canal, Generalleutnant
Fritz Bayerlein formed two Kampfgruppe
using Pz. Gren. Rgt. 901 and 902 from his
Panzer-Lehr Division.

The first Kampfgruppe came under the command of Major
Welsch, Kdr. of Pz. Gren. Rgt. 902. It was divided into two
sub-groups (*Gruppen*). The first sub-group or Gruppe Kuhnow, made up of I./Pz.Gren.Rgt. 902 (Kdr.: Major Kuhnow),
of I./Gren.Rgt. 897 and of 8./Pz.Rgt.130 under Leutnant Peter,

Above from left to right.
Hauptmann Philipps, Kdr. of Pz.Gren. Rgt. 901.
Major Brandt, Kdr. of Pz.Pi.Btl. 130.
Major Welsch, Kdr. of Pz.Gren. Rgt. 902. *(BA)*

was to attack to the north of Pont-Hébert with the capture of Cavigny as its objective.

The second sub-group, or Gruppe Böhm, setting off from Les Hauts Vents, comprising II./Pz.Gren.Rgt.902 (Kdr.: Hauptmann Böhm), 6./Pz.Rgt.130 under Hauptmann Ritshel, 7./Pz.Rgt.130 under Oberleutnant Kues and a company of Pz.Pi.Btl.130, was to get hold of Le Rocher.

The second Kampfgruppe under the command of Oberst Scholze, Kdr. of Pz.Gren.Rgt.901, was also divided into two sub-groups. The first sub-group or Gruppe Philipps comprised I./Pz.Gren.Rgt.901 (Kdr.: Hauptmann Philipps) and 9./Pz.Gren.Rgt.901 equipped with 150-mm self-propelled guns. Several Panthers mainly from 3./Pz.Rgt.6 were to open the way for them. Its mission was to drive the Americans from Le Dézert then to take Saint-Jean-de-Daye. Fallschirm. Aufkl-Abt.12, remaining in its positions to the east of the Saint-Fromond road, would cover the right flank.

The second sub-group or Gruppe Schöne comprised II./Pz.Gren.Rgt.901 (Kdr.: Major Schöne) and Panthers from 2. and 4./Pz.Rgt.6. It would set off from Le Hommet Wood to take Le Mesnil-Véneron.

As soon as these objectives were reached, the two Kampfgruppen would meet up at Saint-Jean-de-Daye and break the XIXth US Army Corps offensive once and for all.

The 9th Infantry Division vs. Kampfgruppe Scholze

The chief-of-staff of the 1st Army had been right to assign the 9th Infantry division, reinforced with CCA, to the XIXth Army Corps since Kampfgruppe Scholze counter-attacked in the sector assigned to that particular division. Unfortunately he could not have known that the Panzer-Lehr would attack before dawn. He thought that the Lehr elements were simply going to reinforce the units already in the line. As a result, the 39th and the

47th Infantry found themselves facing Panzers and their Panzergrenadiere without support. The 1st and the 2nd Bns of the 39th Infantry Regiment, positioned on either side of the D8 road, took the full brunt of Hauptmann Philipps' Gruppe. The Panzergrenadiere moved forward aboard SPWs equipped with anti-tank guns such as the 37-mm Pak 35, the 75-mm Pak 40 or even with flamethrowers, advancing on either side of the road, along the Les Champs de Losque – Le Dézert axis. They felt protected by the Panthers of 3./Pz.Rgt.6 under Hauptmann Schramm who opened the way for them.

The crews of the 9./Pz.Gren.Rgt.901 self-propelled guns were all on the alert, ready to let off their 150-mm guns at any Shermans that would appear. Hauptmann Philipps ordered the crews to be extremely mobile to preserve their freedom of action which was vital should they have to break off. Encouraged by the progress of Gruppe Philipps which had advanced for four hours without any hitches, Generalleutnant Bayerlein sent him the divisional reconnaissance battalion, Pz.Aufkl.Abt.130, under Major von Fallois as reinforcement. For the moment it was still night.

Soon the GIs of the 1st Bn of the 39th Infantry would be fighting these new adversaries, superbly equipped with heavy weapons and armoured vehicles. Hauptmann Philipps took advantage of the presence of the reconnaissance battalion who were skirmishing with the GIs to put together a new plan so that he could head towards Saint-Jean-de-Daye. His objective seemed within reach.

Placed in reserve at La Charlemagnerie, the GIs of the 1st Bn of the 47th Infantry Regiment were surprised to see Panthers from I./Pz.Rgt.6 rushing straight for them, supported by the Panzergrenadiere from II./Pz.Gren.Rgt.901. This was the group commanded by Major Schöne. They had left the D8 to steal very skilfully between the 39th and the 47th Infantry where there was a gap almost half a mile wide.

The 3/47th Infantry who were emplaced opposite Le Hommet Wood were expecting the worst. The sounds of the fight which was thundering on behind made them think that they would eventually be isolated. Indeed it was not long before they learnt that all contact with the 47th and the 69th Infantry

Oberst Scholze
Scholze was a veteran of the Battle of Verdun during which he was awarded the Iron Cross 1st Class when a Leutnant in the Inf.Rgt.391. He was recalled by the Reich on 1 October 1937. He was made a Hauptmann and CO of 10./Inf.Rgt.9 then quickly rose to Major when he took charge of II./Infanterie-Lehr-Regiment. In 1940 he was in command of II./Inf.Rgt.900 which he led a year later in Russia with the rank of Oberstleutnant. When he instructed Pz.Gren.Rgt.901 from 28 December 1943, he was by then an Oberst and held the German Cross in gold. His regiment was subordinate to the Panzer-Lehr. Nominated to serve on the military mission to Rumania, he left Pz.Gren.Rgt.901 on 19 July 1944. In January 1944, he was in command of the 20.Pz.Div. with the rank of Generalmajor. On 23 April he was killed in action and on the same day, his wife and five children were killed during the bombing of Potsdam. *(Photo: J. Charita)*

Regiments had been lost. It was too late when their CO, Lieutenant-Colonel Donald C. Clayman realized that his battalion had advanced too far; he was obliged to move his headquarters to safety towards La Caplainerie.

The Panzers had now run into the 1st Bn of the 47th Infantry, cutting it off from the 2/39th Infantry which was defending Le Ferrey, the northern sector of Le Dézert. This battalion's situation became even more critical when the Panzergrenadiere from I./Pz.Gren.901 (Gruppe Philipps) threw themselves at it, letting off all they had. The two battalions of the 39th Infantry, positioned on either side of the road found themselves completely cut off. The Philipps Panzergrenadiere rushed into the 39th's First Aid station and captured some GIs who in the hours to come were to get in the way.

Suffering heavy losses and finding it increasingly difficult to hold their positions, the 1st Bn of the 39th Infantry fell back to the entrance to Le Dézert.

Three Panthers advancing through the burning village turned off to the left in the direction of Le Perrey to support the Panzergrenadiere attacking the farm there.

For the time being the counter-attack by Gruppe Philipps was turning out to be devastating. It was causing havoc along the 39th Infantry Regiment's lines of defence and Le Dézert was in its hands.

For Major-General Corlett the situation was getting alarming; he had to admit that the enemy had thwarted his plans.

It was clear to him that Generalleutnant Bayerlein was a brilliant tank officer and that his officers were just as good. But were their successes during the early hours of the day not due to good fortune or just simply Chance?

Indeed, Generalleutnant Bayerlein discusses this in his Memoirs. He points out that before launching his two Kampfgruppen against the Americans, he knew nothing of the enemy's situation and that the German units engaged earlier knew nothing at all of the American positions either!

Luckily the fighters from the 366th Fighter Group thwarted Generalleutnant Bayerlein's plans. The Panthers belonging to Gruppe Schöne were on the point of getting hold of La Charlemagnerie in the 1st Bn of the 47th Infantry's sector and found themselves one behind the other on the D257 road. They offered prize targets for experienced pilots.

In spite of some drizzle the planes were ordered to take off. They had to destroy a blockhouse in the Saint-Lô sector. As they approached their target, the P-47 pilots swept down to a height of 100 feet then spotted the column of tanks. The Germans had not seen the Jabos. The column was heading towards La Charlemagnerie on D257. This road was only 18 feet wide and its deep ditches were overflowing with water. It was nightmarish for the Panzerschütze who had to inch forward with a tank nearly 11 feet wide. If one of the Panthers was hit there would be the inevitable traffic jam. Moreover they would not be able to get over into the fields on either side of the road because of the high bank... suddenly the crews of the nine Flak guns spotted the fighter-bombers and tried to shoot them down. Their guns were on the highest point in the sector, near La Fauvellerie. In spite of the weather conditions and the AA fire, the pilots decided to attack the Panzers. It was 9 am. According to the official 9th US Army Airforce report, dated 28 July 1944, they destroyed 75% of the tanks and disorganised the rest. In another report, it was noted that 13 out of 14 tanks were destroyed. Soon the pilots were out of ammunition and returned to base to reload.

A GI who has rushed forward from under cover has been fired at. A few tenths of seconds later he will throw himself to the ground then get back in his hole.
(National Archives)

They took off immediately again to attack the rest of the column which was about 300 yards from the 1/47th Infantry's front line. Seven Panthers at most were destroyed on the narrow D527. The rear of the armoured column was jammed by two tanks at a standstill astride the road. There was no way of turning round. Dozens of Panzergrenadiere were killed by the P-47s' strafing.

Some of the tank commanders rounded up the Panzergrenadiere seeking shelter in the hollows of the hedgerows. The counter-attack must continue. Several Panthers managed to get into and through the all-too-rare entrances to the fields on either side of the road. The Panzergrenadiere immediately jumped onto the tanks and hung on while the 45-ton monsters swerved along with their 12-cylinder Maybach engines roaring. Two Panthers probably belonging to 2.Kp. under Leutnant Scholz, "Ursula" and "Elna" headed to the left while other Panthers belonging to 4. Kp. under Hauptmann Jahnke set off across the fields to the right heading for La Caplainerie.

9th Reconnaissance Troop scouts brought news about the 39th and 47th regiments disastrous situation to Major-General Eddy who consulted with Corlett.

Decisions had to be taken rapidly because the German were consolidating their breakthroughs, that by Gruppe Philipps being now more than a mile deep. All the 9th Division's units placed in reserve had to reinforce the threatened battalions. To re-establish the lines rapidly, Corlett called up the 899th Tank Destroyer Bn which immediately spread out its A and C companies in the most exposed areas.

The orders given were the following: the 1st Bn of the 47th Infantry, which had to abandon La Charlemagnerie, joined the 3rd Bn, still located in front of Le Hommet Wood. It was accompanied by four M10 tank destroyers assigned to it for this move.

The 2nd Bn of the 60th Infantry, which had remained in its positions to the south of Graignes, now had to take up the front line of the 2nd and the 3rd Bns of the 47th Infantry. These two battalions put themselves into a defensive position on the D8 road, thus cutting Kampfgruppe Scholze's retreat. The Kampfgruppe's two sub-groups thus found themselves cut off and surrounded everywhere by the 9th Infantry Division.

Finally, the 3rd Bn of the 39th Infantry, busy up until then guarding the all-important crossroads situated to the south of Saint-Jean-de-Daye, left for La Sellerie in order to stop Major Schöne's Gruppe's advance. This Gruppe had already been slowed down by the terrain and vegetation.

So as not to get in each other's way, the Panzergrenadiere had to split up to advance. Major Schöne was getting more and more worried because his divided forces increasingly exposed and weakened his Gruppe.

The improving weather made visibility better for the 366th Fighter Group pilots. Another 9th Airforce document indicates that the pilots were aloft and operating for the third time that day. "*After destroying the targets they had been assigned, the formation noticed Hauptmann Philipps near Le Dézert. SPWs and Panthers from 3./Pz.Rgt. 6 were subjected to low-altitude attacks.*" This may

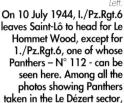

The Distinguished Unit Citation, which was pinned above the left hand breast pocket.

Below.
These two GIs from the 39th Infantry are lying in ambush on the heights near Cherbourg. Although outside the time frame of our study, this shot shows an anti-tank grenade mounted on the left man's rifle muzzle. Like the other soldier, he is carrying a large canvas bag over his shoulder used to transport the ammunition.
(National Archives)

explain why three Panthers left the D8 in the centre of Le Dézert to head for Le Perrey. None of the Panthers was destroyed but their crews did not know that the 899th's tank destroyers had been rushed to the rescue of the GIs at La Charlemagnerie, la Caplainerie and Le Perrey and as far as south of the D8.

The M-10s from the 899th Tank Destroyer Bn under Major Lorance distinguished themselves. First of all, A company left Saint-Jean-de-Daye then split up as follows: one group remained in reserve at La Sellerie, the second took the road leading from La Sellerie to the D8, leaving a handful of tank destroyers who branched off to the right, in the direction of La Fauvellerie; the others took the D8 then headed straight for Le Dézert where the 1st Bn of the 39th Infantry was on the point of being overwhelmed.

A report which accompanied the award of the Distinguished Unit Citation to A Company says: *"Out-numbered in men and materiel, the M10 crews were on the point of being overwhelmed by the armored infantry of II./Pz.Gren.Rgt.901. It was still night. Calmly the men of A Company remained steadfastly at their posts waiting for the Panzers.*

When they opened fire they realised that the flashes from their barrels not only attracted the artillery and the Panthers but also the anti-tank guns and the light guns equipping the Panzergrenadiere's SPWs.

When dawn broke, the crews saw that their 76.2-mm can- non were not able to pierce the Panthers' frontal armour. It was therefore only by attacking them on their flanks that they would be able to destroy them, but only after manoeuvring through the bocage."

Precisely. The report was accurate, as borne out in the field when we visited the area with some of the inhabitants of Le Dézert. The tank destroyers left the D8, heading for the hedgerows situated to the south of the road. Three Panthers were leaving Le Dézert and shells ricochetted off their armour.

Prudently, the crew of Panther "414" also left the D8 pursuing the M10 which had just disappeared. They warned the other two tanks following them. The two Panthers immediately went down the slope heading towards an isolated house which the tank destroyers were approaching. The Panzergrenadiere hung on determinedly to the tanks' structure. The Panthers seemed to want to cover them, but a GI, guessing what the tank was up to, grabbed hold of a bazooka and ran across the field to get under cover in a stream that was deep enough. The tank got into range of the anti-tank weapon. The GI opened fire piercing the armour and bringing the tank to a standstill in a fraction of a second. The Panzergrenadiere who were hanging onto the tank superstructure apparently got away unharmed.

The loss of this Panther discouraged those following. They tried to slip away towards Le Dézert or Les Bois. Taking advantage of the Panzerschützen's confusion, Lieutenant-Colonel H. Price Tucker from the 1st Bn of the 39th reinvested the village getting as far as a hundred yards from the church. GMCs were brought up to form a barricade in the middle the D8.

The GIs from B Company (1st Bn) of the 39th now under reasonable cover opened fire on the Panzergrenadiere whilst the shells continued to fall around them. In the end the anti-tank guns came to the rescue. They could do nothing against the Panthers but they were effective against the SPWs. Two M10 crews got in touch with the infantry from the 2nd Bn of the 39th near Le Perrey where Lt.-Col. Frank D. Gunn's CP was set up in a farm he had transformed into a stronghold. Suddenly they spotted the Panthers coming their way from Le Dézert. A duel started between the tank destroyers and the Panthers. One on each side was lost and the other two Panthers, who were being shot at, did not survive long; in the end both in turn received direct hits. To the GIs' surprise, both wrecks were recovered by the Germans! Looking for further targets the two TDs left Le Perrey. The GIs entrenched in the farmhouse feared another attack by the enemy who seemed to be outnumbering them. Their fears turned out to be justified when they saw two Panthers accompanied by Panzergrenadiere

Panther 215 was the subject of a demonstration for American troops. This means Panthers from 2./Pz.Rgt.6 were engaged along with those from 3. And 4. Kp. Among the infantrymen there are two men wearing Air force uniforms, who can be seen on the following shot too. According to the Signal Corps, this photo was taken on 19 July 1944 near Le Dézert. It would be a very good bet that it is on the D 257 secondary road, two hundred yards at most from La Charlemagnerie and La Caplainerie. Leutnant Scholz, CO of 2.Kp. was killed the same day.
(National Archives)

The generic shoulder patch for Tank Destroyer battalions.

Below.
An M-10 from company C/899th Tank Destroyer Battalion.

approaching. There was a fierce exchange of shots from both sides. Faced with unwavering opposition from the GIs under Lieutenant-Colonel Gunn, the attackers fell back. It was about 3 am.

At daybreak, a Piper Cub observation plane circled over Le Dézert. It gave the GIs of the 9th Infantry Division hope. The artillery would get into action in the next few minutes. The axis of Gruppe Philipps' attack, the D8 road, very quickly became impracticable for the Panzergrenadiere. Philipps divided his forces into two. The first went round the D8 passing to the south, heading for C company and the second headed for Le Camp then Saint-Jean-de-Daye.

Despite losing a Panther to the south of the D8, the Panzergrenadiere stubbornly resisted the GIs from C/39th who had to fall back to the north. Supported by the tank destroyers it was not long before they started to recapture lost ground.

Hauptmann Philipps himself led the second column to the north of the D8. A Panzergrenadier just like all his men, he carried on advancing with his SPWs full of motorised infantry, with a handful of Panthers opening the way for them. Having reached the track leading to La Fauvellerie, he ordered several tanks to use it to get to Saint-Jean-de-Daye, so that he would double the likelihood of reaching his objective. Le Dézert

was now behind him.

Hauptmann Philipps arrived in sight of the Le Camp crossroads. On his left were La Caplainerie and La Charlemagnerie. It was at this moment that the Panthers from 2. and 4./Pz.Rgt. 6 crossed the fields after leaving the sinister D 257. Normally the tanks from 2.Kp. were heading west, and those from 4. Kp. east, trying to join up with Gruppe Philipps.

On Kdr. Philipps' right was La Sellerie, a few hundred yards from Saint-Jean-de-Daye. A radio message informed him that ten or so Panthers from 4./Pz.Rgt. 6 had broken away from the column at La Caplainerie to come and open the way for him in the direction of Saint-Jean-de-Daye.

Hauptmann Philipps told his men to get ready for the last attack. He was unaware of the presence of C company of the 899th TD Bn who had joined up with the 1st Bn of the 47th Infantry spread out between La Charlemagnerie and La Caplainerie. As seen earlier, the TD company had to move up with this infantry battalion and join the 3rd Bn of its own regiment located in front of Le Hommet Wood.

The tank destroyer crews patiently watched the road from La Charlemagnerie to La Caplainerie, waiting for the imminent

arrival of the Panthers; their engines could be heard, getting louder.

A Panther edged round the bend. The German crew had no idea what was in store for them. Suddenly there was an explosion. Their tank was hit and they retaliated, hurling one shell after another at the M10 .

The latter's armour could not resist the Panther's 75-mm shot. The M 10 was probably too far away from the Panther when it fired and the American tank crew was either killed or seriously wounded. Another M10 crew, witnessing the scene, took its revenge by firing ten shots at a Panther. The shocks were so violent that the crew were not able to stop their tank from slipping off the road into the ditch.

The screaming motor and accelerator told the M 10 crew that the Panzerschütze were desperately trying to get their tank out of the muddy ditch. In vain. It remained where it was in spite of the driver's efforts. There was only one thing left to do: get out as quickly as possible. The crew did not go far: the GIs from the 1/47th Infantry captured them later in a farmhouse.

A hail of 76.2-mm shells put an end to the leading tank, "Ursula," whose engine compartment caught fire turning several Panzergrenadiere into human torches. The survivors fled in the direction of the hedges or threw themselves into

Left.
A and C companies/899th Tank Destroyer Bn landed on Utah Beach on 6 June 1944. The remainder of the battalion arrived on the 10th and 11th. Its TDs supported four infantry divisions including the 4th. They were then attached to the 9th in the Cotentin Peninsula. The 2nd platoon of C Company destroyed a large number of heavy guns which were preventing the 2/47th Infantry from advancing along the Cherbourg - Gréville axis. It was the first unit of the 899th TD Bn to obtain the Distinguished Unit citation. The battalion was rewarded with a week's rest and was then called back on 11 July to break the Gruppe Schöne attack. Four of its men were killed in the fighting.
(National Archives)

Above.
1st Lieutenant Henry W. Collins on his P-47 "Glamour Girl."
(Photo Sam Sox Jr)

1st Lieutenant Joe F. Richmond on his P-47, christened "Hey Bernice!"
(Photo am Sox Jr)

Top right.
The insignia of the 366th Fighter Group. This unit was formed in England at the beginning of 1944. It carried out its first missions along the French coast in March 1944. It was engaged on 6 June 1944 to disrupt the rear of the 7. Armee, attacking mainly motorised columns and artillery. Its activities increased when it had a base within the operational zone of the 1st Army to which it was assigned.

the stream. Then it was Elna's turn: it took three direct hits on the left side. The Panzergrenadiere still perched on top of it jumped to the ground, pursued by the infantry's gunfire.

The duel between the M10s and the Panthers raged all around la Charlemagnerie and La Caplainerie. Near La Charlemagnerie, another Panther was hit by several Shermans from F/32nd Armored Regiment, which had arrived in the meantime. The tank crews kept an eye on the surrounding countryside as the GIs continued raking the bocage. Most of these tank duels took place at point-blank range. For its heroic conduct, C company of the 899th Tank Destroyer Bn was awarded the Distinguished Unit Citation, just like A Company.

With a Panzer IV leading, the armour from 4./Pz.Rgt. 6 under Hauptmann Jahnke joined Philipps' SPW column. The two COs discussed their plans for a brief moment then the

(Continued on page 72)

9th Airforce pilot in Normandy

This lieutenant has an A-11 flight helmet, B-7 goggles, an A-14 oxygen mask with T-44C microphone. The general issue wool trousers and shirt, worn with service shoes, are the basis of the flying uniform. The leather A-2 flying jacket is adequate for medium to low altitude missions. A whistle has been attached to the zipper tab, it would come handy for attracting the attention of friendly troops if shot down. Even during low altitude strafing missions, the B-8 back type parachute saved a number of pilots struck by Flak. The regulation pistol is carried on the belt inside the leather holster, two magazines are in the twin-cell pocket on the left side. The leather B-3A gloves are much sought after for their comfort.
(Reconstruction by Militaria Magazine, article by Gregory Pons in issue 237)

A PHOTO REPORT ON THE 11 JULY 1944 FIGHTING AT LE DEZERT

Above.
This famous photo shows two Panthers destroyed on either side of the D 257. It is most likely that the one on the left was hit by a fighter and that the second tipped into the ditch while trying to drive past it. The road was only 18 feet wide and the second tank could not get past which explains why the crew had to use the side of the road to move forward. But the machine's forty-five tons and the water-logged ditch were responsible for it getting stuck.
(National Archives)

Centre.
Returning to the same spot, we noted that two cars which wanted to go past each other had to slow down and estimate quite carefully whether they could or not. One false move and one of them would fall into the ditch which is always full of water. It is evident that reconnoitering the terrain would have prevented the I./Pz.Rgt.6 crews getting themselves into this trap. Unfortunately for the Panzer-Lehr soldiers, they were rushed to engage the enemy as soon as they arrived.
(Photo T. Guilbert)

Above and below.
Caught in the trap along the lane to La Fauvellerie, this Panther called "Chrystel" has lost its right running gear. An M10, lying in ambush in the field whose gate can be seen on the left, had waited until it turned its back before opening fire. When we showed this photograph to Mr André Letemplier, he recognised the spot immediately and he took us there. The site is just as it was. Mr. Letemplier knows each and every road and track in this sector and he was an invaluable guide.
(National Archives)

Left.
"Chrystel" had also been photographed on 10 June 1944 at Mondaye. His nickname is visible on both pictures, painted above one of the hull vision slits.
(ECPAD France)

According to André Letemplier, these other two Panthers were also in the La Fauvellerie lane. They tried to reach Saint-Jean-de-Daye, in an attempts to avoid the departmental roads. "Ingrid" seems to have been abandoned by its crew. It is quite likely that it was the target of American pilots. The 10 ft 9 in wide tank takes up almost the whole width of the road. Note the second Panther in the background. This track is even narrower than the D257 and there is no ditch. These two Tanks most probably belonged to 4.Kp.
(National Archives)

Below.
The attack of Gruppe Philips and 4./Pz.Rgt. 6 towards la Sellerie. The American engineers built a landing strip in the area after the fighting and much of the roads and tracks are not the same today.
(Research and graphics by Frederic Deprun)

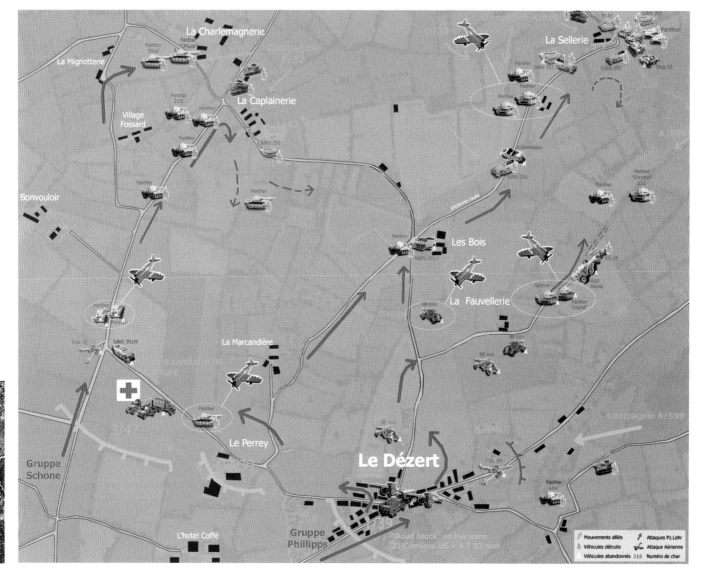

THE FATE OF "URSULA"AND "ELNA"

There are two versions concerning the demise of these two Panthers on 11 July 1944. A local witness, Monsieur Clergeot, states they were destroyed to the south of the D8, near his house as told in the main text.

However, matching period photos with the actual area, which had extensively changed since the war, made us think differently. Furthermore it seems only one tank was actually destroyed on this spot. Another picture exists that shows the machine together with buildings in the background, but it belongs to a private collection we could not access.

As for us, we have a detailed report concerning the destruction of two Panthers in the La Charlemagnerie area which corresponds to that of "Ursula" and "Elna," and confirms that the engagement took place in this sector. The two Panthers met their fate as follows: the crews who were lucky enough to get off the D257 by using the gates into the grazing land headed towards la Charlemagnerie or la Caplainerie. Carrying Panzergenadiere on their hulls, the two tanks headed straight for La Charlemagnerie which the GIs from the 1/47th Infantry were attacking backed up by M10s. The tank destroyers spotted the two tanks and succeeded in manoeuvring without being seen. "Ursula" was hit three times on its left side whereas "Elna," less than two hundred yards away, started to swivel its turret

towards one of the M10s. Too late, the other beat her to it and "Elna" was in turn hit. But the question as to where these two tanks were located remains unanswered.

Above and left.
Both these pictures of "Ursula" were taken by the Americans soon after the battle. One of the soldiers from Pz.Gren. Rgt. 901 lies on the rear deck. Three armour-piercing shells hit the side of the German tank, which went up in flames immediately.
(National Archives, F. Deprun collection)

Right.
After the dead infantrymen's bodies had been removed from the hull, Ursula was loaded on a heavy wrecker's trailer and taken to the wreck yard at Isigny. The rear side of Elna can be seen in the foreground.
(3rd Armored Division Association)

PzKpfw V ausf. A, "Ursula," befehl Panther of I./ Panzer-Regiment 6 seconded to the Panzer-Lehr Division, destroyed at La Charlemagnerie on July 11, 1944.
(Research and illustration by Frédéric Deprun 2007)

Above.
Just as with "Ursula," Panther 425 was recovered and transported to the wrecker's yard at Isigny. It belonged to 4./Pz.Rgt.6. In the background is Pz. IV 898 of the 8./SS-Pz.Rgt.2.

Right.
The second Panther destroyed either near La Charlemagnerie or to the south of the D8, was "Elna." Note the 76.2 mm shell impacts on the hull side.
(National Archives)

PzKpfw V Panther ausf. D "Elna," command tank of I./ Panzer-Regiment 6 seconded to the Panzer-Lehr Division, destroyed at La Charlemagnerie on July 11, 1944.
(Research and illustration by Frédéric Deprun 2007)

Another Panther from the 4.Kp. This shot of Panther 414, taken to the south of the D8, at the entrance to Le Dézert, on 11 or 12 July 1944, proves that the 4.Kp.'s tanks were used during Oberst Scholze's counter-attack. Note the design of the turret numbers, which are identical to those of '425' on previous page. Other photographs show that it was destroyed in this field. Mr Clergeot very clearly remembers the impact made by a bazooka rocket, fired by a GI hiding in a stream. It is worth remembering that the information presented in the text about how the different companies were engaged seems much clearer on paper that it actually does in the field. We noticed that when a company was mentioned, machines belonging to other companies were attached to it. For example, we learn that the 3./Pz.Rgt.6 preceded Gruppe Philipps to Le Dézert. Then we find a 4.Kp. wreck on the side of the D8. It seems quite likely that all operational Panthers were parcelled out in groups to different company commanders. For example Hauptmann Jahnke who was in command of 4./Pz.Rgt.6 probably found himself with tanks belonging to other companies so that he could make up his strength.

(Patton Museum)

Right.
Panther 200 passing through Saint-Lô on 10 July 1944. It belongs to Leutnant Scholz, the CO of that company, who was killed the following day.
(Archives départementales du Calvados)

Above and right.
Panther 321 being towed in a forest near Saint-Lô. Apparently the 3.Kp. was the only one from I./Pz.Rgt.6 to use the D8, between Le Hommet d'Arthenay and Le Dézert. But when it got as far as Le Dézert, three of the tanks branched off to the left towards Le Perrey where they outflanked the GIs of the 2/39th. Their objective was to reach St. Jean-de-Daye. A tank destroyer platoon from A Company of the 899th Tank Destroyer Bn intercepted them and a duel started with the Panthers. One machine on each side was destroyed. Although they had been hit, the other two Panthers fell back under fire.
(Photo Sturm and Drang)

SPWs moved aside to let the tanks open the way, towards La Sellerie. There was only half a mile to go before they were in sight of the village but for the Germans the distance turned out to be never-ending: they were under fire from the GIs in E Company of the 39th who opened up on the column. The Americans were dug in further back from the road and were easily able to shoot the Panzergrenadiere perched up on the tanks. The bazooka teams reduced several half-tracks to heaps of scrap metal.

Without infantry back up, Jahnke's tanks took pot luck and advanced towards La Sellerie at full speed. Hauptmann Jahnke was not very far from Saint-Jean-de-Daye when the leading Pz. IV barely avoided shots from an M10. The German crew replied immediately and destroyed the tank buster from the 3rd platoon of A/899th. The other tank destroyers went into action and the Pz. IV was set upon by the American crews. With the leading tank at a standstill, the following Panthers could not advance towards Saint-Jean-de Daye. The Pz. IV had no chance of getting out.

Hauptmann Jahnke now feared the worst for his Panthers and ordered his tank commanders to fall back to a field located at the fork at La Sellerie. The spot was surrounded by hedges and would conceal his tanks while they waited for Gruppe Philipps. Unfortunately the Panzergrenadiere were still fighting it out with E Company from the 39th on the Le Camp – La Sellerie road. It was impossible to make it across the last 500 yards which would enable them to join up with the tanks and reach their objective.

Below.
An M5 American light tank. These fast and nimble machines, however vulnerable, were used for reconnaissance missions within tank battalions.

Below.
This SdKfz 251/1 of 4./Pz.Gren.Rgt. 901, which fought at Le Dézert on 11 July 1944, was destroyed during Operation Cobra. Note the regimental sign on the bonnet. This 8-ton armoured personnel carrier had a crew of two, with one MG at the front and rear.
(Research and illustration by Frédéric Deprun 2007)

Watching this in his command post, near the D8, colonel Flint, CO of the 39th US Infantry Regiment, grasped the opportunity as it was offered to him. By launching a counter-attack in the direction of La Sellerie, he would be able to stop the Panzer-Lehr outright by destroying the tanks hiding in the field to the south of that village. He ordered the men of the 3rd Bn of the 39th to take La Sellerie with the support of the 3rd platoon of C/899th TD Bn. and three Shermans from G company of the 32nd Armored Regiment.

Colonel Flint's initiative enabled his improvised task force to get hold of La Sellerie then to tighten the noose around the fields where Hauptmann Jahnke's Panthers and one Sturmgeschütze from Pz.Jg. Abt. 130 under Major Barth were hiding.

The tank destroyer crews got the better of six tanks, but the hedges prevented them from getting the other seven which retired towards La Caplainerie, leaving behind them six smoking carcasses silhouetted against the sky.

Meanwhile the Panthers which had been with Hauptmann Philipps and which had taken a narrow track in the direction of La Fauvellerie progressed

Above.
One of the Panthers from I./Pz.Rgt.6 destroyed in July 1944. It has lost its tracks and has burnt out which prevents us from reading the turret number. Unfortunately the date of the photograph is not known. However, the narrow, muddy roads and the greenery recall the conditions under which the Panzerschütze fought the tank destroyers. In the foreground, an SdKfz 251/7 from Pz.Pi.Btl.130. This vehicle carried two small assault bridges. Its armament consisted of two machine guns (MG 34s or 42s) and a Pz B39 antitank rifle. Its crew comprised seven or eight sappers.
(National Archives)

very slowly. The road was rather sinuous and narrow and they could only advance with a great deal of caution.

The Panther called "Chrystel" which was at the head of the column was being observed quietly by the crew of an M10 lying in ambush in a field. Its muzzle was pointing towards the gate of a small meadow leading to the track. Just as the Panther appeared, the tank destroyer fired several shells at its side. With its left track jumping violently the German tank tried to escape. Two other Panthers, one of which was called "Ingrid," were also stuck. Only one managed to get out of the trap by leaving the tree- and hedge-lined track. It ground an embankment down with its tracks sending earth up all over the place then rushed across the fields. It did not get very far before being destroyed like the others.

In the shelter of orchards, copses, embankments and hedgerows, small groups of GIs from the 1st Bn of the 47th were burning with a fire that not even the wildest Panzergrenadiere from I./Pz.Gren. Rgt. 901 could smother. The support of the tank destroyers and the two platoons of Shermans would make sure they would win. Their morale was excellent.

Suddenly the attention of the tank unit leader, Captain Kahn of the 32nd Armored Regiment was caught by the seven Panthers from 4./Pz.Rgt.6. These were heading straight for the Le Camp crossroads where several hours before they had met up with Hauptmann Philipps' column. Still under fire from the GIs in F company of the 39th, the Panzergrenadiere followed the Panthers.

There was a risk of the situation becoming critical for the 1st Bn of the 47th, positioned at La Caplainerie. Captain Kahn's crews were alerted in record time. Their turrets swivelled straight for the Panzers. Then the P-47s appeared. It no longer mattered if the Sherman crews could see or not. Everyone opened fire on the Panthers or on the supposed Panthers! Bazooka teams launched rocket after rocket at them. All the soldiers wanted revenge for some comrade lost in the fighting.

An M10 made the mistake of firing at a Panther from too

Below.
Two bazooka teams from the 9th Inf. Div. succeeded in destroying a Panther on 11 July. One of these belonged to the 1/47th and the other to the 1/39th Infantry.
(National Archives)

far away. Its shells just ricochetted off the armour. The 75-mm barrel thundered lethally. The shell went straight through the tank buster. In turn the Panther finished its course after advancing a hundred yards or so, struck by another TD. The bocage war was pitiless.

The Panzerschütze, however, did not give up because they believed that their world would not survive defeat. But the events which followed would make them change their minds about ideology. A tank destroyer emerging from behind a thicket took a Panther by surprise as it was moving along a track followed by the others. It took ten shots fired at zero elevation before the Panther was killed. This was too much for the Panzermänner, who realised that the game was up. They were outnumbered by far by the M10s and Shermans. The Panthers had a lot of difficulty manoeuvring so they could fall back on Le Perrey. Only three managed to escape, the other two got bogged down in the waterlogged ditches.

According to the 899th Tank Destroyer Bn after action report, it would seem that 12 Panthers and one Pz.IV were destroyed on 11 July 1944. In another document, the tally is 14 tanks and one self-propelled gun destroyed.

Oberjäger Paul, of 4./Fallschirm. Aufkl-Abt. 12, placed on the right of Gruppe Philipps, recalls: *"In case of an attack, we had mined the sunken lane facing us. It was my job to eliminate any sharpshooter or artillery observers. According to what I had been told, several enemy sharpshooters had destroyed one of our Panzers (…)*

At around midday, wave after wave of fighter-bombers came over attacking our Panthers. Our counter-attack was very soon halted and our tanks fell back on their original line. (Editor's note: Paul was wounded in circumstances that he does

not explain.) *I will remember it all my life. It was my birthday the day before. I was carried in a tent section by two comrades who took me 500 yards to the rear, behind the first aid post. I was cared for, then evacuated to Rennes where I had my right leg amputated. Several days later, I was sent to the Luftwaffe hospital at Clichy, near Paris."* According to Oberleutnant Blauensteiner, chief-of-staff to Generalleutnant Meindl, on 29 July 1944 Fallschirm. Aufkl. Abt.12 was reduced to company strength. Its survivors went through the Falaise Pocket, to the west of the Dives on 19 August 1944.

Towards 16.00 Oberst Scholze's two Gruppen were no longer capable of making any further progress against the American lines. The noose was tightening around them. Hauptmann Philipps' Gruppe found itself surrounded with a handful of its men left. Most of them had been killed, wounded or taken prisoner. The Kdr. of I./Pz.Gren.Rgt.901 was forced to surrender. He did not yet know that there were only twelve of his Panzergrenadiere left alive and they were in charge of forty or so GI POWs from the 9th Infantry division. Under the command of Oberfeldwebel Schlabach, they managed to reach their lines. This exploit earned him the German Cross in gold. It is not known what happened to the forty Americans.

According to Helmut Ritgen, a historian and veteran of II./Pz.Rgt. 130, Gruppe Philipps had about 214 men left…

Powerless, twenty or so Panthers from I./Pz.Rgt. 6 remained stymied by the artillery to the west of Hommet wood. Their presence would most certainly have enabled Generalleutnant Bayerlein's counter-attacks to succeed. But now it was too late. The die was cast. The Panzergrenadiere from II./Pz.Gren.Rgt.901 and the Panthers had nothing else to do but return behind the LXXXIV A.K. lines. To get away from the fighter-bombers and the tank destroyers, they abandoned their half-tracks. The enemy infantry was now combing the area. And falling back turned out to be something of an adventure, if not downright impossible, all the more so that the American artillery did not stop bombarding the D8.

SS-Obersturmbannführer Wisliceny wrote the following after

Above.
Leutnant Roeder's platoon in the II./Pz.Gren.Rgt.901 was equipped with three Sd Kfz 251/16s from HQ company. Two of them were destroyed on 11 July 1944 in the 120th Infantry sector. Delivered at the end of January 1943, the vehicle carried 154 gallons of fuel which enabled it to "spit" out eighty 2-second blasts with each of its two flamethrowers. This half-track was also armed with two MG 34 machine guns.
(Private collection)

the war concerning I./Pz.Gren. Rgt. 901's attack: *"The half-tracks belonging to the 901's SPW battalion and a group of Panzers were engaged to the left of my unit. They drove in the enemy lines but were almost wiped out by the Jabos, the tanks and the artillery. Only one Feldwebel and 35 men returned."*

Taking advantage from a period of clear weather which lasted until the evening, the American fighters returned in strength. The pilots had been ordered to wipe out all the Panzers in the VIIIth and XIXth Army Corps' operational area. The situation now turned in favour of the 9th Division. The 39th and 47th Infantry Regiments regained their initial positions and at the end of the day, the pilots claimed 22 tanks destroyed.

The 30th Infantry Division and Kampfgruppe Welsch

While the Philipps and Schöne Gruppen were dealing with two regiments of the 9th Infantry Division, Kampfgruppe Welsch

Below.
One of the Shermans from the 32nd Tank Bn of the 3rd US Armored division destroyed on 11 July 1944. Its right track has been rolled up and placed on the front of the hull. As for the right one, it has been cut near the rear left hand sprocket wheel. An M31ARV is going to tow it to the rear. This scene took place near Le Dézert.
(National Archives)

Infantry Regiments.

First of all Gruppe Böhm left the Les Hauts-Vents sector to attack the 3rd Bn of the 120th Infantry, entrenched at Le Rocher.

It was 5 am and the night was very dark. Alerted by the sound of Pz. IVs and SPW engines which were approaching his command post, K Company's CO alerted his men. Soon after, other companies in the battalion were put on the alert.

At the sight of the Pz. IVs under Oberleutnant Kues (a Panther according to the 120th's history) which were using the road because of the drenched land, the bazooka teams from K Company got ready for action. Their comrades checked their ammunition and their weapons. The leading tank was hit by a rocket. It caught fire but the crew managed to bail out. The Panzerschütze had hardly set their feet on the ground when a hail of grenades fell about them and exploded, killing one and wounding the others.

The three other Pz. IVs and an SPW crammed with Panzergrenadiere continued on their way at full speed towards the 3rd Bn's command post. They were concentrating so much on their objective that they went past the destroyed Panzer without even noticing it.

Led by a battalion HQ officer who opened fire with a jeep-mounted machine gun, the GIs stepped up their firing. They noticed suddenly that one of the Panzer IVs had left the road, its crew thinking it might get away from the American gunfire by vanishing into one of the hedge-lined fields.

The 7.Kp. Panzerschützen's reaction was the right one but did not take into account the waterlogged earth. One of their tanks got stuck in the mud and the Panzerschützen tried in vain to get it out. A bit further away an SPW also bogged down. Both immobilised, they were quickly destroyed by the Americans who quite evidently took advantage of the situation.

In spite of these heavy losses, Hauptmann Böhm from II./Pz.Gren.Rgt.902 followed up his attack by launching his SPW flamethrower platoon under Leutnant Roeder. This officer was killed in his vehicle; a second SPW was also put out of action. Other half-tracks reached the American positions. The Panzergrenadiere jumped down from them to rush at the GIs who fired non-stop. There was hand to hand fighting and the maul was bloody and pitiless, with a lot of killed.

It was as if the 3rd Bn of the 120th Infantry's front line had caught fire. There was fighting going on all over the place. In an ambush set up by a platoon of Panzergrenadiere, the GIs got out of their depth, five of them being captured (although they did not waste time getting away during the next scuffle…).

Although roughly handled by Hauptmann Böhm's counter-

launched its Kuhnow and Böhm Gruppen in an attack on the right wing. The line of defence between Pont-Hébert and the D8 to the south of Le Dézert was held by SS-Kampfgruppe Wisliceny who pinned down the 119th and 120th

Above and top, right.
This Sturmgeschütze III belonged to the Fallschirm-Sturmgeschütz-Brigade under Hauptmann Gesteuer. According to the chief-of-staff of the Fallschirmjäger Korps, Blauensteiner, each battery in the brigade had three StuG IIIs and three Sturmhaubitze 42s. Five Sturmgeschütze were destroyed in June and July. Their losses were very heavy in the Falaise Pocket however.

Top, right.
Wearing headphones with a paratroopers' helmet seems to be a problem... It is clear that the tank commander will have to remove his helmet to use the radio.
(Frederic Deprun)

Right.
These sappers in Panzer-Pionier-Batalion 130 of the Panzer-Lehr Division are passing through a Normandy town during the summer of 1944. Note the tactical insignia and the L for Lehr painted higher up and almost illegible. This is one of the two Sd Kfz 251/9 which equipped the 3.Kp. This half-track was armed with a 75-mm Kwk 37(L/24) short-barrelled gun.
(Frederic Deprun)

attack, the 3/120th Infantry destroyed five Pz. IVs and four SPWs including that of Oberleutnant Graf, CO of 7./Pz.Gren.Rgt.902 who managed to get out alive. Sixty or so Panzergrenadiere were captured. Kampfgruppe Böhm did not manage to break through anywhere on the 3rd Bn's front.

Oberleutnant Kues' last Pz IVs withdrew under the protection of II./Pz.Gren.Rgt.902's soldiers sheltering in their SPWs.

The sun was not yet up before the Gruppe under Major Kuhnow, Kdr. of I./Pz.Gren. Rgt. 902 headed for la Coqueterie. Its objective consisted in taking Cavigny with the support of the tanks from

8./Pz.Rgt.130 under Leutnant Peter.

Five of his Pz. IVs (Panthers according to the 119th's report) in the 8./Pz.Rgt. 130 had already got through the 3/119th Infantry lines. Unwittingly, the Panzerschütze were approaching that regiment's 2nd Bn command post, abruptly waking the GIs up asleep in their foxholes. The alert was given.

Crammed with armoured infantry, the SPWs surrounded the sector in a pincer movement. The five Pz. IVs followed the road in single file, as

fast as possible and firing all the time. The leading tank came level with an anti-tank gun positioned on the side of the road which its crew could not see because of the dark.

Staff Sergeants Steele and Womack had begun to point their gun and were almost ready to shoot at the tank just like they did in training. The Panzer was now at less than 50 yards-range, but its muzzle had already turned and it fired first.

Womack was wounded. Steele,

Sherman M4A1 of the 743rd Tank Battalion. This version has the older 75-mm main gun, which armed the majority of US Shermans in Normandy.

Above
This American casualty is on a plasma drip. The medics have slipped a tent pole into the spade handle so that they can suspend the bottle. Note the stretcher-carrying jeep in the background.
(National Archives)

unhurt ran to a Jeep armed with a heavy machine gun, into which he jumped then opened fire at the Panzer which was still shooting the place over.

Suddenly the Mark IV got a direct hit, an anti-tank shot had just struck home on its side, the tank was immobilised. Meanwhile Womack had got up. He led a bazooka team, went round another Pz. IV busy firing shot after shot. The rocket was loaded with skill into the tube then it shot out in a blaze. The Pz.IV in turn was destroyed. This tank belonged to Leutnant Peters, CO of 8./Pz.Rgt. 130. The 119th Infantry's history mentions: "*Lieutenant Wilson sent off a patrol against the enemy. He and another man fought the enemy infantry in hand to hand fighting. Wilson continued to repel the enemy forces until he was wounded and his soldiers had run out of ammunition.*"

Gruppe Kuhnow had lost five Pz. IVs and 21 men including Leutnant Peters. It was not yet midday...

Major-General Corlett then attempted a masterstroke. Taking advantage of the fact that Gruppe Böhm was now weakened and on the defensive, he wanted to launch a powerful counter-attack towards Les Hauts Vents or even Hill 91. In order to do this, Colonel Roysden, the new CO of Combat Command B, would join the 2nd Bn of the 119th Infantry which would protect his tanks, then together they would take Hill 91.

At around midday, two companies of the 33rd Armored Regiment and the 823rd Tank Destroyer Bn situated to the rear, near Cavigny, got under way. Their progress was suddenly interrupted by the firing from Sturmgeschütze hidden on the east bank of the Vire. These guns were feared by the Americans

and there was nothing else to do but call in the artillery. A few moments later 105 and 155-mm shells started falling and silenced the tanks of Hauptmann Gersteuer, CO of Fallschirm. Sturmgeschütz-Abt. 12. His SP guns branched off towards the east.

The Shermans continued moving on, but they were attacked again. This time by Pz.IVs from 7./Pz.Rgt. 130 waiting for them near La Belle Lande. The tank crews from the 33rd Armored Regiment really fell into a trap. The German crews wanted revenge. They moved rapidly and accurately, operating like robots. Their 75-mm shells struck American armour. Six were destroyed. The Panzerschütze had avenged the death of Leutnant Peter.

Colonel Alfred V. Ednie of the 119th Infantry could not wait any longer for the Shermans. It was 3 pm and the 1st and 2nd Bns had not yet attacked. 30 minutes later, both battalions moved forward without support from the 33rd Armored Regiment. To the GIs' surprise they only ran into light opposition. At 8 pm they were ordered to set up their positions for the night.

The Veterans' Association of the 119th Infantry reports what happened on 11 July 1944: "*The artillery started bombarding the 1st Bn's sector. The men were dug in along the hedges. Suddenly a shell fell right onto a hedge, into a foxhole. From his own position, Sergeant Spencer J. Smiley could just make out the weak cries from the men the explosion had buried under the churned up earth. He left his shelter to help them in spite of the artillery, and started digging with his bare hands then with his helmet to get them out . He stopped only when the blast from an explosion*

knocked him over. He managed to get two men out alive and saw that they needed medical care. He took the most seriously wounded over his shoulder and then headed for the first aid station. He was only able to carry him a few yards before a shell burst bowled him over. He died from his wounds. It was his bravery that gave us the will to fight.*"

At 4.10 pm, the 16./ "D" (SS-Kampfgruppe Wisliceny), positioned along the 33rd Armored Regiment's line of attack, was assaulted by nine Shermans. The Pioniere, huddled up inside their foxholes put up with heavy firing. The armour continued approaching, threatening the front held by SS-Obersturmführer Macher's company. Faced with this firepower and without heavy back up, Macher was obliged to fall back. Later on, when they had reorganised, they started close quarter fighting against the tanks. Two were destroyed, one by SS-Oberscharführer Ellwanger with a magnetic mine (Hafthohlladung), his last act of bravery.

Just like the GIs, the Pioniere of Macher's company accomplished many heroic deeds. SS private Gengelbach lost his right hand from an explosive bullet and found himself isolated. He nonetheless managed to rejoin his group on the front line. SS-Unterscharführer Meier-Northeim threw himself at the Ameri-

cans with no thought for his own life then finished them off with his pistol and stick grenades.

With cool-headedness, SS-Unterscharführer Laessig jumped from the top of a hedge to take a group of Americans who were only a yard in front of him. He gunned them all down with his Mauser 98K.

SS-Oberscharführer Ehm and SS-Rottenführer Förster were continuously engaged on the front line. They covered the company commander all the time and were always there where needed. Alone once in his CP, Obersturmführer Macher was attacked by 17 GIs. Bullets whistled all around him: one grazed his helmet, another hit him in the shoulder but he was saved by his men at the very last minute.

At the end of the day SS-Obersturmbannführer Wisliceny decided to make his Kampfgruppe fall back some 500 yards since it was no longer able to hold the line between the Le Hommet – Le Dézert road and the Pont-Hébert road. He asked Macher to place his Pioniere on the right wing which was more under threat than the left.

Once again the "Das Reich's" trouble-shooters found themselves at the heart of the battle. Already, during the day, this company had re-stabilised the SS-Pz.Pi.Btl.2's lines.

The war diary of the 16./ "D" closes the account of the day's engagement in these terms: "*This hard fighting reminded our men of what they had known on the Russian front. We had to face soldiers who showed untold courage and who observed the code of honour.*"

Colonel Roysden's Shermans got hold of Hill 91 which had been used as an observation point by the Germans since the beginning of the offensive. It was an undisputed victory for Major-General Corlett's XIXth Army Corps. His troops set up defensive positions rapidly in case of new counter-attacks.

As Colonel Roysden correctly forecast, the enemy reacted rapidly. Coming from the south east, elements from Gruppe Böhm headed in his direction. Fortunately, communications between CCB and the artillery were excellent and very quickly, the enemy was subjected to heavy shelling.

"*The redoubtable Panzer-Lehr, which was in a powerful counter-attack stance, found itself on the defensive during the night of 11-12 July 1944. Its two Kampfgruppe had lost almost 500 to 700 men, i.e. half their strength*", General Bayerlein admitted. More than 20 Panthers were destroyed (13 were claimed by Thunderbolt pilots). This figure includes probably those which were destroyed in the VIIth US Army Corps' operational zone and therefore belonged to I./SS-Pz.Rgt.2. They were engaged in countryside where visibility was no more than 200 yards. "*Light tanks would have been more effective*", Bayerlein reports "*but I did not engage them because I had been told that the sector was much more suitable for tanks than the Caen region.*"

As for Helmut Ritgen, he completes the Bayerlein information: "*344 wounded from the two Kampfgruppen were sent to the nearest field hospital. Ten Panthers and eight Pz. IVs were lost as were their crews. Among these losses were two officers, Leutnant Peters and Leutnant Stöhr as a well as the platoon commander of the Flammpanzer from Pz. Gren. Rgt. 902 (…)*".

Above.
Oberleutnant Peters, CO of 8./Pz.Rgt. 130 was killed in the 120th Infantry operational zone, on 11 July 1944.
(H. Ritgen)

Below.
This Panzer IV of 8./Pz. Rgt. 130 fought north of Pont-Hébert on 11 July 1944. Five of the company's tanks were destroyed there. As for 841, it was struck off during Operation Cobra.
(Research and illustration by Frédéric Deprun 2007)

THE 30th US INFANTRY DIV

TAKING ADVANTAGE OF THE TERRIBLE BLOW delivered to the Panzer-Lehr Division the previous day, General Hobbs launched the whole 30th Division into the attack. The 117th and 120th Infantry advanced slowly without encountering stiff resistance, but the 119th Infantry was severely put to the test by the enemy, located to the east of the river.

Above.
This M5 light tank with its stabilised canon can fire on the move. Although it was produced since 1942, it still gave worthwhile service in the reconnaissance units in Normandy.
(National Archives)

Right.
The Pont-Hébert bridge became a nightmare for the soldiers of Combat Command B of the 3rd US Armored Division and those of the 119th Infantry. Terribly distressed by the unending German artillery barrage and by the fierce defence put up by the different groups of Grenadiere, the Americans had to show great determination before they succeeded in getting hold of Pont-Hébert.
(National Archives)

Leaving their departure lines at 9 am, the 1st and 2nd Bns of the 119th Infantry Regiment were able to progress without casualties owing to the 10-minute intense artillery preparation. Less than an hour later, the GIs from the 2nd Bn entered La Belle Lande which had cost them so much the previous day.

The battalion commander reported this success to the regimental commander, Colonel Ednie, who ordered him to establish his position half a mile from Pont-Hébert. He was promised tanks and a platoon of infantry from the 3rd Bn to protect the bridge in case the Germans counter-attacked.

The GIs from the 2/119th were very quickly subjected to fire from German artillery, preventing them from reaching the La Belle Lande – Pont-Hébert road. Several soldiers were wounded. The terrain they occupied was a perfect target for the Kanoniere.

At midday, the 2nd Bn GIs' attention was caught by the number of smoke bombs swaddling the bridge. In spite of the German artillery intensifying its shelling, the American battalion commander left his shelter to get a closer look at the bridge zone. *"The Krauts are counter-attacking!"* he shouted. A radio operator got in touch with Colonel Ednie who tried to reassure him, promising that the 3rd Armored Division tanks were on their way and that the artillery would be supporting them.

This counter-attack was led by Major Brandt, Kdr. of Pz. Pi. Btl.130. During the night, his unit had moved up to reinforce Gruppe Kuhnow which had repositioned itself slightly to its left, to the south of the Les Haut Vents - Pont-Hébert road. Brandt brought with him one of his engineer battalion companies together with 2./Pz. Jg. Lehr-Abt. 130 who established a line of defence 500 yards to the north of the town.

As soon as he got there Major Brandt met Leutnant Claasen from 14./Gren. Rgt. 897 (Kgp. Kentner) to whom he had entrusted the defence of the bridge.

At daybreak, with his units in position, Major Brandt learned that a group of infantry from 352.I.D., situated to the east of the Vire, was supposed to be arriving shortly to take part in the counter-attack together with the Jagdpanther IVs from 2./Pz. Jg. Lehr-Abt.130 and some Pz. IVs from II./Pz. Rgt. 130.

But the American artillery with its 155-mm cannon was

Above.
While a company commander and his platoon leaders are checking their maps at left, their men take a break. Two soldiers in the middle, their backs to the camera, bear the horizontal white stripe of NCOs on their helmets.
(National Archives)

ION AT PONT-HEBERT

quicker off the mark. No less than eight battalions got their guns firing, in a terrible din echoed by the region's hills. The shells fell on the east bank of the Vire, where 352. I.D. was gathering.

CCB's armour finally arrived. They rushed in the direction of the bridge without being spotted. But inevitably this did not last long: Leutnant Claasen's 14./Gren. Rgt. 897 saw them. They waited for the American tanks to get within good range of their 75-mm Paks then they opened fire.

Several Shermans were destroyed under the eyes of the 2/119th Infantry who were powerless to help. For one interminable hour, hell shrouded Pont-Hébert.

The GIs got to almost 300 yards of the bridge before the enemy artillery halted them. This time it was 122-mm and 155-mm guns. These were the Russian and German guns of Art. Rgt. 266 firing.

Suddenly the GIs could not believe their eyes. They saw

six Panzers reaching the Haut Vents sector, heading straight for them. Fortunately the radio was working perfectly. The artillery was called up again and several minutes later, the six Panzers were caught in the trap. Two of them were destroyed by explosive shells and the others scarpered to get under cover.

Even though the situation was critical, Colonel Ednie ordered the 2nd Bn to advance towards

Below.
The experience of the first few weeks of fighting in Normandy led to several innovations that would help Americans progress in the tangled terrain at a lower cost in human lives. This M4A1 of the 743d Tank Battalion has been fitted with large 'horns' on the hull front to dig large holes in the base of hedgerows. These were filled with explosives charges by engineers to blow up the obstacle (also see on p. 85).

Pont-Hébert and the 3rd Bn to try and capture the town.

Major Brandt now knew that he could only count on the Grenadiere from 352. ID. He ordered his Pioniere, supported by a few Jagdpanthers to resist the American onslaught as stubbornly as possible. One American platoon was nearly completely wiped out. Worse: the officers from C Company disappeared one after the other under fire from the German artillery which continued bombarding the heights situated to the east of the river. The most senior man remaining was Sergeant R. Day.

This is an excerpt from the 119th Infantry Regiment report: *"During the artillery barrage, a shell fell directly into a foxhole, killing two men and wounding a third. Suffering from shock from his wounds, the survivor did not realise that the other two were dead.*

While heading to the first aid station, he heard someone calling for help. Shocked, blinded by his own blood, he succeeded in finding the wounded man who couldn't see and was helped by another GI.

Private Dechiaro guided him to the first aid station, helping him to get up and drop to the ground with each artillery explosion. He protected him with his body when the splinters whistled around them. When he reached the station, he refused to be looked after preferring to help and take the medics back to the where the wounded were."

In spite of support from the artillery and from Combat Command B of the 3rd Armored Division, the 30th Division infantry regiments were in no state to reach their objectives.

Pont-Hébert remained in the hands of Major Brandt and the SS-Kgp. positioned mainly in front of the 120th Infantry Regiment which spread itself out, parallel to the north of the Le Hommet - Pont Hébert road.

The 120th Infantry did not gain any ground. However, it did manage to drive off two counter-attacks by SS-Obersturmführer Macher's Pioniere company.

Below.
Fifteen inhabitants of Pont-Hébert were killed and many buildings destroyed before Pont-Hébert was finally liberated on 14 July 1944 by the 119th Infantry of the 30th Infantry Division. This American division had already attacked this town several times.
(National Archives)

A short while later, Macher left for Le Hommet where the command post of Oberst Scholze, Kdr. of Pz. Gren. Rgt.901, was located. The latter informed him that according to SS-Obersturmbannführer Wisliceny's plans, his company had to hold the sector that was most under threat from the 9th Infantry Division. He said that Pz. Gren. Rgt.901, which had been weakened by the previous day's losses, could no longer hold this portion of the front.

The arrival of Macher's Pioniere on the right wing of Kampfgruppe Scholze enabled the Panzergrenadiere to shorten their front while waiting for the reinforcements to come from Pz. Jg. Lehr-Abt.130 under Major Barth, together with a company of Pz. Pi. Btl. 130. Generally speaking, a war of attrition of sorts took over for the whole day. The GIs no longer had to face the powerful counter-attacks of the previous day because the Panzer-Lehr was now considerably weaker.

In spite of his division's weakness, Generalleutnant Bayerlein divided his Kampfgruppe into a multitude of smaller groups each supported by a tank. He recalls: "*The main line of defence was made up of support points ten yards from each other.*

The crews of the Pz. IVs, Panthers or Sturmgeschütze were camouflaged with very great care – it was an art in which they were past masters. All the square, angular shapes of their tanks had to disappear under leaves which were replaced as soon as they started to wither. Except in dire need the engines were cut.

Behind the front line, only two or three tanks, a few Granatwerfer and a group of Panzergrenadiere were held in reserve, ready to intervene. All the lanes and paths which the enemy might use to get near us were mined by our sappers."

General Hobbs told Major-General Corlett of XIXth Army Corps about his plan. He envisaged a completely new tactic for the following day, but the units next to his 30th Infantry Division, the 9th and the 35th Infantry were too far away from his flanks. The 117th Infantry Regiment, under Colonel Kelly, which for the time being had remained too far back in relation to CCB, would have to describe an arc in order to turn south, with la Terrette on its right flank.

As for the 119th Infantry, it had to take Pont-Hébert. All these arrangements were confirmed during the night of 12-13 July.

FIGHTING EAST OF THE VIRE

Above.
During the night of 9 to 10 July 1944, General Baade was ordered to send his 137th and 320th Infantry Regiments to relieve the 29th and the 30th Divisions in the La Meauffe sector. At 5 am the two regiments took the road leading to the front whereas corps artillery bombarded the German positions for an hour. We can see here one of these columns of GIs from the 35th Division.
(National Archives)

Below.
These two Engineers are going to blow up a hedgerow with two shells cases stuffed with explosive each, after a tank had punched holes in the base of the hedgerow as explained next page.
(National Archives)

TO THE EAST OF THE VIRE, the 29th and 35th Infantry Divisions were in position, ready for the final offensive against the capital of the Manche department.

The right wing of the 29th was held by its own 115th Infantry Regiment which was spread out between Hill 108 (not included: in the zone attributed to the 35th Infantry division) – Bourg d'Enfer – north of La Luzerne.

This last place was occupied by the 116th Infantry which was deployed diagonally up to La Bloterie. The third infantry regiment in the "Blue and Gray," the 175th Infantry, was in reserve. To the left of the 29th division was the 2nd Infantry division, in the Vth Army Corps, and on its right, the 35th division which had arrived two days earlier.

New tactics had been evolved to advance in the bocage. It was no longer a matter of following the lanes where enemy machine guns, lying in ambush, could wipe out a whole column of GIs in a minute. These troops had been trained to advance in dangerous and unknown terrain in a different manner.

Each infantry battalion was supported by an engineer company. Alone, small teams made up of one infantry platoon and one from the Engineers, were backed up by a tank and opened the way. Instead of following the roads and lanes, they went through the hedges which were cut open by a tank fitted with large "shears," called the "Cullin device" after its inventor, welded onto the front of the tank. In no time, it tore through the brushwood firing its machine gun at the same time, then entered the field behind the hedge, followed by the infantry.

Some tanks were fitted with sharp-pointed posts attached to the hull front. These were only used when embankments were very high. With a leap forward, the tank planted the posts in the base of the hedgerow then reversed, leaving two large holes in which the engineers

then placed TNT charges stuffed into 105-mm shell cases, and blew up a passage. Once there was a breach in the hedge, the tank slipped through the hole, at the same time opening fire; then the crew kept an eye on the field sweeping it with its armament.

With this support, the infantry could then deploy in the field and cross it. If there was no response from the Germans, the operation was repeated with the next hedge. Otherwise the tank opened fire on the enemy positions until the Germans were all killed or fell back. Like this, the GIs advanced much more slowly than on the previous days but on the other hand there were far fewer casualties. The 747th Tank Battalion was attached to the 29th Infantry Division to support it with its advance on Saint Lô.

Opposite the 29th and the 35th Infantry Divisions were the II. Fallschirmjägerkorps under Generalleutnant Meindl which, it must be understood, was in a critical situation. The Chief-of-Staff of this paratroop army corps speaks about the situation in a statement dated November 1950: *"In mid-June, the German High Command gave up its plans for attacking towards the coast because of growing pressure from the Allies. However it ordered us to hold our front. Generalleutnant Meindl asked for a flexible line of defence to be established in order to save lives, but his suggestions were continually ignored. As a result, the 3. Fallschirmjägerdivision lost between 300 and 400 men with every day's fighting. It was soon vital to plug the gaps with the army corps reserve. There were no troops left to occupy the positions in the rear let alone fortify them. As soon as they arrived, the Fallschirm. Aufkl-Abteilung 12 and the Fallschirm. Stug. Brigade 12 were assigned to 3. Fallschirmjägerdivision.*

Because the situation was becoming dramatic, the High Command made up two Kampfgruppe from two other divisions. These tactical groups were intended to support the 352.I.D. whose forces were dwindling at an alarming rate.

The following units moved up to the front on 20 June

1944: *a regiment from the 353.I.D., reinforced by artillery pieces* (Author's note: Kgp. Böhm – 980 men) *and at the beginning of July another regiment from the 266.I.D. (Kgp. Kentner). The sector where they were engaged was continually reduced, to the detriment of the 3. Fallschirmjägerdivision. As a result, this division was obliged to gather in all the men from the rear of the lines, even the Pioniere, and commit them to the front line."*

Although the 3. Fallschirmjägerdivision had lost a third of its strength fighting the 29th Infantry Division, it must be remembered that these soldiers had been superbly trained and were led by officers of high military worth and ability. Their devotion to the National-Socialist cause was as strong as that of the Waffen-SS.

The night was so dark that the GIs, huddled in their holes could barely make out the thick outlines of the hedges which were just near them. The men on guard at the well dug-in company HQ were on edge, listening carefully, frightened that the Germans would come at them along the sunken lanes which at the moment were plunged in deepest darkness. Each soldier spent the night waiting for the attack planned for 5 am. The hours ticked slowly by. Suddenly at 1am the night was torn by white lightning and shattered by the shots from German 105-mm artillery pieces and 88-mm Flak guns. All the shells fell on the 115th Infantry. When the bombardment ceased, the mortars took over, concentrating in particular on the 1st Battalion's position.

The Pioniere from the 15./Fallschirmjägerregiment 9 (15./FJR 9) took advantage of the fact that the GIs were all huddled up in their shelters to open a breach in the barbed wire which was blocking the way. Once this was

done, the I/FJR 9 paratroopers slipped through the breach then rushed at the GIs who, alerted by the firing of small arms, raised their heads, wide-eyed. They could still not see anything, but they could hear terse orders in German. Suddenly they were seized

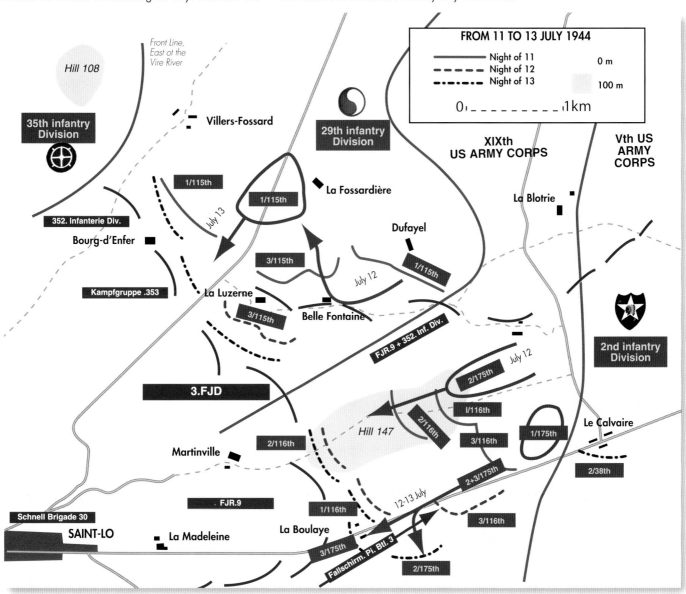

Hill 108

Front Line, East of the Vire River

35th infantry Division

Villers-Fossard

29th infantry Division

XIXth US ARMY CORPS

Vth US ARMY CORPS

FROM 11 TO 13 JULY 1944

	Night of 11	0 m
	Night of 12	
	Night of 13	100 m

0 _____ 1km

1/115th

1/115th

La Fossardière

La Blotrie

July 13

352. Infanterie Div.

Bourg-d'Enfer

Dufayel

1/115th

3/115th

Kampfgruppe .353

July 12

La Luzerne

3/115th

Belle Fontaine

FJR.9 + 352. Inf. Div.

2nd infantry Division

3.FJD

2/175th

July 12

2/116th

I/116th

3/116th

1/175th

Le Calvaire

Hill 147

2/116th

Martinville

1/116th

2+3/175th

2/38th

Schnell Brigade 30

SAINT-LO

FJR.9

3/175th

12-13 July

3/116th

La Boulaye

La Madeleine

Fallschirm. Pi. Btl. 3

2/175th

Paratrooper scouts are walking down a narrow dark lane. Their expressions are taught. There is tension on both sides. Death could loom at any time. Nobody was safe from a burst of machine gun fire.
(BA 101 I/584/2152/24)

Major Friedrich Ludwig Herbert Alpers

Alpers was born on 25 March 1901 in Sonnenberg. Before entering the parachute arm in February 1944, he was a state lawyer. After the death of Major Stephani in the Falaise Gap, he took command of the regiment. On 3 September 1944, he was seriously wounded at Quévy le Grand Mons, then according to different versions, he was killed or committed suicide. The soldiers who fought under him were unanimous in saying that to the end he had remained a worthy officer who was close to his troops.

with panic. Shadows wearing bowl-shaped helmets rushed towards them.

The objective of the Fallschirmjäger was to eliminate the artillery spotters positioned on the heights. But before reaching them they had to sweep aside the three companies from the 1st Bn of the 115th under Major Alpers.

Major Johns of the 1st Bn of the 115th Infantry wrote about this engagement after the war: "*Nobody knew exactly how many there were of them. Most of the soldiers in the forward positions had their heads down during the artillery barrage; some of them opened their eyes wide to see what was going to come. A Company confirmed that the German paratroopers came from the left of the regiment and that they took C Company to task and fought them for most of the night. Then they managed to get rid of the A and D Company command posts. They fired into the foxholes along the sides of a winding road and threw grenades all over the place. I heard they had flame throwers but I never met anyone who had seen one...*"

Although the I./Fallschirmjägerregiment 9 did not indeed have any flame throwers, the 15.Kp. of the regiment had five when it was first fitted out.

Luck was on the Fallschirmjägers' side. They had unwittingly attacked along the junction between A and B companies. The CO of A company, blinded by a grenade, lost consciousness. The GIs who were around him did not even have the time to look after him before the Germans threw themselves at them shooting like madmen. Completely overwhelmed, they abandoned their command post and fell back. In a few minutes, two Platoons of A Company found themselves isolated then wiped out mercilessly. B Company's situation was just as desperate. It found itself scattered and its different platoons could do nothing but fight just as ferociously as the enemy in order to save their skins. There was no longer any coordination. It was every man for himself.

The mortar positions located further back from the front line were also attacked by the German paratroopers who gave no quarter. It was more the surprise than the strength

of the attack which disoriented the American soldiers. The mortar crews' salvation lay in flight. Alerted, Colonel Goodwin Ordway Jr., CO of the 115th Infantry, ordered heavy weapons to be positioned to the rear of his 1st Bn. This turned out to be vital as there were no reserves available for the moment. While waiting for these to arrive, the soldiers of the 1st Bn were alone.

In position on the left wing of this battalion, the CO of the 116th infantry radioed his company commanders: "*Be ready for an enemy attack, the 115th's lines have been driven in.*"

But the Germans did not show up. They were content to fire harassing shots which caused thirty casualties among the Americans; at the same time the GIs from the 2nd Infantry division, positioned in front of Bérigny were also bombarded, before being attacked by two paratroop companies from Fallschirmjäger-regiment 5, reinforced by Pioniere.

The attack against 1/115th Infantry

Once again, surprise favoured the Germans but it did not last long. The Americans we‹re not slow to react violently and push back their attackers. They were ready for the time intended for the offensive and for their mission: taking Hill 192.

Major Johns tells how that terrible night ended: "*It was a savage maul all night. I remained in radio contact most of the time with B and C Companies, but I had no idea where A company was. We found their platoons in the morning still at their posts with German dead all around them; the attack had in fact been stopped by the mortars and by all those who had been rounded up by the men who remained cool-headed.*

Battalion HQ remained out of touch with the regiment and artillery for almost an hour. A German patrol which had ventured into our lines had cut the lines and the radios which were being serviced were silent.

Regiment only found out about our predicament at 2 am. It was then that we called our artillery which immediately bombarded the valley. At the beginning of the

Above.
**Another shot of the paratrooper reconnaissance troops.
The sidecar in the foreground will soon have to be
pushed to avoid making any noise.
The bicycle seen leaning against the bank
was still the best means of transport.**
(BA 101 I/584/2152/24)

*engagement, somebody captured a German whom he
brought to Battalion HQ. The man told us that there were
three paratrooper companies and another of engineers,
fighting as infantry and that each company had on average 110 soldiers. It was about the strength that we thought
we had in front of our front line…*

*Luckily enough for us, the enemy attack moved over
to the right. Every one of us in the CP had an M1 rifle
and a hole near the hedge for shelter."*

Finally the German paratroopers were forced to fall
back because their losses were too heavy. Indeed, 87 of
them had been killed. Their boldness had not paid off.

As for Major Johns, who had lost a quarter of his
strength, he had to reorganise his battalion. He informed
Colonel Ordway that his men would not be ready for
the offensive.

Just before this offensive, five battalions of artillery
from the XIXth Army Corps opened fire on the enemy
lines. At 6 am on 12 July, the 2nd Bn of the 116th Infantry
jumped off. The 1st and 3rd Bns followed at a distance.
As the Americans approached the first hedge, German
machine guns went into action and did not take long to
put repel them. The Fallschirmjäger had set up their positions along the whole hedge length. Bravely, one of the

**This sunken lane could be the one the Fallschirmjägers
were using on the previous photograph.
A team of American linesmen are laying
a telephone cable. On the left a soldier can be seen
placing a cable in a tree.**
(National Archives)

Above.
These Fallschirmjäger are spying the enemy from a hole dug into the hedgerow bank. Note how the PK has walked back to take the picture. An American corpse lies in the foreground.
(BA 101 I/586/2215/25)

American company commanders harangued his men who threw themselves at the wall of branches. But their momentum was very quickly broken. A GI paid this charge with his life by stepping on a mine. Unfortunately, there were others. The GIs had not yet received the order to fall back before they were subjected to accurate fire from 88-mm Flak guns and mortars.

Despite all his efforts, the CO of the 2nd Bn of the 116th Infantry, Major Sidney V. Bingham, Jr., was quite unable to get his bearings in this green hell. The German gunfire was coming from Saint-André-de-L'Epine and from the Martinville ridge (Hill 147). A Sturmgeschütz had also been spotted to the north of the Saint-Lô road.

Major Bingham contacted the artillery by radio and two minutes later, extremely accurate shots fell on the Saint-André-de-l'Epine sector and also on "their" hedge. The mortars of the 92nd Chemical Mortar battalion distracted the artillery on Martinville ridge; meanwhile a few Shermans hurried away towards where the Sturmgeschütz had been spotted and this was

eliminated shortly afterwards.

Under this bombardment, the German artillery fire became sporadic. This enabled the engineers to clear the mines, under the cover of the infantry while it waited for the signal to set off and clear out the hedges. It nevertheless took them some very brutal hand-to-hand fighting to succeed in doing this.

The next obstacle they met was a flooded lane and, to cap it all, it was mined as well! They discovered the mutilated corpses of German soldiers here and there; their comrades had not had the time to take them away with them, such was the pressure they were under.

There's no denying that the artillery prepared the ground for them. In all, it took five hours for the GIs in the 2nd Bn of the 116th Infantry to get through six hedges with tank support!

In the end, Major Bingham's infantry was able to go past the perfect ambush positions which had already been abandoned by the retreating German paratroopers. In exploring other hedges where lay more corpses,

Right.
In a narrow path between fields, German paras have gathered all sorts of equipment. Among MG ammunition cases can be seen American light machine gun tripods. It is possible the crews barely had time to take away the gun before leaving their position.
(BA 101 I/586/2215/27)

the Americans continued to advance, fighting sporadically. All resistance where the II. and the III./ Fallschirmjägerregiment 9 joined was eliminated. Finally the GIs came into sight of their objective, Hill 147, located near Martinville. Gradually, the 3rd Bn advanced on its left flank to give it the necessary backing.

It was only at midday that the 1st Bn of the 115th Infantry got going in turn. Its CO, Major Johns, had a lot of trouble keeping up with the other two battalions.

Colonel Ordway deployed his regiment on either side of the Saint-Lô road. The 1st Bn was on the left, coordinating with the 116th. Its objective was to take La Luzerne. But to do that, the linchpin at Belle-Epine had to be taken first. On its left, the 3rd Bn advanced along a narrow corridor between La Luzerne and the Saint-Lô road. As for the 2nd Bn, it was progressing towards Le Bourg-d'Enfer, situated to the west of the Saint-Lô road.

The soldiers in Colonel Ordway's 115th Infantry marched slowly in the bocage until midday without coming across any real opposition. Once the 3rd Bn was in position to the south of La Belle-Epine, the 1st Bn under Major Johns took the village and the heights to the east of the village. A Company led the attack against the village. C Company which was holding back was standing by to intervene.

At 5 pm the 1st and 3rd Bns were still engaged. Two assaults were carried out but Colonel Ordway did not think they were satisfactory. No less than 13,000 shells were fired at the German positions which still resisted. At 8 pm, the 2nd Bn was attacked to the west of the Saint-Clair – Saint-Lô road. The fighting lasted until dusk.

Major-General Gerhardt, commanding the 29th Infantry Division, called in his reserve regiment because the coordination between the regiments which he had committed was unsatisfactory. Moreover, after the 116th Infantry branched off to the west, it lost all contact with the 2nd Division situated its left flank. In the Le Calvaire sector, which it had abandoned there was now a gap which the Germans could use to their advantage.

The 2nd Bn of the 175th Infantry Regiment was sent to this zone while the other two battalions got together on the division's left wing.

Major-General Gerhardt's objective was to encircle Saint-Lô by closing all the roads leading to it and controlling all the heights. But deep down, he hoped that the Germans would leave the town before they were completely surrounded, thus saving lives. He was not entirely satisfied with the ground his regiments had gained because they could not yet launch an attack to take Saint-

Above.
The Flammenwerfer 41 was widely used by the 3.Fallschirmjägerdivision. This paratrooper is equipped with the most effective version and of course the most widely produced. It comprised two bottles arranged horizontally. The upper one was filled with fuel and the bottom one with nitrogen. It weighed 39 lb in all and had a range of 25 to 30 yards
(BA 1011583/2144/45)

Below.
**This StuG III has been destroyed near Martinville by the 29th Infantry Division. It belonged to the Fallschirm. Sturmgeschutz-Brigade 112.
A second tank seemed to be in front of this one.**
(Frederic Deprun collection)

Lô, as he wished. The German lines in the 116th Infantry's sector had however been pierced.

The 2nd US Infantry Division and Hill 192

That day's real victory was the 2nd Infantry division's taking Hill 192. These heights were the key to the area to the east of Saint-Lô. They stretched from east of Bérigny to the village of Saint-Georges-d'Elle.

Engaged since the 12 June in front of this Hill 192, the GIs in the 2nd division had lost more than 1,200 of their comrades. They had been lured into a static war which recalled the First World War. On the right of this formation, Saint-Georges-d'Elle had seen heavy fighting and had been taken, lost and retaken several times. It was impossible for the American soldiers to get close to, or even into, the area surrounding Hill 192 because the German defences were too strong. The paratroopers in FJR 9 of the 3. Fallschirmjägerdivision were entrenched in hundreds of dugouts hidden inside or below the century-old hedges. Their front stretched from La Luzerne – Bretel – La Belle-Fontaine (II.Btl.) – L'Epine – Saint-André-de-L'Epine – Cloville (I.Btl.) – Hill 192 (III.Btl.)

The losses in II./Fallschirmjägerregiment 9 were heavy. In the 5.Kp. the 'Spiess,' Hauptfeldwebel Oppermann, was wounded. The 5.Kp. commanded by Oberleutnant Schloesser for the time being, lost one of its platoon leaders, Feldwebel Wulff who was hit in the stomach by shrapnel.

In the 6.Kp., at La Luzerne, the platoon leader, Oberfeldwebel Dichtel and Medical Feldwebel Knops were wounded. In the 7.Kp., Medical Feldwebel Bodo Paulet was wounded. The platoon leader, Feldwebel Pölkow was killed.

Finally in the 8.Kp., Stabsfeldwebel Küsserer, platoon leader Oberfeldwebel Leiterhold and Feldwebel Siesserl were all wounded.

The unit positioned on FJR 9's right was FJR 5 under Major Becker which was spread out along the line Saint-Georges-d'Elle – Hue – Ivon – La Saferie – La Taille – up to La Croix rouge, along the Bérigny road.

The German positions were so carefully camouflaged that their location was barely visible on aerial photos. Risky patrols by GIs were sent out to locate these positions and the heavy weapons on the front line, but most of the time, they were ambushed or went down lanes densely sown with antipersonnel mines. The invisible sharp shooters reigned over the area like lords and masters.

An officer from the 2nd Infantry Division recalls that a handful of "green devils" with a machine gun was capable of pinning down a whole unit when it crossed a field.

Without being able to give precise details as to the whereabouts of his company, the 4./Fallschirm. Aufklärungs-Abteilung 12, Oberjäger Paul gives us a realis-

This photo series was shot between 7 ☐
10 July 1944 on Departmental road 6 betv
Saint-Lô and Saint-Clair-sur-Elle. Following
reorganisation of the front, the III.Flak Korps
a small part of the Gruppe Höne were atta⬚
to the Panzergruppe West. The 13. Flakdivis
reinforced by the Flak-Sturm-Rgt 1 and the ▯
Jagd.-Gr. Höne was subordinate to the 7. Ar▯
On the evening of 6 July, Oberstleutnant F
personally received instructions from 7. Ar▯
"You are going to secure the roads immedi⬚
with one or two of your Abteilungs trained fo
this task. Your Flak can fire on ground targ⬚
needs be. They will position themselves in ▯
of the lines whilst at the same standing by ⬚
withdrawn to the rear of the army. Luftflo▯
approves of these decisions. The Army Gro⬚
understanding our difficulties authorises ▯
Abteilungs to move about."

1. Slightly further back of the D6, thre
Flak gunners are eating. Their frying ▯
is placed on an 88-mm shell basket. 1
right hand man's helmet is camouflaç
(BA 101 I/494/3396/16)

2. When they finished, the gunners
camouflaged their 88-mm Flak with
branches; the barrel is pointing dowr
road, ready to fire. These soldiers are
the sector assigned to the
3.Fallschirmjägerdivision.
(BA 101 I/494/3396/16)

3. We can see here a Grenadier lyin₵
ambush in a fox hole with his
Panzerschreck pointing in the directic
the road. He is a few dozen yards fr⬚
the 88-mm Flak gun. During this par̶
the Battle of Normandy, cooperation
between the various arms was vital. ▯
happened that tactical groups were
made up of units from both the Heer ▯
the Luftwaffe.
(BA 101 I/494/3396/22)

4. Another pose for the Grenadier se⬚
on the previous photo. He has uses ▯
captured American goggles to proteɾ
him when firing the weapon. This is ⬚
88-mm Raketenpanzerbüchse 43
('Offenröhr'). This rocket launcher wɾ
fact inspired by the American M1
Bazooka. However, the Offenröhr w▯
rather cumbersome with a length of ⬚
10 ins and a weight of 20 pounds. T̶
was the reason why the second mod▯
was created in 1944. The one on thi₵
shot was produced the year before. ▯
RpzB 43 had a range of 150 yards. ▯
(BA 101 I/494/3396/23)

5. The section commander is watchin⬚
the D6 with a pair of binoculars. The
carriage has been thoroughly
camouflaged and it blends perfectly ▯
the hedges which line the D6. The
signpost shows us that the D96 is on ▯
right. La Luzerne was only 400 yard₵
away and Saint-André-de-L'Epine, 2 ▯
1/2 miles away. The gun is therefore
pointing towards Saint-Clair-sur-Elle. ▯
(BA 101 I/494/3396/32)

6. This gunner has kept his Mauser 9⬚
during the camouflage operation. Th̶
situation remained tense in spite of t̶
apparent calm.
(BA 101 I/494/3396/33)

7. Because the situation evolved rapi̶
this 88-mm Flak is still on its wheelec
mount even though it is ready to fire.
There was not enough time to set it
directly on the ground. Note the rear
mudguard of the Sonderhänger 201 ▯

tic account, evoking the difficulties and the terror set up by the sharpshooters on both sides.

"Our battalion had been ordered to hold an area surrounded by hedges and to protect a road along which our supplies would come. A sunken lane ended up directly on the American front line and lost itself in the thick forest. Hidden on top of the escarpment lining one side of the road, I watched from my Fuchsloch *(foxhole)* with my rifle fitted with telescopic sights. I watched the sunken lane but also the tops of the highest trees which could hide a sharpshooter or artillery spotters. This situation lasted for about two days until a machine gun opened up with tracer bullets. I was not sure whether or not I had been spotted. Once I had located the enemy and his machine gun, I aimed carefully then with a bullseye, I destroyed the water-cooling system of the Browning machine gun.

The bullet ricochetted and finished right in one of the crew's face. After that we had a bit of peace and quiet. During the night we went to see the result of my shot. The corpse of an American soldier lay near the machine gun. But we had no time to think about this as we had to continue our Scharfschützen *(sharp-shooting)* missions."

In the same area as the photos on page 88, a few dozen yards away, a tank of II./SS-Pz. Rgt. 2 is waiting, ready to support the Fallschirmjäger. On both sides it was the same way of fighting: a handful of soldiers supported by a tank. It was the most effective and the least deadly tactic in the bocage.
(BA 101 I/586/35)

Fortunately the GIs had had the time now, after a month of fighting to get used to this hedgerow type of war. The engineers had organized the front line by reinforcing it with barbed wire. The forward positions were closed in, protected by logs, sandbags and mines. Radio contact between the divisional units was by means of a signals company which had unrolled more than 75 miles of telephone cables. For two weeks now, the GIs had been relieved in turn to be trained in the rear. They were drilled specially for the capture of Hill 192. They learnt how to work as a team. As the soldiers of the 29th division had done, they had to learn how to coordinate their efforts with the engineers and the tank crews so that they could get through the hedgerows and at the same time avoid casualties.

The shell containers have been stocked behind the piece. (BA 101 I/494/3396/34)

8. Another rear view of the 88-mm gun. All gunners are at their stations. The historical context which these AA guns were in on 11 July at 05.35 was the following: on the right flank II.Fallschirmjäger-Korps was being subjected to intense bombing. American reconnaissance approached Bérigny and Saint-Georges-d'Elle, only six miles from this gun. At 9 am, the Americans attacked Saint-Georges d'Elle

ON DEPARTMENTAL ROAD 6

and Saint-André de l'Epine. However, the artillery and the mortars of the II. Fallschirmjäger-Korps managed to drive them off. But it was only putting off the moment of reckoning. (BA 101 I/494/3396/37)

9. With his Mauser held against his arm, the Flak soldier is waiting. The mission for this 88-mm Flak crew was doomed to fail. Indeed on 18 July, the II. Fallschirmjäger-Korps abandoned Saint-Lô. Let's allow Generalleutnant Schimpf to end this report: *"I set up the rest of my division which represented simply the strength of a regiment in the sector of Saint-Germain-d'Elle – Bérigny – Couvains. Because of the lack of artillery pieces, the Flak-Abteilungen engaged as anti-tank guns were sent partly to the rear of the front."* (BA 101 I/494/3396/39)

"Ike" talking to an NCO of the 2nd Inf. Div. The divisional insignia representing the head of a Red Indian was remembered by the German paratrooper veterans. Many of them were scared stiff of them because these soldiers were very skilled with knives. This division was formed in October 1917 in France under the command of two Marine Corps Generals. It was engaged for the first time in 1918 at Bois Belleau, Soissons, Blanc-Mont and during the Argonne offensive. Its valour earned it the French Croix de Guerre fourragère. When WWI ended, it left for Fort Sam Houston, Texas where it remained for 23 years.
The division landed on 7 June 1944 on Omaha Beach, it fought for six weeks in the hedgerows then took part in the difficult capture of Brest in September 1944.
(National Archives)

As the days went by, the GIs started getting more and more on edge. They were developing their aggressiveness. They thought of nothing else but capturing that Hill 192. But each time a date was set for the offensive, bad weather set in and the attack had to be called off. Finally the offensive which they had all been waiting for so long was announced for 16 July 1944 at 6 am.

Several hours before the attack was set off, a surprise raid called "Kersting" was carried out by a group of 150 Fallschirmjäger. Kersting was nothing but the name of the CO of 5./Fallschirmjägerregiment 9 who had been killed a few days earlier.

Furtively, the Stosstrupp (assault troop) slipped behind the 2nd Division's lines. The whole front seemed to be inert. There was no noise, not even a rumbling engine. The Fallschirmjäger managed to penetrate beyond the enemy frontline without being spotted. They ran towards a high earthen wall where some of the group got their breath back.

A veteran of Fallschirmjägerregiment 9, Rudi Frübeisser takes up the story: *"On the given signal, an animal cry, the Stosstrupp jumped over the wall as one. They discovered a sunken lane where an American company's position was set up. There was a terrible hand to hand fight. It was difficult to tell friend from foe; the shouts and the swearing alone guided us. The spades and other tools clinked and fell upon the GIs helmets. Shooting was not possible. Soon the wounded comrades would have to be taken away. Oberjäger Ziehlke of the 3.Kp. fired a shot with his Leuchtpistole at point blank range into the chest of an American.*

The whole sector was ablaze and the GIs fled the fighting which was going on here and there. In the heart of the engagement, some hills were lit up by whitish lights hanging from little parachutes which drifted slowly to the ground. Soon we could see just as if it were daytime.

Oberjäger Nüsser violently kicked the chin of a Negro [1] who was kneeling in front of him, with his jump boots as if it were a football. Although he was kneeling he was just as big as Nüsser. Suddenly Jupp screamed. He had just been hit in the hip. His legs gave way under him. He continued to advance on all fours. Suddenly an American leapt after him and tried to hit him with a stone. Holding his pistol in his hand, Jupp squeezed the trigger and the bullet hit the American in the chin.

The American artillery began bombarding the sunken lane. The Fallschirmjägers immediately tried to break off. As far as possible, they tried to take the dead and wounded with them, even though enemy fire was getting heavier as the shock group got closer to its starting position."

Without knowing it, Rudi Frübeisser had just been subjected to the initial effects of the terrible artillery preparation that heralded the start of the 2nd Infantry Division's offensive. Hill 192 vanished behind a cloud of smoke, dust and explosions.

Crushed by the 25,000 shells which were fired, it seemed impossible for the German paratroopers to sur-

vive such a cataclysm.

According to the 2nd Division's history, this preparation was described as the best organised barrage of the whole of the European campaign. The firing plan included eight artillery battalions.

Each firing zone was delimited by a different colour corresponding to a letter on the maps distributed to the GIs in the two regiments who had to attack. In that way, they could guide themselves with some measure of precision. These colours were supposed to guide the aircraft who had to bomb Hill 192. But the pilots were again victims of the bad weather which meant poor visibility for them. Their participation was cancelled when some P-47s just missed strafing some GIs from the 38th Infantry Regiment.

According to the plan, the 23rd Infantry under Colonel Jay B. Lowless, would approach the heights from the east between Saint-Georges-d'Elle and La Croix-Rouge where the paratroopers from the I./FJR. were dug in.

As for Colonel Ralph W. Zwicker of the 38th Infantry, he launched two battalions straight against the III./FJR 9 while the third came in from the west. Shortly afterwards, the soldiers from this regiment supported by two companies from the 741st Tank Battalion and some engineers, dealt with the hedges by blowing passages through

---

1. *In their books, several former German paratroopers mention Black American soldiers in the front line. In reality, Black troops were at the time assigned mostly to support units (artillery, engineers) and the supply services, and there was none assigned to any of the 2d Division's organic units...*

Opposite page, top right.
Using a tree trunk for support, this BAR gunner is ready to open up in a field. Reality or reconstruction, we will never know. Whichever it was, this picture shows us a daily scene from the front as all these GIs experienced it.
(DITE/USIS)

Below.
The 2d Infantry Division shoulder patch.

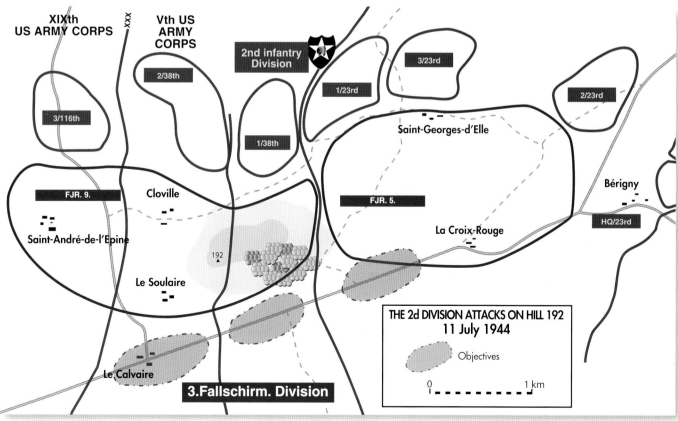

XIXth
US ARMY CORPS

Vth US ARMY CORPS

2nd infantry Division

3/23rd

2/38th

1/23rd

2/23rd

3/116th

1/38th

Saint-Georges-d'Elle

Bérigny

FJR. 9.

Cloville

FJR. 5.

HQ/23rd

Saint-André-de-l'Epine

La Croix-Rouge

192

Le Soulaire

THE 2d DIVISION ATTACKS ON HILL 192
11 July 1944

Le Calvaire

3.Fallschirm. Division

Objectives

0   1 km

them, completely bowling over the enemy who very often was hiding behind.

The first line of defence was very quickly disrupted and the Fallschirmjäger had no choice but to huddle in their holes to escape the thousands of shells which were falling everywhere. They stubbornly refused to come out of their positions even when they where overwhelmed. Some of them did not hesitate to open fire on the GIs even if there was no chance of them getting away. Generally, the artillery did not succeed in breaking their resistance. Burrowed in their hole, dug deep into the ground and skilfully protected, they still preserved all their determination to resist. When the GIs went past their positions they sneaked out of their holes and fired behind the GIs'

backs. The most difficult obstacles to get past were the fortified "strong points;" these comprised a heavy gun, like an 88-mm Flak canon and a few paratroopers dug in nearby.

As with most platoons in the 38th Infantry, that of 1st Lieutenant Reynolds was taken to task by artillery, automatic weapons and small arms. A report about this officer can be read in the archives of the 2nd Infantry Division. *"First of all, First Lieutenant Reynolds hesitated then bravely advanced towards the enemy to reconnoiter a route for the tanks. Constantly under fire from the front and the sides, he crawled along a hedge then reached a position held by the enemy which was machine-gunning his men.*

With no concern for his own safety, Lieutenant Reynolds killed three Germans and forced the fourth to surrender. This act of bravery enabled his soldiers to advance without danger. By his courage, skill and his heroic devotion to duty, Lt Reynolds acted in the greatest tradition of the armed forces."

The Fallschirmjägers' losses were heavy. Helmuth Struppel confirms this in his narrative: *"The tanks reached us by firing through the hedges. Sharpshooters also caused losses. The Americans used HE ammunition which caused terrible wounds. At about 10 am, we were ordered to withdraw because we could not hold out in our positions any longer. I had a wounded man in my machine gun nest. So I started to help him walk with some of the others. A shell exploded next to us. The wounded man was hit again by shrapnel, this time in his side. Another piece hit my MG tool kit then ricochetted whistling close to my chest. That day I must have escaped death more than a hundred times.*

At 11.15 I was the last man in my platoon. Car-

This monument dedicated to the 29th Infantry Division stands today at Saint-Clair-sur-Elle. The names of the localities liberated by the division are engraved: Couvains, La Luzerne, La Meauffe, Le Mesnil-Rouxelin, Moon-sur-Elle, Saint-André-de-l'Epine, Saint-Jean-de-Savigny, Sainte-Marguerite-d'Elle and Villers-Fossard.
(T. Guilbert photograph)

Above.
These Fallschirmjäger have set up a machine gun post hidden behind an earthen bank. This is a captured American .30 calibre Browning. As a veteran of FJR 9 recalls, "There was an acute lack of weapons and ammunition from 11 July onwards so we had to make do with recovered weapons in order to continue fighting."
(BA 101 I./582/2103/18)

Opposite page, top.
There were many booby traps along the road to Saint-Lô. The German sappers were past masters in the art. Here a jeep has just run over a mine. As its tyres have been taken down, this is probably a staged shot for instructional purposes, as the other picture.
(National Archives)

Opposite page, bottom.
All the German sappers' equipment picked up by the American army as it progressed was recovered, analysed and identified. There was also information and instruction for the American troops. All the objects on the two blankets have been classified by category. In the left-hand part the following can be read, from top to bottom: German Tellermines, Bangalore torpedoes, German grenades, Booby trap charges, German firing devices. In the central part: French anti-tank mines and hand grenades, American fuses. On the right-hand side: American anti-tank mines, German "Schu" mine, German "S" bouncing mine, Russian stick grenade.
(National Archives)

rying my MG, I crawled through the enemy lines then came across a comrade who imitated me and showed where one of our wounded comrades was whom he wanted to fetch. The tanks were getting closer. Crossing a field without any cover at all, we were subjected to heavy artillery fire. I expected any moment to get a direct hit. My nerves were cracking and I was not alone. The shells continued falling for several hours. It was hell. There were only thirty or so men left of the 170 men in our company."

Although the Americans were advancing slowly, they were doing so effectively thanks to radio which ensured there was coordination between the infantry and the artillery.

The same could not be said for the German battalions under Major Stephani and the HQ of Generalleutnant Schimpf. Contact was lost. The telephone wires were severed by shrapnel.

The storm continued as day was breaking. E Company of the 38th Infantry was certainly the unit in the 2nd Division which ran into the heaviest resistance during the day. Once the artillery fell silent, its men were engaged on Cloville. The destroyed houses were still burning and all the German positions seemed to have been wiped out. But this was only an impression. Suddenly machine guns cross-fired, tearing the morning mist. A handful of GIs tried to escape from the bullets whistling all around them and ran towards a hedge. The leader of the 2nd Platoon ordered his men to hit the ground because the mortars were targeting the hedge. They were caught in the middle.

Fortunately the GIs from the 3rd Platoon gave them covering fire. For the moment the situation was critical and neither of the platoons was in a position to overcome the German resistance. The fume-laden air got to the soldiers' throats.

Rudi Frübeisser from the III./Fallschirmjägerregiment recalls: *"…then several Typhoons appeared in the sky and attacked our supposed positions and the sunken lanes with their rockets. Part of the brushwood and the grass very quickly caught fire. The CO of 13.Kp., Leutnant Josef Glaser was seriously wounded in the face and stomach by shrapnel. The Americans were increasing their bombardment, to be sure of hitting all our shelters. Then groups of B-24 bombers started to approach and then dropped their bombs like a carpet where our regiment was supposed to be."*

The leader of the 1st platoon of E Company of the 38th Infantry decided to take the 80 or so paratroopers who were holding out against him from behind. Covered by a Sherman, mortars and BARs, his men went round the village following a hedge, out of sight of their adversaries who were busy shooting at the other two platoons. Soon and to their great surprise, heavy artillery fire fell upon the German paratroopers; several GIs who had bravely got closer gunned down some of them. Attacked on both sides at the same time the Germans raised their arms an hour later. There were only fifteen of them left.

Meanwhile, the infantry of the 2nd Bn of the 38th Infantry whose objec-

THE FALLSCHIRMJÄGER ADVANCE

1. A Fallschirmjäger is advancing cautiously through an abandoned village, holding his Mauser 98 K.
(BA 101 I/584/2160/7)

2. A Panzerschreck team is following the road but taking care to melt into the shrubs along the building.
(BA 101 I/584/2160/10)

3. They pause for a moment probably waiting for the order to advance. They have got rid of their equipment which is particularly heavy. The soldier carrying the rocket launcher has removed the cumbersome shield which weighed almost 4 lb, raising the total weight of the Panzerschreck to 17lb.
(BA 101 I/584/2160/12)

4. The two paratroopers set off again. Note the rocket containers carried by the second soldier. Each of these boxes only contained two rockets weighing 7 lb. The gunner holds one, giving a total firepower of five shots a minute. The barrel had a life of 1,000 shots maximum.
(BA 101 I/584/2160/14)

Left.
"Lying down in the grass hidden behind the leaves, two GIs from the 2nd Inf. Div. are about to open fire with their light machine gun," is the Signal Corps original caption. From a reliable source, it happened twice, once on the American and once on the German side, that a machine gun lying in ambush in such circumstances managed to wipe out an entire company as it was crossing a field.
(National Archives)

ing over our positions, they strafed us with their machine guns then returned to launch their rockets while groups of American infantry got closer to our positions; there was hand to hand fighting in several places.

The adjutant of our 2.Kp., Herbert Breit was wounded in the eyes by a phosphorus bomb. He was taken to the rear. In the 3.Kp. under Hauptmann Engelhardt, there was close quarters combat. Little paratrooper Helmut Seetzen was fighting with a huge Negro who stabbed

Right.
The air and bombing attacks did not get the better of the paratroopers' resistance even though their losses were very heavy, as Helmut Struppel remembers: *"There were only thirty men left in my company of 170 men."*
(Dite/Usis)

later. There were only fifteen of them left.

Meanwhile, the infantry of the 2nd Bn of the 38th Infantry whose objective was to attack the heights from behind, had to fight house by house to clear Le Soulaire. They had to help E Company which found itself under fire from an armoured car of Fallschirm. StuG. Abt.12 and a Pz IV. The two vehicles were perfectly camouflaged. Powerless, E Company was trapped in Cloville and its ruins. But a Sherman from the 741st tank Bn came and got them out by destroying the two German tanks all by itself.

Rudi Frübeisser of Fallschirmjägerregiment 9 remembers: *"We could hear the roaring of tank engines then an order from the company "Steady, tanks are approaching." We dug up the Panzerfaust and Panzerschreck which had been buried in the earth after all the explosions. We loaded the machine guns then we waited. Meanwhile Major Stephani accompanied by a group of runners and Leutnant Willi Geck went round the front lines. The signals detachment which had laid cables again had re-established contact with the companies.*

Several Shermans managed to breach the regimental lines. Some of them, equipped with flame throwers sprayed our positions. Hard luck for the wounded who could not run. Sometimes, the Fallschirmjägers, scorning death, managed to destroy the tanks by blowing them up with explosive charges. Once again, the twin engined fighter-bombers intervened in the ground fighting. Fly-

Right.
**A morbid scene during the Battle of Saint-Lô: the bodies of paratroopers are carried away in an American 6 x 6 trucks wagon to a provisional cemetery.
The officer on the right is a Hauptmann. Could this not be Hauptmann Erwin Köhnlein from the staff of FJR.8, who was reported missing?**
(National Archives)

him in the back. When Helmut fell, the Negro grabbed a stone to bash his skull. At that moment Gefreiter Nowack shot him with a machine pistol and he fell on top of the body of the little paratrooper."

At about 5 pm several groups of GIs from the 2nd Bn of the 38th Infantry started to cross the Saint-Lô – Bayeux road. There was no reaction from the Fallschirmjägers. The Shermans emerged to take up their position in front of the infantry. But when they reached the road, the 75-mm Paks barked and the Panzerfaust croaked; the tanks turned back and the infantry responded. These exchanges lasted for almost two hours until the Germans fell back, leaving the road open for the 2nd Bn.

It took ten hours for the first companies of the 1st Bn

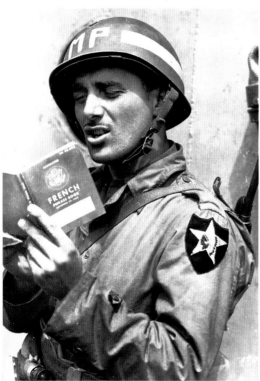

This MP from the 2nd US Inf. Div. is learning simple sentences in order to communicate with the French civilian population. Although they were acclaimed as liberators, relations between the Americans and civilians were not always good.
(National Archives)

Despite the intervention of the American artillery, the Fallschirmjäger clung on to their positions. Furious, Lieutenant-Colonel Frank T. Midden of the 1st Bn had to give up the idea of taking the last three hundred yards which would enable him to take the heights completely. An all-out attack against that type of opposition would be suicidal. The GIs set themselves up defensively for the night.

On the left wing of the 2nd Division, the 1st Bn of the 23rd Infantry had attacked from the road situated to the west of Saint-Georges-d'Elle. At the beginning, the Shermans had advanced fairly easily but then they ran into uneven terrain cut by hedges which slowed them down considerably. The paratroopers from Fallschirmjäger-regiment 5 took advantage of the situation to harass them and as a result the American crews were content to stay at a distance and support the infantry with their guns.

A Company which had gained some ground went along the Saint-Georges-d'Elle road. But the unit's momentum was broken by enemy fire coming from the houses. The fighting rapidly became very harsh and a number of American soldiers were killed. Lurking in the shadows, the Shermans were ready to support the attack of the 1st Platoon which was regrouping. It had not gone 30 yards when the impacts from mortar shells made the earth tremble. Several Granatwerfer teams from 13./FJR. 9 had waited for the right moment before opening fire. Then it was the machine guns which targeted the Americans.

The GIs could not get through that wall of fire and they suffered terrible losses. They tried to shelter in the ditches by desperately digging holes. From a distance the Shermans continued firing without letting up. If they advanced they risked being shot at by the Panzerfausten. The other two tanks were contacted by radio and a manoeuvre was organised with the 2nd and 3rd Platoons of A Company to get the 1st Platoon out of the trap. The GIs launched the attack against the first houses.

The presence of the two Shermans from C Company of the 741st Tank battalion made matters worse for the Fallschirmjäger. They nevertheless held on to several houses though it was not long before these collapsed under fire from the 75-mm shells of American tanks, which were as close as a hundred yards.

houses though it was not long before these collapsed under fire from the 75-mm shells of American tanks, which were as close as a hundred yards.

The Fallschirmjägers' losses were getting heavier and heavier. Many were caused by the two tanks. Moving up behind the two machines, the GIs shot any enemy soldiers who showed themselves. The paratroopers who succeeded in escaping from the houses were gunned down in the copses or in the hollows of the hedges.

Sergeant William C. Stanley had just realised that the leader of the 3rd platoon had been seriously hit. He decided to replace him and to muster the remnants of the 1st platoon. The objective of A company had almost been reached. In spite of the losses, it headed south towards the Saint-Lô – Bayeux road.

The hours continued to tick by, very trying for the GIs of A Company because German mortars were showering them with 81-mm shells. Finally, the sudden arrival of elements from the 3rd Bn made the Fallschirmjäger bound from their holes. Machine guns crackled on both sides, stick and fragmentation grenades flew through the air and exploded.

All American troop movements were followed by paratroop spotters set up in a sort of wooden tower installed on the top of Hill 192. From there they could even see Omaha Beach…

Major Kurt Stephani, Kdr. of FJR 9 had set up his command post half a mile from Hill 192 and was not always in touch with his company commanders. The artillery was so violent that he could not even think of sending runners. The paratroop officer had experienced this type of situation in Italy; he therefore wanted to avoid sending his men to certain death…

The fighting was particularly bitter. During a hand-to-hand engagement, the Co of the 10.Kp., Oberleutnant

Hans Grundmann was hit in the head by shrapnel.

Leutnant Ingenhofen, a veteran of Crete, Stabsfeldwebel Reinert, Oberfähnrich Kuhl and Feldwebel Mund were captured during this fight; the CO of the 11.Kp., Hauptmann Matula was also captured with one of his platoon leaders, Fähnrich Willmes (ex-flying personnel) and Feldwebel Mühlstedt. In the 12.Kp., platoon leader

Above.
On 18 July 1944, this Fallschirmjäger, a prisoner in the operational zone of the XIXth US Army Corps, has lost all his pride. He will not be able to prevent forgetfulness drowning the intense love he had for his country. While waiting for better days, he will be interned in England or in the United States. Note that this soldier is wearing jack boots and not jump boots. From June 1941 onwards, the paratroopers were no longer used in their airborne capacity but rather as an elite infantry unit.
(Dite/Usis)

Left.
These GIs have just captured a trench in which they have found abandoned equipment. One of them is examining a broken 98K. It seems probable that its owner broke it on purpose before surrendering.
(Dite/Usis)

Right.
Very well camouflaged in a hedge, this 75-mm Pak 40 anti-tank gun is waiting for American tanks. The gun is ready to fire. The layer on the left is checking the sights whereas the gunner on the right is standing by ready to load a new shell into the breech. The "75-mm Panzerabwehrkanone 40" was capable of destroying any Allied tank. With its 75-mm L/46 canon it could pierce 132 mm of armour at a distance of 500 yards.
(BA 101I/582/2120/7)

Leutnant Hartmut and Fähnrich Heigel were killed as was Feldwebel Johann Böm.

In the 13.Kp., Feldwebel Siegfried Hagen and Kurt Müller fell.

In the 14.Kp., Feldwebels Keletat and Blum as well as platoon leader Oberfeldwebel Diebrich were seriously wounded. There were many more wounded in the III.Btl. mainly due to grenade splinters. The doctors and their aids worked flat out, till they dropped. The paratroopers who were still in condition to fight had to drive back the Americans and re-establish their positions; in order to do that, they had to destroy the tanks as well. Those driving along the sunken lanes and hedges were easier prey than the others.

"To succeed, the Fallschirmjäger threw grenades without them exploding onto the turret hatch in such a way as to attract the tank commander's attention. Then when he opened the hatch, they would fire with their Very pistols or throw bunches of stick grenades through the opening; the tank would start to smoke then it would catch fire shortly afterwards; the earth always started to quake when there was an explosion", says Rudi Frübeisser.

Here and there shells fell on the manholes which disappeared in a whirlwind of earth and dust, throwing up burning debris into the air. The officers and the Fallschirmjäger threw themselves body and soul into this exhausting fighting. They were sometimes lifted bodily into the air by the blast of the explosions. The tanks and the Jabos did not stop attacking their positions. When the growl of the engines got closer, the paratroopers had no choice but to seek shelter in their pits or shelter behind a wall and wait for death. Some of them went mad; if only the Americans would stop throwing phosphorous grenades! Some of these were recovered, as were weapons and ammunition, off dead or wounded GIs. The fighting carried on.

With the artillery bombarding their lines, it was impossible for the paratroopers to bring a single ammunition crate forward. If the fighting lasted any longer, the Fallschirmjäger would soon be running out of ammunition completely.

In the end contact was re-established and Major Stephani asked each of his battalion commanders what the situation was.

mann Meyer (III.Btl.) to fall back on the La Luzerne and la Barre-de-Semilly sector. While moving to his next command post, Major Stephani lost one of his best officers, Hauptmann Mierisch, who was wounded.

After defending their sector hedge by hedge and field by field, the II./Fallschirmjägerregiment 9 paratroopers withdrew back to their second line of defence set up along a line from Saint-Lô - Bérigny.

In the move, 147 of them were captured by the 2nd Division. In order to get away from the American pressure Hauptmann Karl Meyer's battalion obtained the support of a divisional reconnaissance battalion, the engineers battalion under Hauptmann Beth and a few assault guns from Fallschirm. StuG. Brigade 12.

Once the situation was stabilised, all these units set off again to face the 23rd Infantry Regiment. The paratroopers of II./FJR.8 under Hauptmann Josef Krammling took back part of Hill 192 for themselves. As for the II./FJR 9 under Hauptmann Meyer and the I./FJR 5, positioned on the Saint-Lô – Bérigny road, near La Croix Rouge, they blocked the Americans who could not advance a single yard.

Oberfähnrich Fritz Preuffer's Werfers of the 4.Kp. had some success during a skirmish at La Taille.

During the night of 11 to 12 July 1944, the GIs from the 2nd Infantry Division were subjected to artillery fire and bloody counter-attacks which were all driven off. During one of these, the new CO of I./FJR 9, Leutnant Hans Witschaker, was killed by a bullet in the head. He was immediately replaced by Leutnant Arnim Stoerz who in turn also received a bullet in his head while climbing into a position. In the Kp.2, Oberleutnant Frisch took command of the unit when its CO, Hauptmann Lepzig was mortally wounded. Fate hit again and Frisch was killed too. The role of company commander then fell to Leutnant Radom. Unfortunately not for long, for he too was put out of action by a serious wound. In 8./FJR 9, Adjutant Kuesserer and platoon leader Leiterhold were wounded and in the 9.Kp. it was Hauptmann Karl Friederich Rieschel who was killed bringing up supplies.

The Kdrs. of the three FJR 9 battalions, Major Alpers, Hauptmanns £ Ladwig and Meyer discussed the situation with Major Stephani.

They were terribly exhausted. All night, in the regimental command

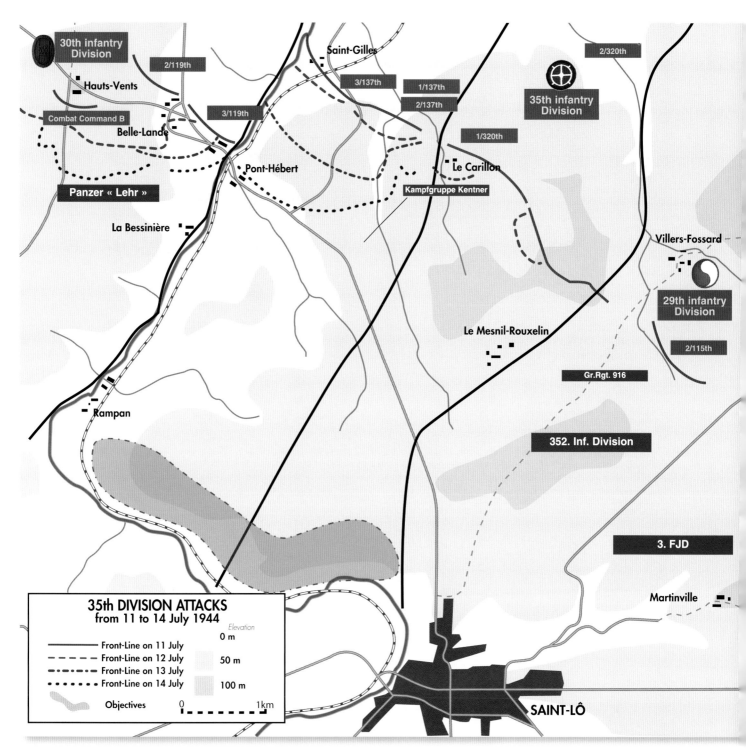

35th DIVISION ATTACKS
from 11 to 14 July 1944

Elevation	
Front-Line on 11 July	0 m
Front-Line on 12 July	50 m
Front-Line on 13 July	100 m
Front-Line on 14 July	
Objectives	0 ———— 1km

Labels on map:

30th infantry Division
2/119th
Saint-Gilles
2/320th
Hauts-Vents
3/137th
1/137th
3/119th
2/137th
35th infantry Division
Combat Command B
Belle-Lande
Pont-Hébert
Le Carillon
1/320th
Panzer « Lehr »
Kampfgruppe Kentner
La Bessinière
Villers-Fossard
29th infantry Division
Le Mesnil-Rouxelin
2/115th
Gr.Rgt. 916
Rampan
352. Inf. Division
3. FJD
Martinville
SAINT-LÔ

Having left the Saint-Pol de Léon – Roscoff sector on 12 June 1944, Kampfgruppe Kentner moved to the north of Saint-Lô. Its stages were via Pommeret (1st day), Tramain (2nd and 3rd), St Samson (4th), Lourmais (5th and 6th days), la Croix-Avranchin (7th), Sourière (8th and 9th days), St Samson (Normandy, 10th day). Its columns were attacked several times by aircraft but also by the French maquis which killed nine men and an NCO; an officer and five Grenadiere were wounded. The Jabos destroyed two of their 20-mm Flak guns. From 25 June 1944, Kampfgruppe Kentner was attached to 352.I.D. Its mission was to hold two miles of the front, from a point situated about 300 yards from the Le Mesnil-Rouxelin – Moon-sur-Elle to the River Vire, between Rampan and La Meauffe. It therefore took over the sector of Gren. Rgt. 914 which had just been placed in the 352.I.D.'s reserve to the east of Les Ifs.
(BA 101 I/583/2130/27)

Right.
These paratroopers and spotters are climbing a makeshift wooden ladder to get to their improvised observation post. From there they will be able to watch the countryside and warn the artillery about American troop movements. Strangely enough, the man in the foreground has a bayonet hanging from his belt whereas he is carrying a slung MP 40. This scene is typical of the fighting in July 1944 in the Saint-Lô region. This photo was taken by P.K. Czirnich and published in *Der Adler* at the end of June 1944.
(BA 1011/582/2101/4)

Ladwig and Meyer discussed the situation with Major Stephani.

They were terribly exhausted. All night, in the regimental command post, they tried to reorganise the battalions and find means of relieving the soldiers so that they could sleep. From time to time they heard the cries of the wounded who had been gathered in the first aid posts. Dr Kurt Schmidt tried his best but there was not much that a single doctor could do with all those casualties.

Now there were reports coming in with the runners about the terrible losses the companies had suffered. Fallschirmjägerregiment 9 had lost almost 600 men! As for its Kdr., he put forward a higher figure: 1,000. How and where could Generalleutnant Meindl dig up any reserves? Too many weapons and too much equipment had been lost. In spite of all this hard fighting, the 3./Fallschirmjägerdivision had in fact only lost 20% of its strength mainly due to the excellent positions the paratroopers had set up. Rudi Frübeisser confirms: *"Against severe odds, the front line positions were restored. Many shelters were dug in the banks. We covered them with planks and rafters and piled these with earth. Up until then these shelters had been effective during the bombardments. Some Jägers volunteered to bring back the bodies of their dead comrades to an assembly point. Then during the night, they were transported to the heroes' cemetery, designated thus by Major Stephani, near La-Barre-de-Semilly, 3 miles east of Saint-Lô. When night fell, we saw the grass and the hedges in the region burning just as if it were the steppe again!*

What did the night hold in store for us? Would the Amis [2] come at us again?"

The 35th US Infantry Division is coming…

During the night of 9-10 July 1944, Major-General Baade of the 35th Infantry Division ordered the 137th and 320th Infantry Regiments to place themselves on a line starting to the east of the Vire, the north of La Meauffe, passing through La Rivière and stopping at La Nicollerie. Within 24 hours, the two units were ready for the 11 July offensive.

These GIs came across the same difficulties as the soldiers of the 2nd and 29th Infantry Divisions: hedges, sunken lanes, departmental roads littered with traps laid by the Germans, who were as usual determined to hold their positions. Although they turned out be hard fighters, they did not consider themselves to be political soldiers like the Waffen-SS and the paratroopers. These troops belonged to the Heer, the regular army.

The war however was still on and the men on both sides did their soldier's duty. On 11 July 1944, the 1st and 2nd Bns of the 137th Infantry followed "Highway 3" which the Grenadiere had mined and along which they had set up machine gun pits. This deadly fire caused a lot of casualties among the GIs. As if small arms were not enough, the Germans opened fire now with their artillery and some Flak guns.

Vigorous action by assault groups had to eliminate

---

2. *Amis is the abbreviation for Amerikaner, and the nickname given by the German soldiers to their foe.*

KAMPFGRUPPE KENTNER	
Strength	
Officers	60
Other ranks	3020
Hiwis (Soviet POW auxiliaries):	150
Equipment	
MP 40 SMG	200
M. Granatwerfer (mortars)	15
Flammenwerfer	6
Panzerschreck	30
Faustpatronen I	150
Faustpatronen II	160
2 cm FlaK	9
5 cm FlaK	5
7,5 cm PaK	6
I. K. H. r.	6
sFH (f) (15,5 cm)	12

these strong points one by one, sometimes with hand-to-hand fighting. With unparalleled savagery, the adversaries even went so far as to shoot each other at point blank range.

The American infantry christened this road "Death Valley Road" because of the number of Grenadiere they killed, but also because of the number of their comrades whom they left behind there.

When they came in sight of La Meauffe, they discovered a village in ruins, each house turned into a bunker. The road was only temporarily safe, announced Colonel Layng of the 137th Infantry. The fighting lasted for longer than an hour. The elements of Kampfgruppe Kentner were crazily audacious. They had decided they were going to drive back the attackers.

Kampfgruppe Kentner came from the 266.I.D. which had been stationed in the Saint-Pol de Léon sector in Brittany until 12 June 1944. The division had been separated in two distinct groups. The first was sent to Brest and the second to north of Saint-Lô which it reached on 23 June. It was Oberst Kentner, Kdr. of Gren. Rgt. 897, was in command.

The tactical group was made up of Rgt. Stab/Gren. Rgt. 897, Stabs Kp. 897, I. and II./Gren. Rgt. 897, 13./Gren. Rgt. 897, 14./Gren. Rgt. 897, the I./Pi. Btl. 266, the III./Art. Rgt. 266 and Kol. Baumgärtel. When the Kampfgruppe was engaged against the 335th US Inf. Rgt., it was reinforced by II./Gren. Rgt. 899 and II./Gren. Rgt. 898.

While the first two battalions of the 137th Infantry were preparing for a new assault, the 3rd Bn was placed in reserve and were getting ready to intervene at the most critical points of the La Meauffe sector.

In the end it was the artillery which dealt with reducing the enemy defences. By radio an observer gave the exact positions of the fortified houses, then one minute later a salvo fell upon these. The infantry took over to clean out the last German positions, killing or capturing the defenders. The GIs discovered with some surprise that Kgp. Kentner's Grenadiere's morale was still good in spite of their age (between 32 and 36 years old).

Once La Meauffe was captured, the 1st Bn of the 137th did not pause. It was stopped again at Saint-Gilles which was bitterly defended by other Kampfgruppe Kentner elements. These Grenadiere waited for the Americans steadfastly because they knew they were safe inside their defences, superbly set up by the Osttruppe conscripted a short while beforehand. They established a strong point around and inside the village church as well as in the chateau. The walls of these buildings dated back to the 18th century and were unbelievably thick.

The Germans opened fire when the GIs were 200 or 300 yards from these historic buildings. The German

Above.

This paratrooper Leutnant has got hold of a face mask to camouflage himself better. This was quite unusual for Normandy and this item of equipment can only be a regulation item issued by the Luftwaffe against the cold, or made locally. It is quite likely that this officer had covered his helmet with straw in large quantities just for the reporter.
BA 101 I/586/2218/7)

infantry had never been better prepared. MGs, placed in the bell tower, decimated the GIs in the 1st Bn. Infantrymen lying in ambush behind the cemetery wall opened fire through holes which had been made earlier. Faced with this unexpected opposition, the Americans withdrew in a thick cloud of smoke. Two hours after this fight which took place at the entrance to the village, the GIs were still blocked and more than fifty of their wounded had to be evacuated. The battalion commander succeeded in getting in touch with the regimental HQ which sent the 3rd Bn up in reinforcements. Towards 6 pm the XIXth Corps artillery went into action in support when the two battalions went into the attack.

The commander of the 137th Infantry, Colonel Grant Layng was seriously wounded by machine gun fire. Brigadier-General Sebree, Major-General Baade's second in command, replaced him immediately. But there

**Major Stephani, Kdr. of Fallschirmjägerregiment 9 on the right, with Generalleutnant Meindl (in field cap, centre). Stephani was a reserve officer before the war, then he was committed for the first time with the rank of Leutnant in Jägerregiment 75 of the Lw. Jg. Div. on 10 October 1941. He was then CO of the 8.Kp., the machine gun company. A year later he was a Hauptmann and Kdr of the reconnaissance battalion of the XIII. Flieger-Korps. T his unit became the Fallschirm-Aufklärungs-Abteilung 12 in February 1944.
On the first of the same month, he was appointed Kdr. of Fallschirmjägerregiment 9. Seriously wounded during the breakout from the Falaise Pocket, he died at the Chateau de Perre at Ecorche, where there was a British field hospital. Kurt Stephani had been awarded the Iron Cross, 1st and 2nd Class, the General Assault badge, the German Cross in Gold on 5 June 1944 and the Knight's Cross posthumously, on 30 September 1944.**
(J. Charita)

Major-General Baade during the fighting in July 1944.
(National Archives)

Divisional insignia of the 35th US Infantry. Division.

was more and more bad news. Lieutenant-Colonel John. N. Wilson, commanding the 219th Field Artillery Battalion was killed together with his liaison officer.

In spite of the artillery bombardment and the numerous assaults made against the village from both sides, the infantry was incapable of eliminating Kamfgruppe Kentner's positions. The GIs of the 137th Infantry noticed that the Germans fired their mortars every time an artillery barrage started, so that the GIs would think that it was their own artillery which was causing their casualties. This trickery which also took place in various parts of the front demoralised the American troops.

The following figures concerning the losses suffered by the 137th Infantry during the fighting for Saint-Gilles give an idea of the amazing resistance put up by Kampfgruppe Kentner: 12 killed, 96 wounded and 18 missing. Only three Grenadiere were captured, all the others were killed.

Informed about all this in a report from Brigadier-General Sebree, Major-General Baade decided to launch an attack for the following day (12 July) with the support of the 654th Tank Destroyer Battalion and his division's reconnaissance troop.

The cloud-laden sky gave the Grenadiere some hope; if it was going to rain soon it would mean bad visibility for the pilots, the TD and Sherman crews. Alas, not one drop of rain would fall.

The noise from the engines of the much-feared armour got closer. To defend themselves, the Germans had only 81-mm mortars and their small arms, useless against these steel carapaces. They did not even have any Panzerfausten.

As soon as they saw the tank destroyers, they opened fire. The radios asked for support from the 88-mm Flak guns placed to the rear. Relentlessly the tank destroyers headed for the positions held by Oberst Kentner's men, who found themselves isolated one after the other. Desperate and powerless, they had to face these tanks that stopped to fire a few 75-mm shells very accurately. Then approaching the church, they did not hesitate to fire at point blank range at this magnificent building dating back to 1718.

Under such conditions, buildings with historic significance no longer counted. Only one thing was important for the soldiers: survival. If a church had to be destroyed, it was destroyed.

Bolstered by the tank destroyers, the GIs followed in their tracks, ready to take their revenge. They managed to surround Saint-Gilles but it took them more than three hours to overwhelm the Germans who gave in when Oberst Kentner learnt that one of his strong points situated half a mile away to the south had been eliminated by an American battalion.

Major-General Baade was not really satisfied with the capture of this village. He thought his 35th Infantry Division was just not advancing enough. His battalions lacked coordination because of communications interrupted by the intense artillery barrages and the scrubby lanes they had to use. Subjected several times to mortar and machine gun fire, they had been pinned down more than once

Major General Paul W. Baade

A veteran of WW1 in which he led a regiment of the 81st Division, Baade studied four years in several service schools from 1919, then four more with the Chief of Infantry staff. A Brigadier General in 1941, in 1942 he became executive commander of the 35th Infantry Division on the California coastline. A Major General in 1943, Baade instructed his unit in various training areas. The 35th landed in France on June 8, 1944 and was committed at once in the Saint-Lô sector. Baade led his GIs all the way to the Elbe in 1945, without respite during 11 months of combat.
(National Archives)

Below.
Leaning on her rabbit hutch this peasant woman watches an infantry column going past. As the signpost attached to the hedge indicates, there is only one way: towards the front. The horizontal stripe painted on the back of the helmet of the soldier in the foreground shows that he is an NCO. He has been issued with an M3 submachinegun for close quarter fighting.
(National Archives)

HEDGEROW FIGHTING
EAST OF THE VIRE
12 July 1944...

A VETERAN of FJR.9, Rudi Frühbeisser wrote about the early hours of this day: *"In the end, at first light, the fighting stopped. Suddenly American medics emerged from a column of stretcher-bearers carrying the wounded. Among the wounded were some of the paratroopers from our regiment.*

The Americans were bringing up medical equipment and supplies. It was not possible however for them to treat all the wounded as there were so many. Moreover their ambulances could not get through along the roads littered with the wrecks of the tanks our Fallschirmjägers had destroyed. In spite of all that, the white-smocked American medics still took care of our wounded.

Major Stephani, back from his command post on the heights near le Calvaire, was holding his head in his hands, his eyes filled with tears. He had just discovered the terrible sight in front of him. He had the same leather coat he used to wear in Russia. He could not stand losing men in his regiment. If any of his officers or paras were killed, it was as if a part of himself had died. What was still important to him, even if his regiment was bled to death, was to have tried to save as many of his men's lives as possible, with the help of his officers. Generalleutnant Meindl, Kdr. of II. Fallschirmjäger-Korps, a friend of our regiment, was told by phone about the casualties. Major Stephani who was called away for a meeting of corps officers was still terribly upset.

The supply vehicles drivers, driving like madmen, came up as close to the positions as possible, just where the medical column had been a short while earlier. Equipment, food, weapons and ammunition were handed out. It was all carted away, back to the positions, but some of it was however taken to the rear to avoid it getting destroyed.

Hill 192 found itself partly in American hands for the second time. The terrain captured was barely a mile deep. The casualties they suffered to reach our positions were higher than those of the regiment - 3 000 men." (the total losses computed by the author are as follows: 69 killed, 328 wounded and 8 missing).

The division's front now extended from La Chapelle towards La Luzerne – St-André-de-l'Epine, then towards a lane situated 700 yards to the west of Hill 192. From there, the line continued up to La Taille (excluded), 200 yards from the St-Lô-Bérigny-La Soulaire road, to the south of the road leading to La Riberaie wood in the direction of Le Perron – east of St-Pierre-de-Sémilly.

The 29th Infantry Division and Hill 147

"The progress of the GIs of the 116th Infantry Regiment was completely obstructed by a force estimated at 1,500 paratroopers from the 3. Fallschirmjägerdivision under Generalleutnant Schimpf." This is what can be read in the 116th Infantry after-action report. The ground in front of the German positions, along a winding road, had been mined and this constituted an extra obstacle for the infantrymen in Major Bingham's 2/116th Infantry.

The latter had completely underestimated the enemy's strength - which was about 12,000 men – and their grim determination to hold onto their

H.K.L. (main line of defence). He ordered E and F Companies to make a frontal attack, following the Shermans from the 747th Tank Battalion very closely.

The artillery which was supposed to have pounded the German positions to pieces had got the target coordinates wrong. Its 105 and 155-mm guns pounded F Company instead. One of its platoons disappeared and one Sherman was destroyed. The soldiers scattered frantically, leaving the unfortunate wounded to fend for themselves. Those that were not wounded rushed to the rear. Joseph Balkoski in his book on the 29th Infantry Division interviewed Captain Charles Cawthon who gives us the following eye-witness account: *"from the heights, I saw the leading Shermans, followed by infantry, move up into those fields. A courageous GI jumped up onto the turret of one of the tanks to get a better view of the German defences.*

Smoke spread over the battlefield with the sweet, sickly smell of high-explosive shells and which makes one think of death. The infantrymen, quite clearly reduced in number, huddled behind the hedgerows while the artillery, the mortars and the armour pounded the enemy."

In his command post, the CO of the 747th Tank Battalion, Lieutenant-Colonel Stuart G. Fries was furious; he had lost contact with his junior officers! He decided to send liaison officers to give them new directives. But they arrived too late. When one of them came across a hand-ful of Shermans returning to the rear, he asked the Squadron Commander why they were falling back. The reply was very simply *"... because Fries in person told us to!"*

Consternation, stupefaction and questions. It took them almost an hour to work out that a German who spoke perfect English and whose radio was on the same wavelength had ordered the tank crews to turn back...

Fortunately when they captured Hill 192, the 38th Infantry of the 2nd Division considerably weakened the German defensive lay out. Elements of III./Fallschirmjägerregiment 9 nevertheless still repulsed the 2/116th Infantry. Cautiously, Major Bingham's men moved on, searching every hedgerow from which a deadly burst of machine gun fire could cut them down within seconds.

The Fallschirmjäger was a tough opponent, because

of both his fighting worth and his eagerness. Thanks to their camouflaged jump smock and their helmet, they blended perfectly into the bocage and were very difficult to spot.

Once within sight of Martinville, the GIs waited for the order to take the town. But Major Bingham hesitated. He did not know where the neighbouring units were and did no want to throw himself into the lion's den.

He contacted Major-General Gerhardt who ordered him to wait for nightfall. He informed Bingham that the 1st Bn had just driven off a counter-attack by destroying two tanks out of three engaged, but its situation was critical. It was therefore better to wait for the time being, all the more so as the 3rd Bn was not in a state to take the ridge line which stretched out to the south of the

St-Lô – Bayeux road.

Because of this, the 2nd Bn of the 116th Infantry found itself engaged behind the other two battalions. Bingham had to wait until the following day before he could get hold of Martinville, the last stronghold on his way to Saint-Lô. Just over a mile separated the two towns. During the night Bingham asked the 3rd Bn of the 175th Infantry to head for Le Boulay so it would be up in line to attack jointly with his own battalion.

Unfortunately, this plan could not be carried out because the III./Fallschirmjägerregiment 9 paratroopers spotted the 3/175th moving up.

Rudi Frübeisser of Fallschirmjägerregiment 9 continues the tale: *"Brief orders were given to us. We had to stop the Americans' progress by harassing them with our*

fire. The Granatwerfer reinforced our small arms fire. In some spots there was even some close quarter fighting.

Regimental headquarters, with the group of runners under Leutnant Willi Geck, left immediately for the front. For the front-line Fallschirmjägers, these reinforcements were very welcome. Obergefreiter Gössel from Vienna (14.Kp.) was killed. At I.Btl. HQ, Jäger Holbeck was hit in the head and killed instantly. Oberjäger Bira from 3.Kp. was also killed. Although he was looked after by Drs Reuter and Kniebernigg, Jäger Breuer from 3.Kp. died of his wounds. He had been hit by mortar shrapnel in the head. Most of the losses were in the 14. And 15. Kp. With the support of these two companies, it was even possible to recapture a hill in front of La Rocque, 400 yards from L'Epine.

The fighting lasted all day then it petered out at dusk. The positions were established again and improved. The Jägers' foxholes in the embankment had resisted."

As for the 115th Infantry Regiment placed on the right of Bingham's (116th), it had run into problems all day. One of its battalions had attacked much too late. Spotted by the German observers set up on Hill 122, it had

Above.
This model M Marder III armed with a 75-mm Pak 40/3 L/46 has been hit by an artillery shell on its front left. T. This self-propelled 75-mm tank destroyer, based on a Pz. Kpfw.38(t) chassis, equipped the Panzerjäger Abteilungen. This one belongs without doubt to 352.I.D. which had 16 of them.
(National Archives)

This shot shows how the term "Foxhole" means exactly that. This hole dug by a GI is about six feet deep. Note that it is situated on the side of a lane and near a cemetery. Although uncomfortable and small, this position does protect the soldier from shell bursts. The American GIs often used captured German manholes for themselves.
(National Archives)

fallen into several ambushes, one of its platoons being completely wiped out.

What is more, without any armoured support, it was forced to attack along a front almost two miles long. None of its objectives was reached and it was unable to support Bingham's battalion (2nd) which could otherwise have got hold of Martinville. Colonel Ordway who was in command of the 115th Infantry was told off several times during that sinister day…

On 12 July 1944 at dawn, the 2nd Bn of the 116th Infantry Regiment at last managed to reach Martinville ridge without running into any real opposition. But soon afterwards it came under extremely accurate artillery fire; this was the work of the German observers on Hill 122. To stay entrenched on these heights would be suicidal. Gerhardt told the battalion to come down and attack St-Lô alongside the 2nd and 3rd Bns of the 175th infantry Regiment. The CO of this regiment, Colonel Reed, believed in Gerhardt's plan because his unit had the necessary punch to carry it off. The 116th had suffered too many casualties to be able to launch an attack on the town by itself.

Unfortunately, the incessant, accurate bombardment by the German artillery reduced Gerhardt's plans to nothing. The general recognised that the Fallschirmjägers' defence was still formidable. Indeed, despite their losses, the paratroopers carried on with their ambush tactics, made all the easier by the terrain and the countless hedgerows. To the west of the St-Lô – Isigny road, the companies from the 2nd Bn of the 115th Infantry converged on Le Bourg d'Enfer where elements of Kampfgruppe Goth (Gren. Rgt. 916) were apparently entrenched. The astonished GIs discovered that there were no inhabitants in the hamlet: it was quite empty. The battalion commander reorganised his unit, then at about 11 am, he sent it off in the direction of Sainte-Emilie, towards the south.

At midday they stopped for a break, to eat some rations and rest, then set off again. All was going well.

Suddenly it started to rain mortar shells and machine guns started firing; then the artillery joined in. The GIs could not advance any more for the time being because they had reached Oberst Goth's line of defence. Major Clift, the battalion commander, wisely ordered his men to fall back. But they panicked and in total chaos, the 2nd Bn abandoned Le Bourg d'Enfer.

The soldiers in Gren. Rgt. 916 or Kampfgruppe Goth took advantage of this situation to infiltrate where the 2nd and 3rd Bns, which had been stopped by a minefield, met.

Colonel Ordway of the 115th Infantry was furious and reproached Major Clift for having disengaged his unit. Then it was Ordway's turn to be told off by Gerhardt.

Not knowing whether or not he was going to be relieved of his command and replaced by Major Asbury Jackson, Clift succeeded in getting his men under control and back to the starting line.

Meanwhile the 3rd Bn succeeded in getting through the minefield with the help of the engineers; it then reached La Luzerne quickly where it got itself reorganised before continuing southwards. Unfortunately for the Americans, the German artillery supported Oberst Goth's resistance points as much as they could, by showering a hail of shells on the GIs. The Grenadiere of 352.I.D. were also giving them a hard time. As for the 1st Bn of the 115th Infantry under Major Johns, it managed to reach Belle-Fontaine with great difficulty and harassed by artillery and sniper fire – the snipers were totally invisible in the Norman bocage. Its next mission was to reach La Luzerne with the objective of attacking southwards. But the 3/115th found itself blocked in its advance by the Fallschirmjägerregiment 9 paratroopers who had also stopped Major John's GIs, so the soldiers dug in where they were and thus made up the regimental reserve.

The amount of ground gained by the 29th Division at the end of the day was ridiculous and the casualties were heavy: 21 killed and 87 wounded. The 116th Infantry had only advanced about 500 yards and Colonel Reed's 175th Infantry, placed in the rear had lost 60 men just getting into position. In spite of the stream of abuse from Major-General Gerhardt against him, Major Reed was not in a position to comply with his orders because German resistance had stiffened.

Gerhardt was exasperated and thought up a new plan. He ordered Colonel Ordway of the 115th Infantry to attack towards the south. But it was a waste of time. There was still no hope of advancing, even a hundred yards. Some of the traumatised GIs even refused to obey orders!

Gerhardt had to admit that his division's every move was being spot-

ted by the German observers set up on Hill 122. The 29th Infantry Division's attack was a total failure.

Major-General Corlett of the XIXth Corps told Gerhardt in the evening that the plan had not worked because Hill 122 was occupied by the Germans but that once that hill was taken, the enemy would be deprived of its observation post and St-Lô would be taken.

Above.
This 88-mm Raketenpanzerbüchse 54 is examined by three GIs from the 30th Div. It is in perfect condition and all accessories are present: ignition battery, protective shield, and sling.
The soldier on the left is inserting a rocket (RPzBGr 4322 or 4992) into the tube.
(National Archives)

Opposite page.
This Grenadier is getting ready to fire his Panzerfaust. The scene is realistic, except that the launcher is not armed. It was only when the safety pin was removed and the sights raised. Three figures marked on these sights – 30, 60 and 80 – indicated the range in metres. The right way to fire was to place the tube under the right shoulder and then lower the head to read and adjust the range. For longer range shooting, the tube would be placed over the shoulder.
(BA 101 I/721/0375/28a)

THE 30th US I.D. TO THE WEST OF THE VIRE

GENERAL HOBBS HAD NOT yet had the time to indicate when his 117th and 119th Infantry Regiments' attack would start before elements of SS-Kgp. Wisliceny, supported by ten or so tanks from II./Pz. Rgt.130 launched a counter-attack from La Terrette in the 2/117th Infantry's sector.

The regimental commander, Colonel Kelly, was irate. He had promised Hobbs that he could count on him and his men and now, with this sudden attack, there was a risk not keeping his word.

If the Army corps artillery was not accurate enough to break the enemy attack, it was no more accurate when trying to take out SS-Obersturmbannführer Wisliceny's command post which was located no more than half a mile to the south west of Esglandes and used up almost 3,600 shells for nothing!

The 2nd Bn took the full brunt of Wisliceny's attack. Machine gun bursts tore the air several inches above the soldiers' heads. Then the explosions from the mortar shells started to get closer. Soon the artillery firing from the heights could be made out on the other side of La Terrette, firing in the direction of the American battalion.

The GIs had no choice but to wait for two never-ending hours, lying down along the hedges or in the foxholes which

they had taken over from their opponents. They were paralysed by fear.

When they heard small arms fire, the GIs knew the Germans were near and bravely got to their feet to meet them. They refused to be brushed aside by this violent assault.

Their opponents had a reputation for being war-hardened veterans. They may have belonged to the "Das Reich" armoured division and Kampfgruppe Welsch but they were not expecting such a lively response from the GIs of the 2nd Bn.

Granatwerfers now thundered, enabling the Waffen-SS to inch closer. The Pz. IVs of the Panzer-Lehr also advanced, protected by a smoke screen.

The 2nd Bn's CO only allowed his men to fall back a hundred yards, yielding only a single hedge to Kampfgruppe Welsch. Trying to get news of the battalion by radio, Colonel Kelly was told by a junior officer that the attack could be

This Sherman tank is advancing up a slope and thus exposes a perfect target for a hidden German tank-killer. The Panzerfaust could hit anywhere on the lower hull, without exposing the launcher to the main gun or machine guns, which were unable to depress their barrels further.
(National archives)

A 75-mm Howitzer Motor Carriage M8 from the 30th Reconnaissance Troop is leaving Saint-Gilles in July 1944. The short howitzer meant the gun could be mounted in a revolving turret. It was in fact a modified light M5 tank and 1, 500 were produced. One of the Panthers from I./Pz. Rgt.6 is lying in the ditch.
(National Archives)

Below.
One of the rare photos taken in Normandy showing an M3 SMG. Nicknamed the "Grease Gun" because of its shape had a range of 300 yards and could fire at 450 rounds/minute. Its magazine held thirty 45-calibre rounds.
It is worth mentioning that SMGs were not officially part of the Infantry regulation armament, they were however handed out for close quarter or street fighting.
The machine gun is a water-cooled M1917 A1 Browning on its tripod. Note the water pipe fixed to its sleeve. This Heavy MG was operated by the infantry battalion's 4th (Heavy weapons) company.
(National Archives)

broken if the artillery got rid of the enemy cannon situated on the heights to the west of la Terrette. Fearsome artillery duels took place all day long. From the German firepower, the XIXth Army Corps intelligence estimated its strength at three artillery battalions, ie three-quarters of an enemy artillery regiment. There were also 88-mm Flak guns and Panzers dug in hull-deep on the hills.

Other counter-attacks took place in order to force back Combat Command B, but standing like rocks in the middle of the storm, the American tank crews did not yield ground.

As for the GIs in the 119th Infantry, they had got closer to Pont-Hébert, but in the evening they had to admit defeat because Major Brandt's sappers and elements from Kgp. Kentner, which had come up in the meantime, were defending the town ferociously.

On the right wing of the 30th Division, the 9th Division pushed back 17. SS-Pz. Gren. Div. which led to Kgp. Scholze withdrawing to the south of Les Champs-de-Losques. A company of Major Brandt's Pioniere covered the retreating Panzer-grenadiere. His men fought a rearguard action and laid mines at the same time along all the lines of retreat.

Hauptmann Göttsche, with his 12th Paratroop Recce Battalion, which had been recently incorporated into Kgp. Scholze, was ordered to join the II.Fallschirmjäger Korps as his unit was down to a quarter of its strength. To make up for this shortage I./Fallschirmjägerregiment 14 was chosen to join Kgp. Scholze.

From 7 to 13 July 1944, the 30th Infantry Division lost nearly 3 200 men. The last two days were very costly for the 2nd battalion of the 119th Infantry which suffered almost 50% casualties.

At 8 am exactly, the 2nd and 3rd Bns of the 137th Infantry attacked from Saint-Gilles and from Le Carillon. They came across elements of the formidable Kgp. Kentner which resisted them fiercely. They did not know that they had run into two infantry battalions belonging to Grenadier-Regiments 897 and 899.

The French 155-mm guns in Kentner's artillery bombarded the 2nd Bn so heavily that it was in no condition to advance a single yard. The Americans had not spotted at least eight

machine guns nestling in a hundred-yard long hedgerow!

As for the 3rd Bn of the 137th Infantry, it advanced easily for 500 yards without loss before the MGs started firing and the 88-mm Flak guns thundering.

It was hell and the 2nd and 3rd battalions where pinned down. Divisional artillery had to intervene to get them out of this sticky predicament. Two Acht-achts (the 88s) were destroyed.

The 2/137th CO gathered his company commanders to explain his new plan and above all the new tactics they were going to use. E Company was to attack to the right and G Company to the left. Both of them would be supported by a heavy machine gun platoon and an 81-mm mortar platoon. Moreover a tank platoon would be standing by for the battalion.

The tactics consisted of bombarding the enemy's known and supposed positions. Once the steel storm had gone by, groups of five or six GIs would head for the targets which should, in theory, have been blasted to kingdom come, and spray them with their guns as a precaution.

This tactic seemed to get good results since E Company advanced about 600 yards. The regimental commander, Brigadier-General Sebree [1] was all the more satisfied because the two battalions managed to join up. He was getting ready to hurl these units again against Kentner when a counter-attack led by the man himself pushed the 3rd Bn GIs from

1. *General Sebree was the commanding general's executive officer, he took over the 137th Infantry from colonel Layng, who had been severely injured on July 11.*

their positions back to where they had started from in the morning!

At present, what Brigadier-General Sebree feared most was having to retreat even further. Just managing to hold his ground was a miracle in itself. His regiment had made no territorial gain and he had lost 21 killed, 87 wounded and 17 missing during the recent fighting.

As for the 1st Bn of the 320th Infantry, it had not done any better. It was stopped dead in its tracks in the Le Carillon sector by concentrated machine gun and anti-tank gun fire which caused further losses. The situation was just getting worse and worse.

The 29th Division to the East of the Vire

The three infantry regiments in the 29th Infantry Division were now in position to renew their attack on Saint-Lô. They were waiting for the planes to fly over and blast a way through the German lines. But it was raining and visibility was bad. The pilots were hanging around waiting to be given the order to take off. No orders for the moment, with the minutes ticking by and with the infantry needing them! Unfortunately, the bad weather seemed to be setting in. There would be no air support that day.

Only a few machines would fly over the area and it was to drop leaflets. One of these was addressed to Major Becker's Fallschirmjäger.

"Soldiers of Fallschirmjäger-regiment 5!

Hill 192

Hill 192 is your left flank.

Hill 192 is a strong point held by your comrades from Fallschirmjäger 9.

Hill 192 is ours since last night. The men from Fallschirmjägerregiment 9 remained at their positions. But even the best of soldiers were no match for the superiority of our artillery and the deadly fire of our mortars. The foxholes you have taken so much trouble to dig will only give you limited protection.

You will lose all your comrades when we attack.

Fallschirmjägerregiment 9 is about to be wiped out.

The best thing for you to do is to surrender.

Have you talked among yourselves about the Panzers which have fallen back? Like your artillery? Do you think that the trucks will risk coming up to supply you?

Young men from your regiment have already talked about this; they're asking you to join them. To cease resistance is not cowardice but just human common sense. Fighting against such superior forces is not a question of courage but rather of suicide, and for a lost cause.

This is what 142 men from your regiment have understood.

This is a victory for the prisoners who are behind American lines.

If you want to stay alive,

If you want to go home,

Take this advice:

STOP EVERYTHING."

Rudi Frübeisser remembers these tracts: *"Other tracts enticing us to surrender were sent to us. As there was no longer any toilet paper coming up in the supplies, we used them for that."*

The GIs in the 2nd and 3rd Bns of the 116th Infantry Regiment gathering on Martinville ridge for the attack were getting worried. The 747th Tank Battalion Shermans which should have been there in support had not arrived yet.

Their crews were in fact waiting for fuel and ammunition but these were not getting through. Once again, Lieutenant-Colonel S. Fries, commanding the tank battalion, was told off by Major-General Gerhardt.

Lieutenant Purnell was fed up waiting so he gave up on the tanks. He launched his 3rd Bn of the 175th Infantry unsupported towards the heights situated between Le Boulay and La Madeleine. Haplessly, his men left their holes to enter no man's land, overgrown with those cursed hedges the Fallschirmjäger 9's paratroopers favoured so much.

The Americans' courage was just not enough. They had to be lucky enough to locate the "green devils," invisible in their dugouts nestling in the brambly banks. In the end they were joined by some tanks. When gunfire echoed behind them, the GIs assumed that the enemy had changed position.

Major General Charles Hunter Gerhardt

Gen. Gerhardt commanded the 29th US Inf. Div. from July 1943 to the end of the war in Europe. He was the son of a career officer and always remained in military circles; he served with the 89th Division. during WWI.

A stern taskmaster, he overdisciplined and overtrained his soldiers.

There was a joke going around about the man in Normandy which revealed a lot about him. *"Gerhardt has three divisions: one in field, the second in hospital and the third in the cemetery."*

A better leader of men than a tactician, he did not spare human lives and the 'Blue and Gray' recorded the highest losses in any unit ever: 20,111 men. For this reason 'Uncle Charlie' was downgraded after the conflict to the rank of Colonel. With time he returned to the rank of Major-General.
(National Archives)

Moving around across this type of terrain was a nightmare for *both sides.* Rudi Frübeisser recalls this tragic anecdote: *"Without realising it, Leutnant graf von Hellermann suddenly found himself cut off from his platoon. He was alone, desperate. Suddenly he saw an American tank coming his way. He grabbed a Panzerfaust then without even taking shelter in a foxhole, he headed for the machine. He waited boldly for the tank to enter the lane where he lay in ambush. Aiming carefully, Leutnant von Hellermann let the tank get as near as possible and fired at the same moment as the radio operator opened fire with the machine gun. The Leutnant was killed with a bullet straight through the head at precisely the same moment as the hollow charge drove right through the tank.*

Later the Fallschirmjägers in his unit found his body in front of the tank he had destroyed.

Oberjäger Müller was killed in similar circumstances and the turret exploding into the sky marked the end of the fighting."

On their left the GIs from the 3/175th heard the 2nd Bn shooting at the enemy whose resistance was as determined as it was fierce. Indeed it was being attacked by sappers from Hauptmann Beth's Fallschirm. Pi. Btl.3, threatening to encircle them.

Colonel Gill looked at the radio whose silence told him that contact had been lost with the 2nd Bn. *"Today looks as though it's going to be as bad as yesterday!,"* he roared in exasperation.

Now that he was out of contact, Colonel Gill had to take the initiative. He could not carry on to his objective because the German resistance had stiffened too much, so he decided to swerve away slightly from his initial line of attack – Gerhardt was to get angry with this officer for not respecting the orders for the mission…

However, it is possible that Gill's movement worried the front line Fallschirmjägers because the reinforcements were seen heading their way shortly afterwards. This time the American artillery spotted them and bombarded them with phosphorus bombs until the observers signalled that there were no more enemy left in sight.

Rudi Frübeisser recalls: *"At around midday the bombardment lasted an eternity. It was concentrated on our positions as well as on our rear.*

Oberjäger Schweiger and Jäger Mazurek from the messenger platoon (Kradschützenzug) were wounded. In front

of St. Pierre de Semilly, Oberjäger Mayer of the 1. Kp. was killed by shrapnel in the chest and the legs. Four other soldiers in that company were seriously wounded.

In the 2. Kp., Jäger Schulz received an explosive bullet in the stomach. In the 14.Kp., Oberjäger Müller was hit in the lung. The 15.Kp. which was still in its positions at Bretel, making up the northern wing of the regiment, lost Obergefreiter Clippers from Aachen who was killed by a shell."

Colonel Purnell, CO of the 175th Infantry Regiment, who had still not engaged his 1st Bn was given permission by Major-General Gerhardt to position this unit on Hill 101, situated more to the south. If the battalion managed to carry out this manoeuvre it would be able to support the other two battalions in the regiment during their advance. Progress was becoming more and more difficult because of the German artillery which prevented them from getting to the Saint Lô – Bayeux road.

The 1st Bn was on the point of starting off when a message from Brigadier-General Cota ordered it to remain where it was because the other two battalions were out of touch for the time being.

But as the plan was very good, it was up to the 2nd Bn of the 116th Infantry to support the two battalions of the 175th that were already engaged. The 2nd Bn, which was spread out along Martinville ridge, ran into high hedges bristling with rifles that made them suspect that their slightest movement was being watched very closely. This battalion, no more than any of the others, was unable to progress in that green hell. For the day, the 175th Infantry lost 152 men and the 115th another 108 in order to hold the line. One of the companies fought all day to conquer an orchard of apple trees to the southwest of La Luzerne.

Major-General Gerhardt who had spent the last 48 hours giving orders, shouting and harassing his officers, had to admit that his infantry was on its last legs from exhaustion. He ordered several battalions to rest the following day enabling them to celebrate Independence Day - ten days late! As for those stuck at the front, they would stay there until the offensive took up again, planned for the 15th.

Gerhardt took advantage of this pause to visit his men. They were in a sorry state. They were haggard, had hardly eaten anything recently and most especially, they had hardly slept over the last few days. He promised them that they would take Saint-Lô then they would be able to rest. This day of respite enabled both sides to gather up their dead and bury them, as well as the horses and the cows which had been killed which were sinister and smelt foul.

Major-General Corlett of the XIXth Army Corps talked to Gerhardt and Baade. He asked Baade to commit his reserve regiment, the 134th, which would relieve the 115th the following morning. Once this operation was carried out, the GIs in the 134th would organise themselves to take Hill 122 while the 29th division took care of Saint-Lô...

Rudi Frübeisser took notes about his regiment's fight-

Above.
Although often forgotten, the cattle belonging to the Norman farmers paid a heavy tribute to the war. The horses, cows, pigs and other animals which were so precious during the Occupation did not count much compared to strategic considerations. Over all Normandy, the number of swollen carcasses lying in the fields could not be counted. The smell was often horrible and they had to be buried as quickly as possible in order to avoid the risk of disease
(Private collection)

The 29th Infantry Division shoulder patch. Beyond the yin and yang design, the blue and gray colours are a symbol of its regiments' history, which fought on each side during the Civil war.

Right.
Hauptmann Meyer commanded I./Fallschirmjägerregiment 9. He is photographed here by Propagandakompanie photographer Rieder one or two weeks before his death. This photo was published in *Der Adler* on 15 August 1944. Unfortunately, this photo report is not in the Koblenz archive.
(Author's Collection)

ing and remembers: *"All during the day, the II. Btl. held on to its positions despite heavy losses. With evening the battalion's Adjutant, Leutnant Günter Kunzmann who had been in Italy with the reconnaissance battalion, was twice shaken by shells which fell near his foxhole. Twice he found himself buried but managed to get out alive. He thereafter decided to stay outside his hole."*

At dawn the next day a runner brought Hauptmann Meyer, Kdr. of I./Fallschirmjägerregiment 9, the battalion's casualty list. He spoke to him but as there was no reply, he thought his CO was asleep. He tried to wake him but the officer did not react. He jumped down into the trench and shook him. The officer's body just slumped down slowly.

The runner found that Meyer had received a piece of shrapnel in his eye which went through his head and helmet. To honour his memory, his ordnance officer asked his men to fire three salvoes with the guns.

Shortly afterwards the ordnance officer took a sheet of paper from his map case and a pen and started to write:
"On the Western front
Günter Kunzmann
Leutnant
L 50922
Dear Mrs Meyer,
It is my sad duty to inform you that your husband died a hero's death. He was our battalion commander. During the night of 12-13 July 1944 he was killed by shrapnel which fell on our positions. He had bravely led our units during the fighting in the Saint-Lô region.

You cannot imagine the pain felt by all his soldiers.

For us, your husband was not only our CO but 'the old man.' He was for us, from the most senior officer to the youngest soldiers, a man whom we adored and revered.

We buried him with military honours in the heroes' cemetery, Stephani 2, a mile to the south of Le Barre and 2 1/2 miles to the east of St Lô in Normandy.

Your husband was not just a comrade for us but our model so that we could do our duty during the fighting.

We will never forget Hauptmann Meyer.

Our battalion is with you with all our hearts.

Gunter Kunzmann."

THE 35th DIVISION TO THE EAST OF THE VIRE

BRIGADIER-GENERAL SEBREE would not admit defeat. The previous day had been terrible for his 2nd and 3rd Bns of the 137th Infantry Regiment but the time for retribution had come and the means set in motion were impressive.

At 07.30 the batteries of the 161st, 216th and 219th Field Artillery bombarded Kgp. Kentner's Grenadiere's positions for thirty minutes; the gunners were not worried about wasting ammunition.

Meanwhile the 35th Division's assault engineers opened up a passage through the minefields which the GIs from the 137th started to use immediately. Then when the last salvoes echoed away, they slipped through the cover in the fields and the lanes in the direction of the Grenadiere whose fate seemed to be certain annihilation.

Indeed, the situation got worse for the Germans.

Dazed by the artillery fire, they saw that the American infantry was supported by Shermans from the 737th Tank Battalion. Each of the battalions of the 137th was accompanied by a platoon of tanks and tank destroyers.

Kentner's Grenadiere were going to die trying to hold on to a few square yards of bocage or a few tumbledown hovels, especially at La Petite Ferme.

Two brave Panzerschreck two-man teams managed to destroy two tanks. A third Sherman lost its track from a mortar bomb. Eight other tanks were destroyed in the zone where the 137th was engaged by Grenadiere

Above.
After carrying out research to design a 155-mm cannon, the American army created the M114 in 1934. 6,000 were produced till 1945. It was also used by field artillery battalions in Korea and Vietnam. Shell consumption reached its peak during the Battle of Saint-Lô, more exactly between 4 and 15 July 1944. As the high command preferred to expend steel rather than lives, enormous amount of ammunition were fired for any major attack or to destroy enemy troop concentrations. Fortunately the capture of Cherbourg harbour allowed the tonnage of ammunition supplies unloaded to be increased to between 12 000 and 14 000 tons daily!
(National Archives)

from the 352.ID. and from the 1./Fallschirmjägerregiment 14, the first unit from this regiment to be engaged. One of its soldiers, an 18-year old runner succeeded in destroying a Sherman with a Panzerfaust. The following day he repeated his performance but was killed by the tank he wanted to destroy. 55 Grenadiere and Fallschirmjäger were captured.

Covering the front line, the tank destroyer crews opened fire with their machine guns from only a few yards at the hedges, which they sprayed liberally. During the day they destroyed 19 machine gun pits and four mortar positions.

At the beginning of the afternoon, only the 2nd Bn of the 137th US inf. Rgt. had advanced - 300 yards. It managed to evict the enemy from La Petite Ferme, which changed hands several times. The Grenadiere fell back towards la Petite Mare where they came across other comrades, already in position. The Americans spoke here of *"several fortified houses."*

The GIs called up help when they found that the approaches to La Petite Mare were mined. They had to wait for the pioneers who, when they arrived found they had their work cut out, all the more so as the 88-mm Flak guns did no hang around before going into action. The American artillery responded; these duels with shells demoralised the GIS whose ranks started thinning out.

In order to reach the Pont-Hébert – Saint-Lô road, a rather small territorial gain, Brigadier-General Sebree lost 17 killed, 106 wounded and 4 missing.

While the 35th Division was fighting to the east of the Vire, the 119th Infantry of the 30th Division managed to push the enemy back, but not before they had blown up the Pont-Hébert bridge on their way. Fortunately the XIXth Corps engineers quickly built another one. Supported by a platoon of tanks, the GIs in B Company of the 1st Bn entered the town at about midday. The Germans broke off towards the south under heavy fire from the artillery which gave them no respite.

Two important changes in the command structure of the 119th Infantry Regiment were made. Colonel

M. Sutherland replaced Colonel Ednie who was transferred over to the 29th division and Major Robert H. Herlong replaced Colonel James W. Cantey.

The 30th and 9th Infantry Divisions joined up on the right flank of the XIXth Corps, to the south of Le Hommet d'Arthenay. The objective for these two divisions was to reach the Saint-Lô – Périers road.

The Engineers have just erected a bridge at Pont-Hébert. As can be seen, the church has been spared by the artillery because the hills which surrounded the town were much higher. The German observers preferred natural heights to watch the Americans advance from.
(National Archives)

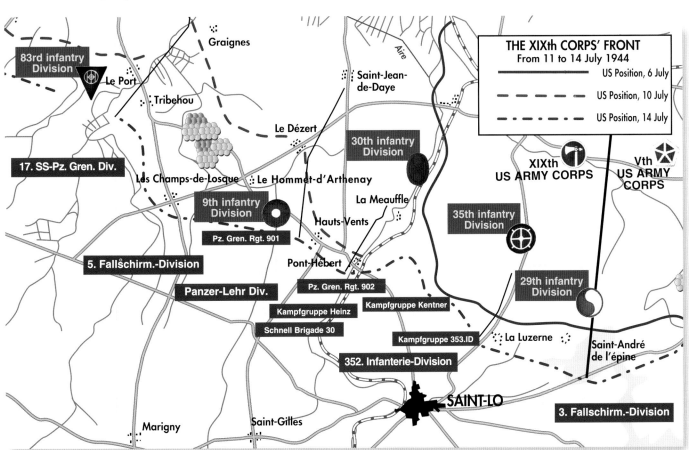

A group of Fallschirmjäger is gathered around Oberfeldwebel Alexander Uhlig, leader of 16./FJR 6 (at right, without helmet). A. Uhlig was admitted to the parachute school at Stendal in 1938, he was then assigned to Fallschirmjägerregiment 1. On 14 January 1940, he became a platoon leader in the regiment, before leaving to train as an aerial observer in several Kampfgeschwader (bomber squadrons). On 1 February 1944, Uhlig was transferred back to the paras with 8./FJR. 6 at Köln-Wahn. On 14 April 1944, he was assigned to 4./FJR. 6 and when the regiment was committed in Normandy, he was company commander of 16./FJR. 6. Engaged in the Raids sector together with the 2. SS-Pz. Div. between July 14 and 26, he was awarded the Knight's cross for capturing 234 GIs of the 90th Infantry division (1/358th Infantry) with the remains of his unit (33 men) and a single Panzer. Alexander Uhlig was captured on 31 July 1944 in the Coutances pocket. His principal awards are: Iron Cross 1st class (11 May 1940) and 2d class (1 August 1943), parachutist badge (7 September 1938), Narvikschild (1 March 1941), Wound badge (28 October 1942), 'Kreta' cuff title (15 November 1942), Frontflugspange für Transportflieger Bronze and Silber (22 December 1942 and 10 January 1943), Beobachter-Abzeichen (8 June 1943) and Knight's cross (29 October 1944).

Since we know the exact unit, it is possible to examine the various uniforms worn within Major von der Heydte's regiment. As to headgear, the Fliegermütze sidecap can be seen together with the 1943 Field (probably worn by a recent reinforcement, 3rd from left). This man was not issued with the camouflaged jump smock but with the simpler Luftwaffe Tarnjacke, as worn by Jäger of the Lw-Felddivisions, and Flak gunners. The para at far right has the same garment, but with the specific para helmet and a camouflaged bandoleer for rifle clips.

The second man from the left carries the same bandoleer, but the earlier pattern in solid blue canvas. All the same, his jump smock is early war, the second type in green material. He is probably a veteran of the Sturmregiment, like Uhlig.

In the background at right, two Luftwaffe soldiers (most likely paras as well, and one with the standard steel helmet) wait in a commandeered horse-drawn waggon.

(BA 1011/586/2215/11)

120

THE 30th DIVISION WEST OF THE VIRE

15 July 1944...

AT DAWN, THE PARATROOPERS from III./Fallschirmjägerregiment 14, who had arrived the previous day to relieve Pz. Gren. Rgt. 902, were subjected to a severe artillery bombardment to the south of Les Hauts Vents. Many of them were killed before even taking part in their first fight.

Leaving Brittany behind, these Fallschirmjäger had walked 112 miles in seven nights before reaching the front. They used horses and carts for transport on their way through Dinant, Pontorson, Avranches, Bréhal, Cérences, Roncey, and Montpichon in the Charantilly sector where the 'Tross' had been set up. The 5. Fallschirmjägerdivision, to which FJR 14 belonged, had no organic motor transport.

It was a recently-formed division (April 1944) and only 10% of its soldiers had ever jumped. In spite of being led by experienced officers, they could not boast elite status like the other paratroop units did. For example, a group of paratroopers from FJR 14 and Fallschirm. Artillerie-Regiment 5, all belonging to small detachments coming from different companies, were intercepted at Plemet, near Londiac by the French résistance, who persuaded them to surrender, pretending that American armoured troops had invested the town (which was not true).

The Kdr. of Fallschirmjägerregiment 14, Major Noster, learning that his regiment was attached to the Panzer-Lehr division, was furious with the High Command for waiting five weeks after the landings before engaging his unit! And under such circumstances, Noster entertained very grave misgivings about his soldiers' ability to stop the 9th and 30th Infantry divisions.

Major Noster was a paratrooper from the early days and acquired a solid reputation when his battalion (I./Fallschirmjägerregiment 2) jumped over Holland in

1940. Seriously wounded and captured, he succeeded in escaping to rejoin the German army.

The American bombardment lasted fifteen minutes then a creeping barrage took over. The more experienced officers knew that the infantry would be following about a mile behind the shells and that they would just have enough time to get ready. Major-General Corlett was being cautious because his observers, once again, could not really give any accurate information about the Fallschirmjäger troop movements.

And yet there were not very many of them: they were still the same platoon of the I./Fallschirmjägerregiment 14 which the 9th Infantry Division had run into the previous day. With unheard of boldness, this handful of paratroopers commanded by Officer Cadet Malade counterattacked, and by some miracle came through. They managed to infiltrate the enemy lines, but their luck could not hold out forever. The Fallschirmjäger came across infantry supported by three Shermans. Melder Stach had already got hold of a Panzerfaust thinking that he could repeat his previous day's exploit. But this time the Sherman won the round: Stach's chest was torn apart by machine gun bullets.

The tank in turn was destroyed by one of Stach's comrades who followed his example. The tank burnt like a torch and the tank crew died an atrocious death.

Officer Cadet Malade broke off the engagement after scaring the wits off the American defenders. His platoon

Above.
These Fallschirmjäger are lucky enough to be riding aboard a truck. Indeed, there was cruel lack of troop transport vehicles. It is probable that these belong to the 3. Fallschirmjägerdivision because the 5. Fallschirmjägerdivision did not have any at all. When they moved up to the front, the regiments in the 3rd paratroop division were only mobile if a third of their strength (ie a battalion) remained behind. Once the first contingents had reached their destination, the trucks went back to fetch the rest.
(BA 101 I/583/2145/7)

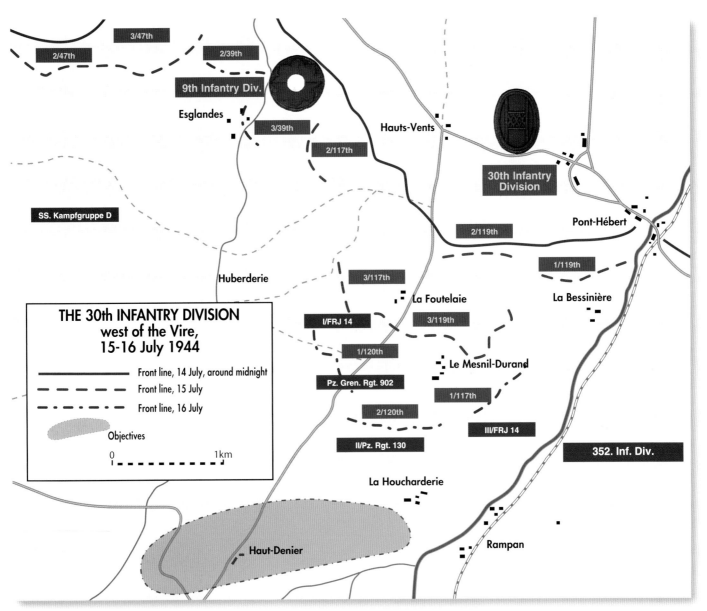

THE 30th INFANTRY DIVISION
west of the Vire,
15-16 July 1944

——————————— Front line, 14 July, around midnight

— — — — — Front line, 15 July

— · — · — · — Front line, 16 July

Objectives

0   1km

Map labels: 3/47th, 2/47th, 2/39th, 9th Infantry Div., Esglandes, 3/39th, Hauts-Vents, 2/117th, 30th Infantry Division, SS. Kampfgruppe D, 2/119th, Pont-Hébert, Huberderie, 3/117th, 1/119th, La Foutelaie, La Bessinière, I/FRJ 14, 3/119th, 1/120th, Le Mesnil-Durand, Pz. Gren. Rgt. 902, 1/117th, 2/120th, III/FRJ 14, II/Pz. Rgt. 130, 352. Inf. Div., La Houcharderie, Haut-Denier, Rampan

Due to the shortages in both gasoline and motor transport, the German still relied on old-fashioned transportation, such as horse-drawn cart or bicycles, quite useful on the narrow Norman paths.
(BA 101 I/ 582/2114/8)

returned to its initial position in the crude foxholes dug beforehand.

The battalion commander, Hauptmann Schmidt got in touch with *Fahnenjunker* Malade telling him to hold his positions at all costs. A veteran of this platoon recalls: *"In front of our positions there were Americans lying there wounded. One of them was crying out for his mother. After a short while the man's cries of agony got weaker then ceased altogether."*

A runner at the company commander's CP waited for the message the CO was writing out. The note was brief: *"Malade, don't be pig-headed, break off."*

Orders coming from different officers in the same battalion were contradictory. Malade had the choice: obey either the company commander, or the Kdr. of the battalion. He chose to obey his immediate superior. His platoon was almost surrounded but nevertheless managed to fall back. It lost three dead and three wounded. Our veteran writes: *"The platoon got together in a sunken lane and marched back to our old positions which we manned again. The whole sector was being shelled and watched carefully by American pilots who strafed us whenever they could. In the positions we found bodies of our own troops, killed by the enemy fighters' dive-bombing attacks."*

The 3rd Bns of both the 117th and 119th Infantry,

Opposite page, top.
In a relaxed manner, these HQ personnel march down a country lane, near some dilapidated farm buildings. One has a Schirmmütze and the other has kept his helmet and gloves despite the sunny weather.

Opposite page, bottom.
The cart (a pram?) supports a large wooden locker, whose large 'Ic' paper tag indicates it belongs to the Intelligence section of a paratrooper unit's HQ. The officer with the peaked cap would then be the intelligence officer of either the 3. or 5. FJD HQ, Hauptmann von Both in the first case, or Hauptmann Georg Passberg for the latter. All the same, *Goliath* could be this officer's code-name.
(BA 101 I/ 582/2114/14 &18)

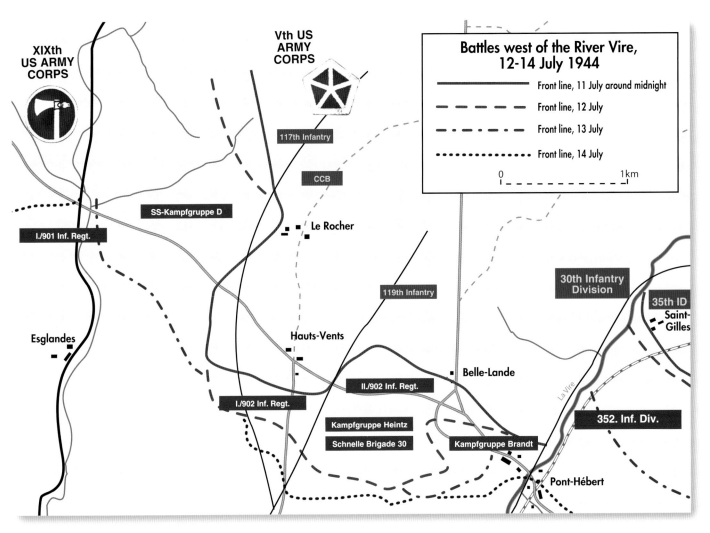

XIXth
US ARMY
CORPS

Vth US
ARMY
CORPS

**Battles west of the River Vire,
12-14 July 1944**

Front line, 11 July around midnight

Front line, 12 July

Front line, 13 July

Front line, 14 July

0   1km

117th Infantry

CCB

SS-Kampfgruppe D

Le Rocher

I./901 Inf. Regt.

30th Infantry
Division

35th ID

Saint-
Gilles

119th Infantry

Esglandes

Hauts-Vents

Belle-Lande

La Vire

II./902 Inf. Regt.

I./902 Inf. Regt.

352. Inf. Div.

Kampfgruppe Heintz

Schnelle Brigade 30

Kampfgruppe Brandt

Pont-Hébert

deployed on either side of the D77 over a length of just over a mile, attacked the remnants of the Pz. Gren. Rgt. 902 under Major Welsch. In order to face the few Panzers and Sturmgeschütze supporting these Panzergrenadiere, the battalions were backed up by two companies from the 743rd Tank Battalion.

The 119th Infantry was engaged between this road and the Vire. The 2nd Bn followed the 3rd, and the 1st Bn was emplaced along the Vire to ensure the east flank of the 3rd was protected. It risked being attacked by the 352.I.D., located to the east of the Vire.

A report drawn up by the regiment says: *"1 Company attacked with two platoons; the 1st and the 4th followed at one hundred yards. After advancing 300 yards, the company lost contact with the unit on its left and the two platoons at the rear lost contact with the rest of the company. German small arms and mortar fire was very heavy.*

The two platoons at the rear tried to join up with the company but after going a hundred yards, they were caught by a machine gun hidden fifty yards away. Shortly afterwards an artillery salvo hit in front of them. Encouraged, the Panzergrenadiere started firing again at the Americans with small arms and mortars. One GI was killed and two others were seriously wounded. A medic, Pfc. Maurice R. Bertrand, seriously wounded in the head, crumpled.

After the machine gun surprised the platoons, the enemy infantry also attacked, trying to isolate them. Pfc. Henry J. Herchel, a machine gunner, located the MG and started crawling towards it underneath the shots, taking a light machine gun with him. When he got 40 yards away he opened fire and wounded the two gunners. Shortly afterwards he destroyed their machine gun.

As a precaution, the two platoons fell back sixty or so yards, behind a hedge where they set up solid defences against the Panzergrenadiere; it was not long before the Germans came up on their left. The GIs managed to contain their repeated assaults then succeeded in re-establishing contact with the rest of the company."

It was very difficult for the infantry to advance because of the stiff resistance the Germans put up; they did not hesitate to throw tanks into the fight alongside their infantry. But the heaviest American losses of the day were not due to small arms fire but to the artillery.

The 117th Infantry had set up its positions between the departmental road and la Terrette, spearheaded by its 3rd Bn; the 2nd Bn, placed on its right wing, pinned down SS-Kampfgruppe Wisliceny located behind La Terrette. This unit was already also engaged against the GIs from the 47th Infantry of the 9th division, half a mile further north.

The 3/117th Infantry was progressing just as slowly as its neighbours on the right. It came under machine gun fire which once the enemy nests had been pinpointed, came under fire from the CCA Shermans. Then Browning bullets dealt with the machine gun crews; the GIs discovered the results when they started advancing again. They saw them half-in, half-out of their holes, lying at the foot of the bank where they had been gunned down just as they were about to fall back.

The greatest threat for the tank crews was from the Paks lying in ambush and their biggest fear was being burnt alive inside their tank. In that case, it was up to the infantry to cover the tanks by getting rid of the anti-tank guns. But when Panzers or Sturmgeschütze showed up, the crews found themselves forced to fight a pitiless duel through the hedges and across the fields, at a range of 200 yards at the most. The one who came out best was the quickest on the draw and who knew how to vanish, only to return and pounce upon his adversary elsewhere. Two Shermans and two Panzers were destroyed during the morning's fighting.

Another fearsome threat was posed by the Panzers which were dug in turret defilade. Their 75-mm shells whistled through the undergrowth like a powerful scythe, tearing trees apart and then finishing their trajectory against a tree trunk, throwing off shrapnel and bits of wood all over the place. Many GIs were wounded or killed in this way.

The presence of the Shermans was reassuring for the infantry, saving a lot of lives by getting rid of the stiffer enemy resistance points; but the tanks also attracted fire from the enemy artillery whose spotters, placed up on the heights signalled their slightest movements. These were the first targets.

There were also tragedies on the 117th Infantry front. The Panzergrenadiere caused chaos with their Panzerfaust. Lying down along the embankments, they fired their rockets at the tanks at less than 100 yards, sometimes even at 60 yards. At that range, they just could not miss and first one tank was set ablaze then a second, then a third and finally a fourth on the east flank of the 3rd Bn.

The mad scramble by Colonel Kelly's GIs appeared however to be paying off. Until the beginning of the afternoon, all hell was let loose

Above.
Coming out of his foxhole covered with planks and dirt, lieutenant CE Thomson of the 117th Infantry (30th Division) is using an EE-8 field telephone. These were always linked to another telephone, unlike the famous "Handie Talkie" which can be seen on the left and right of the photograph. This hand held radio enabled short range voice communication within the company net.
(National Archives)

in the Saint-Lô region. Little by little, the German units started breaking up. It was 3 pm when the GIs of the 3rd Bn of the 117th Infantry caught sight of the houses at Le Mesnil-Durand. They had leapt forward a mile from their start-off line, an accomplishment in its own right.

At the beginning of the evening, Colonel Kelly was ordered to stop his infantry battalions, in order to maintain a solid front line. German armoured counter-attacks were still likely.

C Company from the 743rd Tank battalion immediately left Les Hauts Vents to reinforce the 117th Infantry and the 823rd tank Destroyer Bn, positioned to the west of the departmental road. Moreover this lay-out enabled the 30th Infantry to hold its positions until the following morning. During the night there were several counter-attacks by the Germans but these were driven off.

With great boldness, a group of German soldiers accom-

panied by three Panzers headed for the 120th Infantry's command post; this unit had been placed in reserve. Pfc Henry A. Snotherly and his comrades were busy setting up their machine gun in their position when they recognised the outline of a Panzer as it went past. A hedge separated them.

These three GIs from the Cannon Company could not believe their eyes. They saw the head and shoulders of the tank commander sticking out of the turret, only a few yards away. And he had not seen them, either! In a fraction of a second, Pfc Snotherly shouldered his M1 rifle to aim at the German, but the latter had just spotted him. At the very moment the American squeezed the trigger, the turret hatch closed down over the tanker's head. Alerted by Snotherly, a bazooka team from a neighbouring company ran up. Snotherly and his comrades hurried back because in a few seconds all hell was going to be let loose.

Men from the Antitank company of an infantry regiment are breaking camp. The WC 62 6 x 6 Weapons carrier at the back was used to tow the 57-mm antitank gun M1. The large mound in the middle is a camouflage net for artillery pieces.
(National Archives)

Above.
Lying along the edge of a field, this Grenadier is ready to use his *Schiessbecher* **(grenade-launcher). This device enabled soldiers to launch 30-mm grenades. Special sights were fixed to the rifle so that it could launch grenades over a distance of 250 yards. This ammunition was effective only against light armour.**
(BA 101 I/584/2159/20)

Right.
One of the most common infantry guns, the 75-mm leichtes Infanteriegeschütz 18 can be seen here in its motor-towed version fitted with tyres. There was another version with wooden wheels reserved for horse-drawn units. Although the style of this gun appears out of date (production started in 1927), its maximum range was 3,550 yards with a normal charge and 4 600 yards with the super charge. Most of the Infanteriegeschütz equipped the 13.Kp in the infantry regiments, eg the 13./Gren. Rgt.984 (275.I.D.).
(BA 101 I/583/2130/36)

Above.
This Landser armed with a grenade-launcher fitted to the muzzle of his 98K rifle did not have time to fire it. An American medic is kneeling alongside the German soldier, who has suffered a head wound. In the background, another medic look on, he has turned his field jacket inside out to expose the darker and less visible flannel lining. The soldier at left has shortened the wooden handle of his folding shovel, to make it less cumbersome when attached to the rifle belt.
(National Archives)

Ten minutes later, one of the tanks was destroyed in close combat by the bazooka team. Shortly afterwards the team re-emerged on the flanks of the two other tanks after getting through a hedge and across a lane, disorienting the Panzerschütze who lost another tank. In a flash the two GIs changed positions then attacked the last Panzer which they also destroyed.

Thinking they were being attacked by a large enemy force, the German infantry fell back in disorder. Meanwhile, Pfc Snotherly and his four comrades went back to their original positions aboard a jeep. The danger seemed to have moved on. Moreover, wasn't that a half-track parked on the side of the lane?

The half-track, however, was full of enemy soldiers who were looking right at them. Unawares, the jeep driver put his foot down on the accelerator, expecting to share a few words on the situation with them. The welcome they got was not what they were expecting… at less than thirty yards, bursts of machine gun fire greeted their arrival. By a fluke, Snotherly was only wounded in the hand which was not enough to prevent him from swerving sharply to try and escape the bullets which were hitting the jeep. One of the passengers crumpled up, riddled with bullets. Snotherly did not dare look round. He tried his damnedest. He turned the steering wheel violently heading for a steep bank. The men seemed to lift up into the air with the MGs still firing at them.

When the jeep crashed down in the field Snotherly drove on flat out, without looking back, even to find out what had happened to the two seated at the rear. Unfortunately the jeep broke down, putting an end to the mad ride across the fields and Snotherly was captured. It was then that he discovered, just before being taken to an SPW, that one of the passengers of the jeep was dead and the other wounded.

Snotherly and his wounded comrade thought their last moment had come when they saw the Panzergrenadiere crammed into the half-track which had opened fire at the jeep. They were about to be interrogated when the noise of an engine could be heard approaching, giving them a

bit of hope. It was a jeep towing a trailer-load of ammunition. The men must have been on their way to deliver it to the 3rd Bn of the 120th Infantry command post.

The after-action report takes up the account: *"When the jeep ran into the SPW, the enemy opened up at point blank range, killing two men, Lieutenant Frederick A. Schlemmer, platoon leader in D Company and Private Kenneth L. Cross, wounding two others, Sergeant Francis P. Riley and Sergeant Cecil N. Blankenship. A handful of Panzergrenadiere assembled the prisoners behind the SPW while the rest of the troops headed towards the command post of the American battalion. Snotherly and his comrades wanted to warn the officers at the CP but he was in a tight spot and his situation was then at its most precarious.*

*Then a miracle took place. The two GIs with the bazooka who had destroyed the three Panzers had been attracted by the bursts of machine gun fire, and since they had one rocket left they cautiously headed for the spot, convinced they could score another hit. Luck was on their side that day. The machine guns were now silent but they had got close enough to hear the German's guttural voices. They got closer, bent double, sweating profusely, fear gripping their stomachs. They paused for a moment to catch their breath and saw the silhouette of the SPW, camouflaged with long green and brown zebra-like stripes. They went round a field, followed a dip in the ground then went down the lane where the half-track was parked. They got themselves ready quickly and mechanically. They both went

through the motions, so often repeated, for loading and firing a bazooka. There was no need for a second rocket; the SPW was reduced to a heap of scrap metal with that one shot."

Snotherly carries on with the story: "Machine guns echoed everywhere. In the confusion I crawled towards a bank, and then tried to reach the command post to warn our men. When I got fifty yards from the command post, located in a field, I raised my head. There was enough light still to tell our soldiers from the Germans. These were Germans and one of them saw me. He came to me and hit me several times with his burp gun to get me to stand up. I recognised the Panzergrenadiere who had captured me earlier. He led me to a lane leading to where their CP was set up on the road. I found myself in a hedge-lined ditch where I remained until the following morning, listening to the noise of tanks moving in the area.

I too wanted to have a look at these tanks. But when I raised my head, my guard hit me with the butt of his gun, to force me to lay face down in the ditch.

At that very moment, a German opposite me in his foxhole, shot by one of our men, collapsed and his two buddies behind me raised their hands in surrender. I signalled the German behind me to join his two comrades. When he got up I snatched his machine pistol and got out of the ditch to keep an eye on him and pointing the gun at him. The GI who had shot the German several seconds earlier turned his gun at me thinking I was the enemy; he came over when he saw I was a GI. He got the German out of the ditch.

While I covered the men behind me, one of them ran for it. I tried to shoot him but I didn't know how the gun worked. I pressed the clip release thinking it was the trigger. A little while later, the same German soldier surrendered of his own accord. We handed these Germans over to the 3rd Bn's HQ. In all there were 220 of them."

At midnight, General Hobbs was informed that his division was attached to the VIIth Army Corps under General Collins but that his objectives were still the same.

The 35th US ID to the East of the Vire

Untiringly, Brigadier-General Sebree launched his 137th Infantry Regiment into the attack again. But his men had already been spotted by the enemy observers. The German shells tore up the ground a few hundred yards in front of the departure line, paralyzing the GIs. They knew that

Major-General Butler B. Miltonberger, CO of the 134th Infantry. Promoted to Brigadier General rank and executive commander of the 35th Division, he was Chief of the National Guard Bureau until 1947.
Gen. Miltonberger also authored the official 134th Infantry war history.
(35th Div. Association)

With all its crew's senses on the alert, this Sherman tank is advancing carefully, scouting out ahead, in the deserted streets of a village. Its situation is extremely precarious because a Panzerfaust team positioned behind a window can easily take the machine out in a split second.
(National Archives)

every one of them was being closely watched by a Grenadier who had chosen one of them as his own target… Morale was low. They waited for the steel rain to end.

Under less fire than the other battalions in the 137th, the 3rd Bn advanced victoriously in the La Mare sector by opening up several breaches in Oberst Kentner's lines. The latter sent his remaining reserves but they were unable to prevent the GIs from occupying the terrain up to the Saint-Lô road. When K Company crossed the road, it was 09.10.

Shortly afterwards, Brigadier-General Sebree learnt by radio that this company was in contact with the enemy and that it was impossible to advance; the machine gun fire was far too heavy and accurate. It was obvious that Sebree had sprung the trap Kentner had laid for him, succeeding in cutting off the 3rd Bn from its regiment.

At present Kentner asked Hauptmann Erlenberger, Kdr. of the II./ Gren. Rgt. 897 to launch a counter-attack in order to drive the 1/137th back.

The GIs of the 320th Infantry Regiment who had leapt forward 300 yards took about thirty prisoners. Although his forces were getting weaker, Kgp. Kentner was still a nightmare for the 35th Infantry division which lost 16 killed, one hundred or so wounded and one missing.

Just before the 134th Infantry set off, the XIXth Corps artillery bombarded the German positions which were along the regiment's axis of attack. In turn the enemy artillery opened up. All this din got on the soldiers' nerves; they had not slept during the night of 14-15 July. This attack on Hill 122 was turning out to be a terrible ordeal.

Camouflaged in the woods and the copses, Kgp. Kentner's Grenadiere and the first paratroopers from Fallschirmjägerregiment 14, who had just joined them, were ready to attack the American task force.

This was made up of the 134th Infantry, the 2nd Bn of the 320th Infantry, the 737th Tank Battalion (less B Company), two platoons from A Company of the 60th Engineer Combat Battalion and a platoon of the 654th Tank Destroyer Battalion.

According to the plan, the 134th Infantry advanced on the left flank between the 320th's operational zone and the main road leading to Saint-Clair-sur-Elle. For two hours the task force progressed in a most spectacular fashion, but when the 134th Infantry came into sight of Emilie, they ran into opponents who were quite determined to stay, each house in the village having been transformed into a fortress.

Violent fighting started. Safe behind stone walls, the Grenadiere and Fallschirmjäger surprised the Americans who thought it was only a rearguard unit burrowing in some buildings.

Working their way through the storm of bullets, the GIs had to fight hard to take the village. They had to fall back twice to their initial positions, making bloody trips there and back. In spite of the Americans' efforts, the Germans still held fast. At the beginning of the afternoon, a new plan was drawn up and the divisional artillery opened fire with a barrage that crept inexorably towards the enemy. The GIs followed the hail of steel at a distance and when the 155-mm guns fell silent, the GIs cleared out the remaining resistance points, those which had escaped the shelling. The Garand rifles barked furiously. There was fierce hand to hand fighting here and there.

After waiting for an hour, the battalion commander was finally able to tell his superior, Colonel Butler B. Miltonberger that Emilie had been taken and that it was soon to be the turn of Les Romains.

Encouraged by this success, Major-General Baade asked Brigadier-General Sebree to take over the 134th and supervise the capture of Hill 122. It was about 6pm when he got there. After analyzing the situation, he presented the various officers in the Task Force with a workable plan; they approved his decisions unanimously.

At 8pm the fearsome P-47s appeared, strafing and bombing the enemy positioned on Hill 122, which disappeared in a sea of flames and shouts. The Fallschirmjäger had barely time to get over this devastating attack, get their positions back in order and be ready to face the Task Force's vigorous attack.

At 8.45pm, the artillery started bombarding Hill 122. The 92nd Chemical Mortar Battalion fired more than 7,000 smoke bombs during the operation. As for the 'divarty' of the 35th Infantry division, it used up 11,000 shells… It seemed to last forever for those who were on the receiving end. For the GIs who had to take the heights, this last quarter of an hour before the attack was still much too short. The enemy's strength had been considerably weakened but it was still formidable.

At 9pm sharp, the 134th Infantry regiment (less C Company) launched its attack in the direction of the heights, drowned in a dense cloud of dust which got to the men's throats. The 3rd Bn attacked on the other slope.

The 2/134th Infantry had to take up a defensive stance because German resistance was so stiff. Warned that this battalion was in difficulty, Brigadier-General Sebree sent it some tanks from the 737th Tank Battalion. These appeared on the enemy rear by going round Emilie by the east.

When these tank crews made contact with the infantry, the company commanders of the 2/134th adopted new tactics. From then on, the GIs would move up in small groups with the help of a tank they would guide, so as to fight small separate engagements. So it was that at 11pm, the GIs

from A and B Companies announced that they had got a foothold on the northern escarpment of Hill 122. The German forces had been knocked around a bit and they were now beginning to give ground.

The TDs from the 654th Tank Destroyer Bn which had been following at a distance the groups of soldiers gathered around the Shermans, cleared up what remained of enemy resistance. Immediately informed by the GIs of the 1/134th Infantry that they were reaching Hill 122, the pioneers from the 60th Infantry rushed forward to reinforce their positions with sandbags, barbed wire and anti-

tank mines. Brigadier-General Sebree had thought of everything.

The 35th Infantry Division's advance along the right bank of the river now created a serious threat to the German flank towards Pont-Hébert. Indirectly, it was in a position to support the 30th division which was to attack the following day.

The 29th ID to the East of the River Vire

Major-General Gerhardt's unpopularity now reached new heights. He was very angry because his division was

making no headway in front of Saint-Lô. To him, this was unthinkable. The soldiers, especially the officers, who were in direct contact with him did not enjoy his company that day. He criticised them all day but they could not accomplish more. Unflinchingly, they obeyed orders which most of the time turned out to be impracticable.

Although the 1st Bn of the 115th Infantry under Major H. Jackson had broken the defences of the 353 Infanterie-Division Kampfgruppe located to the east of the D6, it was now prevented from proceeding to Hill 122, situated to the west of Martinville, by Major Stephani's Fallschirmjäger who were just as determined as ever. They had been ordered to hold out because, as they no longer had the support of the Kgp. of the 353.I.D. on their left wing, there was a risk of being isolated. As a precaution, Major Stephani moved his command post to a farm hidden at the end of a valley, near Fumichon.

To make the most of the opportunities, the 2nd Bn of the 115th Infantry joined up with the 1st Bn, and then attacked together over a wide front; and a large bag of paratroopers were captured. It was the best haul of the whole campaign for Saint-Lô. Alas, in order to gain only about half a mile of terrain, Major Jackson lost 20 killed and one hundred wounded.

Supported by Shermans of the 747th Tank Battalion, the 3rd Bn of the 116th Infantry moved along Martinville ridge and headed for La Madeleine in a southeasterly direction from Saint-Lô. They had barely got going when they were subjected to concentrated fire from small arms then, 10 minutes later, from artillery as well. In less than thirty minutes, many men were killed or wounded.

The American observers were unable to locate where the enemy batteries were set up in all the greenery. Later they discovered that there were 88-mm Flak batteries positioned on Hill 101 near La Madeleine. The American infantry were not the only ones to be knocked about. The armour also suffered. They tried to get away from the shells by hiding behind hedges. Seven of them exploded in balls of fire, throwing up bits of burning metal. The hedges were torn apart time and time after again by these shots. The earth trembled. The whole countryside seemed to be on fire. The 3rd Bn's surprise attack had misfired. It was detected before it even got under way.

Noting that the engineers and the Sherman crews were falling back in disorder, the GIs in the 3rd Bn thought that the Germans had broken through and in turn they started to scatter. Then the officers from regimental headquarters together with Sergeant Forbes, the Message center chief, realised what was going on and rushed out of their tents to stop the runaways and send them back to the fight. The men wanted to get in touch with their CO but he had been transferred during the day to the 8th Infantry Division.

To remedy this grave situation, the 116th Infantry CO, Colonel Philip R. Dwyer, requested assistance from Gerhardt. The latter immediately set up an operation to disengage them. He got the 1st Bn of the 116th to intervene and attack on the right wing of the 3rd, and the 2/175th Infantry to attack the enemy in the rear by trying to advance along the Saint-Lô - Bayeux road.

This pincer movement started to pose a threat to the Germans. If the 29th Infantry Division succeeded in taking this linchpin, Saint-Lô would fall into American hands.

Except for the 2nd Bn which was committed, the other two battalions of the 175th Infantry were still positioned on the left flank of the division, holding their positions firmly along the Saint-Lô – Bayeux road. They were subjected to heavy fire from 88-mm Flak guns, but the GIs were well dug-in and just waited for the fighters to intervene.

Judging by the absence of shoulder straps and the metal wings pinned directly to the cloth of his Fliegerbluse collar, this young prisoner belonged to another branch before being assigned to the parachute arm as a reinforcement. There was certainly a shortage of golden yellow patches and he has been asked to remove the original collar insignia. This disposition was also current in the Felddivisionen.
Dite/Usis)

Suddenly a dozen P-47s dived straight at the Flak guns camouflaged on Hill 101. None of the guns escaped their fire. Stunned and half-deafened by the explosions of the rockets, the Flak gunners hastened to the rear under fire from the GIs' automatic weapons. Because of their excellent conduct under fire and to encourage them as well, Major-General Gerhardt sent each of his battalion and regimental commanders this memorandum:

"The division has obtained satisfactory results for today. The advance must be continued whatever the price. At 7.30pm all the division's fighting elements will attack and finish reaching their objectives before nightfall. Each soldier in the division will have to give the best of himself. Fix bayonets, 29th Let's go!"

After disengaging the 3rd Bn of the 116th Infantry, the two other battalions advanced on either side of Martinville ridge which was still held by the Fallschirmjäger who attacked them as they went past. But the GIs stubbornly plodded on towards La Madeleine, their objective. The German strong points tried to stop them but these were getting weaker. The Americans persevered with their efforts and eliminated each strong point then moved on to the next one, twenty yards away, before starting the same cleaning up operation again.

Nothing seemed capable of stopping Lieutenant-Colonel Bingham's soldiers who reached their objective, right next to La Madeleine. Darkness shrouded the place. As a precaution, Colonel Dwyer asked Bingham to remain where he was and set up his positions for the night. The 1st Bn which ought to have advanced alongside him had been lagged behind for some time now. It was blocked less than 300 yards from its starting line. Bingham's battalion was in fact isolated without the support of its heavy company and of one of its infantry companies!

Moreover 45 wounded had to be evacuated and there were only three medics. Bingham still had a radio that worked so he alerted the command post which sent over some plasma during the night by means of a Piper Cub liaison plane.

The Germans had understood the predicament of Bingham's 2nd Bn. A few bold Green Devils came up on the rear of the battalion and succeeded in isolating it by cutting its communications lines. Bingham reinforced his positions for the night, recommending his soldiers not to fire until they were sure of their target since ammunition supplies were getting critically low. With their nerves on edge and their fingers squeezing the triggers, they settled down to wait for an invisible enemy.

Opposite page,.
The machine gunner shoulders his MG 42, pretending to fire for the reporter's camera. The 250-round belt fed into the breech should be held by the ammunition bearer to ensure that it was fed through correctly.

Bottom.
This shots shows a MG-Schütze lying in ambush would look like, note how his bandaged right hand holds the stock to keep the weapon in line when firing. The MG42's firepower was 1,500 rpm, and the excellence of its mechanism and its weight (rather light for a machine gun: 23 lb) made it one of the most effective automatic weapons of WWII.
(BA 101 I/582/2106/23 et 24)

Two of a Tank Destroyer's crew are visible in the open turret while the machine moves at a fast pace. Off-road, this AFV could move at 20 mph and on the road at 30 mph. The 76.2-mm barrel is pointing at the road and a crew member is grasping the turret-mounted .50 Browning machine gun. This TD belongs to the 703rd Tank Destroyer Battalion. Each of the companies was assigned to a different task force in the 3rd Armored Division, the 1st Company to Task Force X under Colonel T.E. Boudinot, the 2nd Company to Task Force Y under Colonel Parks and the 3rd Company to Task force Z under Lieutenant-Colonel Abney. *(Dite/Usis)*

THE 30th DIVISION
WEST OF THE VIRE

16 July...

NOW ATTACHED TO THE VIIth Corps, the 30th infantry Division under General Hobbs launched its 117th and 119th Infantry Regiments against the German lines.

The two unit gained half a mile of ground then the 120th Infantry held in reserve joined them. Once this move had been carried out, the 1st and 2nd Bns of the 120th attacked in turn, each supported by a company from the 743rd Tank battalion.

In spite of lively opposition from isolated groups of Panzergrenadiere under Hauptmann Böhm (II./Pz.Gren.Rgt.902) supported by Panzers, mostly dug in up to the turret, Colonel Birks' GIs managed to advance.

The intelligence of the 30th Infantry Division was now convinced that the German tanks were running out of petrol. Why else would their crews use them as static antitank guns? The tanks in the 743rd Tank Battalion destroyed three of them and the bazooka teams two more.

All the enemy's strong points were wiped out one after another. Nothing seemed to be able to halt these GIs and when they came into sight of Le Mesnil-Durant, the understrength Panzergrenadiere got ready to defend it. B Company of the 117th Infantry following closely on the heels of the 120th took the village and set up its positions on some heights situated to the south.

But at 4 pm Major Noster of Fallschirmjägerregiment 14 ordered Hauptmann Schmidt to launch his I.Btl. against the right wing of the 120th Infantry (to the west of the D77). Schmidt, who had set up his command post in a damaged farmhouse, was not familiar with the situation on the American front, let alone what was happening on that of the army corps to which he belonged. The previous night, he had moved with his paratroopers into the Amigny sector to position himself on the east flank of II./Pz.Gren.Rgt.902.

Exhausted the long march, the Fallschirmjäger were then subjected to a terrible bombardment by the American artillery. This was the fault of a Nebelwerfer battery located on the edge of a wood who opened fire on the Americans for no particular reason. Located by the observers very quickly, the artillery poured down a deluge of steel and fire on the German soldiers.

Hauptmann Schmidt's CP inevitably got hit a couple of times because

his shelter was only a hundred yards from the Nebelwerfer battery. The shooting carried on endlessly.

Once calm was restored, Hauptmann Schmidt asked one of his officers to summon the battery commander of Werfer-Lehr-Rgt.1. A few minutes later a Leutnant came up, clicking his heels. Hauptmann Schmidt coldly ordered him to take his guns elsewhere because his shooting had set the Americans off, retaliating against the battalion and his HQ.

Apparently hurt by the Fallschirmjäger Hauptmann's attitude, the young officer disappeared with his artillery as quickly as he could.

Having already experienced the hell of heavy Allied shelling at Monte Cassino, Hauptmann Schmidt knew that he now had to move. He organised the withdrawal and the CP was set up 600 yards further to the rear, in some woods. This was a wise precaution because the next day, one of his junior officers told him that the farmhouse they had left had been entirely destroyed.

Helmut Wilhelmsmeyer, a veteran of 1./Fallschirmjägerregiment 14 remembers: *"We had just got ourselves set up when our command post was spotted by the Americans. We were subjected to heavy mortar fire. Then the Jabos flew over the woods firing on the off-chance, wasting an impressive quantity of ammunition and fuel."*

Despite this dramatic situation, Hauptmann Schmidt ordered the supply platoon to bring the ammunition to a sunken lane a few hundred yards from the CP. He personally kept an eye on the issue because there were only limited quantities. Now resupplied, the first three companies of the

Above.
A handful of Fallschirmjäger return with this trophy captured from the Americans: a jeep with its trailer, a windfall for these paratroopers who had no transport vehicles.
(BA 101 I/5854/2159/27)

Right.
The HQ commander, a junior officer holder of the German Cross and the Iron Cross First Class, comes out to meet his men and examine the jeep more closely.
(BA 101 I/5854/2159/27)

Previous page, bottom.
This shot was taken by Sergeant PM Larkin of the 9th Air Force, shortly before Operation "Cobra." The scene is taking place in the Amigny sector. The bodies of the crew are lying near their tank: a Panther from I./Pz.Rgt.6. It was destroyed on 16 July 1944 by the 120th US Inf. Rgt of the 30th US Inf. Div.
(PM Larkin)

WERFER-LEHR REGIMENT 1

Below, inset.
The unit sign. Before arriving in Normandy, Werfer-Lehr Regiment 1 had fought in Crimea and Russia. Its Abteilungen were reformed several times over owing to severe losses, especially after Kursk. However Oberst Böhm's regiment had its full complement when it reached the Normandy front in June 1944, as a part of Werfer-Brigade 8. It suffered its most heavy losses when crossing the Seine at the end of August. Böhm was even killed there. This unit fought on during the battle of the Bulge.

Above.
Under the watchful eye of the Gefreiter section leader, the gunners prepare their 15 cm Nebelwerfer 41. The launcher weighs about 1,160 pounds. Its rate of fire was six rockets in 10-second salvoes, max. range was about 4 miles. The original term of *Nebelwerfer* ('smoke launcher') is inappropriate. (Continued on opposite page)

battalion went off into the near-impenetrable bocage. The fourth company remained in reserve. But mortar fire, followed by that of the artillery caused heavy losses among the Fallschirmjäger, particularly in the 3.Kp. and the supply platoon who took the brunt of the attack.

An hour later the bombardment stopped and Schmidt started off again with his Fallschirmjäger who managed to advance over one and a half miles without coming across any strong opposition. The scouts went first to find any possible ways through. Behind them the company commanders waited patiently for their radio messages confirming that all was clear.

Major Noster's strategy worked. His paratroopers surprised the GIs of the 120th Infantry who barely put up any

resistance. Until then all was going well for the Germans. Having reached a position to the north of Le Mesnil-Durand, the paras were then subjected to intense artillery bombardment which stopped their advance in its tracks. The I.Btl.'s baptism of fire marked the men for life.

The counter-attack lost its momentum then bogged down completely. Schmidt asked his company commanders to gather on some heights in order to reorganise whilst waiting for the 4.Kp. to intervene.

But it was now too late for the paratrooper battalion to reach its objectives. The Americans of the 30th infantry division had pulled themselves together. Backed up by their artillery and air force, the Americans got the better of Schmidt's soldiers. The latter asked his officers to pull

Right.
This Panzer IV of II./Pz.Rgt.130 was destroyed in July 1944 by a 75-mm gun in front of the Lemazurier farm, near Le Mesnil-Durant. Its crew was trying to stop the 30th Division. On the same day, the 120th Infantry under Colonel Birks destroyed 16 Panzers, five with bazookas.
(National Archives)

back to their starting points. It was his last order: he was killed a short while later in a skirmish. Other officers also lost their lives in this tragic counter-attack.

Oberleutnant Meissner, the CO of 1.Kp. who on his own initiative took command of the battalion. In groups or by themselves, the Fallschirmjäger got back to their starting line as ordered.

Helmut Wilhelmsmeyer, of 1./Fallschirmjägerregiment 14 evokes the battalion's losses: *"The company commanders, Hauptmanns Gnann, Gaebele and Andresen were seriously wounded. Hauptmann Gaebele had taken a shell fragment in his left thigh and was being helped by Gefreiter Schroder who got him away from the combat zone. Unfortunately this officer died from the amputation which was carried out in the nearest field hospital."*

Worried by the 60% losses in the I.Btl. and by the failure of the mission entrusted to the late Hauptmann Schmidt, Major Noster received orders to support the II./Pz.Gren.Rgt. 902 in a new counter-attack.

The paratroopers from III./Fallschirmjägerregiment 14 under Hauptmann Meissner joined the Panzergrenadiere who had an tank platoon (four Pz. IVs according to the Americans, four Tigers according to the paratroopers).

Hauptmann Meissner was picked to lead the operation. He was a veteran of the campaign for Belgium and the Netherlands, and then Crete and Russia. He feared no

battle and so far victory had always smiled at him. Since the previous night, his four companies had been placed on a defensive line stretching out from the south-east of Le Mesnil-Durand to Pont-Hébert.

Otto Bernhardt, a veteran of Fallschirmjägerregiment 14 tell us that during this change of position, Oberleutnant Rank, CO of the 9.Kp., was wounded in his left arm by grenade. He was sent quickly to a first aid post but lost a lot of blood during the transfer and died shortly afterwards.

The history of the 120th Infantry Regiment gives an account Hauptmann Böhm's attack: *"this was the baptism of fire for S/Sgts Howard E. Callaway and Dewey H. Harris from A Company. They were a bazooka team. No veteran fought as well as those two on 16 July 1944. Seeing enemy armor threaten our troops, the two soldiers got in position under fire from the enemy artillery, mortars and small arms. In a short time, they managed to destroy two tanks. One Panzer at thirty yards to the north was shooting at our troops. Another was approaching from the south. Breaking cover, S/Sergeant Callaway fired twice and destroyed the tank from the south. Then getting up close in front of a Panzer, he fired a rocket which hit the track, bringing it to a standstill. Crawling along the hedges to keep out of sight of the enemy the two men saw the other tank which was still heading to the north again. Having got to within a range of 60 yards they managed to destroy it with a single rocket. A bit later coming across other Panzers they managed to get close while still keeping under cover.*

Getting to within 75 yards and still seconded by S/Sergeant Harris, Callaway destroyed another tank using two rockets. With four tanks out of action, the enemy's resistance was considerably reduced which made it easier for the GIs of the 120th Infantry to advance."

During another counter-attack Lieutenant Pulver saw three Panzers slipping towards his company. He got hold of the radio to call in the artillery. But before the "Long Toms" (the nick-name for the 155-mm guns) could thunder, the Panzers had continued on their way. They were not very far from his men who had not even spotted them.

In desperation, Pulver also grabbed a bazooka and took a GI with him, to carry the rockets. When they got within firing range without being spotted by the Fallschirmjäger who were following the two Panzers, he aimed his weapon at the side and fired. The rocket described an arc then fell onto the tank. There was a moment's silence. The Lieutenant only had time to open his eyes wide before he

Above.
This Fallschirmjäger, probably an NCO, is keeping a watch on the surrounding countryside with his 6 X 30 binoculars. Note his helmet cover which was specially for the paratroopers. This one has the same type of camouflage pattern as his jump smock; it is the second version. The first was solid green, like the earliest smocks. Canvas strips were sewn onto both types so that leafy branches could be slipped through them.
.(BA 101 I/586/2106/22)

saw the Panzer shudder with a huge explosion. The tank disappeared in a cloud of smoke which engulfed the infantry too. Some of them screamed, shouted, gasped. Many of them were wounded in the explosion. The other Panzers started to turn and head for the two Americans, tearing apart the hedges, branches and grinding down the embankments with their tracks. They were not even in line before another one of them caught fire. Lieutenant Pulver and his associate got away discreetly. They only had one thing to do now: get back to the command post.

It is just probable that thirty or so Fallschirmjäger from the first battalion who had got lost might have been involved in that fray.

During this bloody day, the 30th Infantry Division caused the Fallschirmjägerregiment 14 many casualties and put 16 Panzers out of action. Colonel Birks of the 120th Infantry claimed the destruction of eight of them, as well as wiping out a whole company of paratroopers who were exposed in a field.

Shocked by the dramatic events of the day, Major Noster, Kdr. of Fallschirmjägerregiment 14, strove on field telephones to round up his commanders on a line set up to the rear of the front.

At the end of the day, General Hobbs was satisfied with his men's conduct under fire and with their progress. His 119th and 120th Infantry Regiments were holding a perfectly coherent line between La Terrette and the River Vire, and his 117th, positioned on the division's right flank, was in touch with the 9th Infantry Division engaged against Kampfgruppe Wisliceny situated to the west of La Terrette.

At 2 am, SS-Obersturmbannführer Wisliceny ordered his men to get ready to destroy the bridge in case of an attack from the east. It was the only way to protect his right flank since there was no longer any contact with II. Fallschirmjäger-Korps. By doing this, he got most of his strength into the line facing the 9th Infantry Division which was coming from the north of Englandes.

Wisliceny had foreseen events quite well since five Shermans were seen heading for the bridge three hours later. Infantrymen were perched on their decks. A Kompanie-Trupp from 16./"D" assigned to watch over the bridge, let the Americans approach to about 200 yards then opened fire with heavy machine guns. A platoon of Granatwerfers also joined in. The explosions surprised the GIs who were not expecting such opposition. Suddenly an explosion which was more powerful than the others drew the soldiers' attention from both sides. SS-Obersturmführer Macher's sappers had just blown up the bridge.

The leading Shermans were brought to a standstill; the crews waited for new orders when the Pz. IVs from II./Pz.Rgt. 130 started firing at them. The leading Sherman turned into a ball of fire, with a direct hit from a 75-mm shell. Several GIs fell to the ground never to get up again; the others disappeared into thin air, looking desperately for any sort of shelter.

The American assault group was finally forced to fall back or be wiped out. Leaving SS-Kgp. Wisliceny's right flank, the GIs from the 9th Infantry Division made a frontal attack at the beginning of the afternoon. The first assault took place in the sector held by the 1./SS-Pz.Pi.Btl. 2 which gave way under the pressure. It took the support of the first platoon of 16./"D" to fill the breach.

At 17.30, Major-General Eddy concentrated his forces from the 9th Infantry Division in an attack which he considered to be decisive. The sappers from 3. and 4./SS-Pz.Pi. Btl. 2 were rushed in and were not spared either by the infantry or the artillery. Before being overwhelmed some sappers tried to resist with their Flammenwerfer which the GIs feared like the plague. Their MGs were still firing when the GIs reached their positions. Even SS-Hauptsturmführer Schmelzer from 4./SS-Pz.Pi. Btl. 2, the most decorated man in the "Das Reich" Engineer Battalion had to admit that their only salvation lay in retreat. Rapidly out-fought, the Pioniere vanished into the smoke towards the south.

Warned that the Americans were infiltrating his lines, SS-Obersturmbannführer Wisliceny called in his troubleshooter, SS-Obersturmführer Macher, who got together a few dozen sappers and succeeded in filling the gap but not without casualties.

The 9th Division seemed to be bleeding the stubborn SS-Kgp. to death. At about 19.00 it was almost surrounded and supplies were no longer getting through. From now on SS-Hauptsturmführer Hilber and his men would be taking over its job.

General Hobbs now had to do without the support of Combat Command B which had held the Haut Vents sector since 11 July. This armoured unit had been vital in supporting his many attacks until 16 July. In six days' fighting, Combat Command B lost 131 men and 24 of its tanks, mainly by those fatal Panzerfaust rockets.

His tanks were to assemble to the west of Saint-Jean-de-Daye before being attached to the Vth US Army Corps.

The 35th US ID to the east of the Vire

It was hardly daybreak and the GIs from the 1st Bn of the 134th Infantry Regiment were already being subjected to artillery fire coming from Hill 122. Working non-stop at the forefront, the engineers were getting the ground ready by clearing it of mines. Suddenly a huge explosion lit up the summit of the heights. *"The Germans have just blown up their ammunition depot,"* Major-General Baade confirmed to his chief-of-staff, *"a sure sign they're bugging out."*

The commander of the 35th Infantry Division could not have been more wrong. It was in fact an agreed signal for the Fallschirmjäger to counter-attack in the direction of the 1st Bn. They appeared just like ghosts in front of the GIs who quickly pulled themselves together. Keeping cool-headed, they waited for their enemy to be within range before pulling the trigger. Gritting their teeth, with fear gnawing at their stomachs, the first machine gunners opened fire. The first burst cut down three paratroopers.

The GIs fired with precision, hitting home with each shot. Some of the Fallschirmjäger crumpled up but the others kept coming with fixed bayonets or throwing grenade after grenade at the Americans. They shouted to give themselves courage but the Brownings soon cut them down in full flight.

The survivors decided to turn back or to hide in the thickets to escape the bullets whistling everywhere.

Taking advantage of the enemy's confusion, the CO of the 134th Infantry launched his men in an attack against the heights. They ran into isolated groups who tried at all costs to

Above.
An aerial shot of the greenery surrounding Saint-Lô.
(National Archives)

Right.
A GI from the 35th Division on the outskirts of Saint-Lô, on 18 or 19th July. The divisional patch can be seen on his left sleeve. The division entered Saint-Lô on 18 July, after repulsing strong attack in the Emelie sector.
(National Archives)

prevent them from advancing. Stubbornly the GIs progressed, clearing out everything in their path. When they reached the heights, they established defensive positions in case there were any counter-attacks.

This extra effort turned out to be useful for them when the enemy attacked during the night. But the 1st Bn held fast, waiting patiently for the 2nd Bn to rejoin. But it was having difficulty advancing.

During the day, the 3/134th Infantry Regiment was also counter-attacked but these were weak attempts. Kgp. Kentner's forces were dwindling. All his reserves had been thrown into the battle the day before.

During the fighting Hauptmann Erlenberger, Kdr. of II./Gren.Rgt. 897 was killed. This was a severe loss for Oberst Kentner who lost one of his best officers.

The objective assigned to the 134th Infantry had been reached. Its 1st Bn had got hold of Hill 122 and therefore could now be considered as a shock battalion in the XIXth Corps. This undeniable victory opened the road to Saint-Lô directly, but it had cost the lives of 102 GIs with 589 wounded and 101 missing.

The 29th US ID to the east of the River Vire

The position of the 2nd Bn of the 116th Infantry Regiment was unchanged. At dawn on this Sunday morning, Major Bingham and his soldiers were stunned to be so few left with perhaps the worst still to come. For heavy weapons, they only had four 81-mm mortars and four calibre .30 machine guns.

Staff Sergeant Ronald W. Cote, a squad leader in E Company remembers: *"We dug all day to improve our defences. We were hungry and thirsty because when we left the day before, we had only taken two rations each with us. Most of us had eaten it all the night before. During the afternoon, we drank the last drops of water in our bottles. What little conversation there was, was about hunger, thirst and the need to be relieved.*

During the night several of us crawled down the slope to fetch some water in the one or two abandoned houses (…)"

Despite radio communication problems, several contacts were made with the liaison officer of the 111th Field Artillery Battalion. The sergeant in the battalion's radio section, Sgt T/5 Norman J. Lloyd, reported that with a soldier of HQ Company, he had managed to cross the German lines to take information to the officers at the regimental HQ.

Moreover he got them to understand that it was useless to risk soldiers' lives just to restore communications since the battalion was well set in on the heights. Major Bingham who had been expecting an attack at any time all day started to wonder whether or not the Germans were really aware of his isolated situation…

As for the other battalions in the 116th Infantry, it was not a question of getting hold of any more terrain but of hanging on to what had been won the day before.

The GIs in the 1st Bn had to face a German counter-attack coming from Martinville Ridge.

A hundred or so Fallschirmjäger, some of them equipped with flamethrowers, supported by three Panzers threw themselves at the GIs. Although they were exhausted, the GIs left their positions and went forward to meet the enemy who was taken completely by surprise by this reaction. The flamethrowers were of no use because the crews could not get close enough to their targets.

The German counter-attack had failed. Several German corpses lay on the escarpment of Martinville ridge; furious, the Fallschirmjägers asked for mortar and artillery support and ten minutes later, a deluge of steel fell upon the American positions. In spite of heavy losses and more powerless than ever, the Americans held off a second light machine gun counter-attack. The sole Panzer (according

Below.
These two signalmen, (*Funker***) are getting ready to lay telephone cable between command posts. These cables created a lot of problems because they were often severed during the numerous bombardments. When this happened, signalmen had to find the break and repair the line, very often under enemy fire. The cable reel was carried on the back with a special frame and harness. The bag which can be seen on the bottom holds the operating handle. The cable was about 300 yards long.**
(BA 101 I/584/2161/12)

Generalfeldmarschall Rommel (1st left), Oberbefehlshaber der Heeresgruppe B and SS-Oberstgruppenführer Paul Hausser (2nd left), Kdr. of the 7. Armee visiting Generalleutnant Meindl (centre). The scene is taking place in the courtyard of a house at Fervacques, to the north of Tessy-sur-Vire where the II.Fallschirmjäger-Korps' HQ was set up. Oberstleutnant Blauensteiner, Meindl's chief-of-staff, can be recognised, shaking hands with the Heer officer. The bareheaded parachute officer standing back is Hauptmann Götsche, Kdr. of Fallschirm.Aufkl.-Abt. 12
(BA 101 I/584/2162/23)

Bottom.
The same place today.

to another report it was an SPW firing its machine gun and according to a third report, it could have been Sturmgeschütze!) coming along the Martinville road caused them heavy losses by firing into the hedges lining the road and behind which the GIs in the 1st Bn of the 116th Infantry were sheltering. This tank's advance opened up breaches in the positions which could no longer be held. A bazooka team tried to get close to the tank but unfortunately the crew spotted it and it was ruthlessly eliminated. The Panzer seemed to be invulnerable.

Faced with such a critical situation, the young Lieutenant from another unit who had been ordered to take A Company was out of his depth. He preferred to entrust the task to an old veteran, First Sergeant Peterson, who had replaced his company commander for three days now.

He reorganised the soldiers and urged them to hold their positions. Only cool-headedness would get them out of this particular tight spot. A terrible fight got under way.

Trusting Peterson, the GIs fought ferociously but their firepower was no match for the Panzer which was carrying on with its task of dealing out death.

The Fallschirmjägers now realised that the American front line was crumbling. They pressed on, certain of winning the day.

Without an anti-tank gun, 1st Sergeant Peterson knew that his men could not resist for ever. He ordered the men to break off shouting at the top of his voice, trying to yell above the row. The GIs in A Company now tried to escape from the intense Fallschirmjäger fie by vanishing into the bocage, heading for the battalion HQ. Some of the soldiers fell on the way.

When Major Thomas S. Dallas heard the staccato noise of weapons and saw the first GIs running towards him, he understood that A Company was on the point of being wiped out. Among these soldiers was Sergeant

Peterson helped by another soldier carrying a wounded comrade who could not walk.

Dallas managed to stall the rout in his company in less than five minutes. The Fallschirmjäger with their terrible Panzer could appear any moment now. An Oglala Sioux GI kept his head in a most unbelievable way and showed unfailing courage. With Sergeant Peterson he rounded up the survivors and showed them a hedge which was near their old positions, where they would be able to stop the attackers. There were only a few dozen men left in the company when it reached its objective. When the GIs spotted the camouflaged jump suits and the bowl-shaped helmets through the brushwood, their weapons started to rattle. The German suffered heavy casualties. The Panzer went into action.

1st Sergeant Peterson decided that he was going to destroy that tank. He was taking no chances and equipped with a grenade launcher fitted to his Garand rifle, he snatched a grenade which he fitted. Then he sneaked through a hedge which tore his jacket and grazed his hands and his face but fear and tension were so strong that he ignored the scratches.

He went into a field where he found the ideal spot from which he could eliminate the steel monster.

With lightning speed and because he was an expert rifleman, he fired grenade after grenade, six in all, at the Panzer. All were bull's eyes. This time the tank crew abandoned all thoughts of advancing, fearing for their tank and especially for their lives. They fell back leaving the Fallschirmjäger to their fate. Meanwhile the GIs had driven off the enemy, and then retaken their former positions. Shortly afterwards Sergeant Peterson was relieved to see their comrades from B Company coming up to their rescue. Order gained the upper hand. The wounded were evacuated. The losses for A Company were 37 killed and wounded.

The second counter-attack also failed. The Fallschirmjäger had to make do with calling in the mortars and the artillery to harass A Company and the other units in the 1st Bn of the 116th Infantry.

Although the GIs in the 29th Infantry Division maintained their overall positions, they nevertheless suffered alarming casualties. Joseph Balkoski reports: *"The 3rd Bn of the 115th Infantry was reduced to 177 men. Its initial strength was almost 900. E company in the 175th Infantry only had 50 soldiers and one officer left out of 187 men and six officers. One platoon of the 1st Bn of the 115th Infantry which numbered 18 men on 17 July when it was supposed to have 41, finished the day with only three."*

These figures give us an idea of the strength of the 29th Infantry Division which nevertheless was supposed to deliver the final, decisive blow to Saint-Lô. When an officer drew Major-General Gerhard's attention to the state of exhaustion the men were in, the retort was that the Germans were in an even worse condition than the "Blue and Gray." And he was right...

Right.
Generalleutnant Meindl addressing his men. After the war he spoke of them in these terms: *"I will always be ready to speak favourably of my troops' bravery and take full responsibility for whatever I might have said. Following my fundamental principle 'Save as much blood you can,' I went as far as my idea of a soldier's honour allowed me to go."*
(BA 101 I/584/2162/35)

Far right.
On 25 July 1944, the II.Fallschirmjäger-Korps' front was stabilised. Generalleutnant Meindl took advantage of this short respite to decorate his soldiers.
(BA 101 I/584/2162/23)

Below.
His men had not forgotten the date of their commander's birthday. Surprised and moved by his troops' attention, Meindl discovers they have prepared roast veal to celebrate. Later on there was a cake which he shared with his senior officers (seen in another picture from the report). This was therefore 16 July 1944 and Meindl was 52. But it was also on this day that 15 miles away the I. and III. FJR.14 were partly wiped out.
(BA 101 I/584/2158/36)

GENERALLEUTNANT MEINDL'S BIRTHDAY

C
OLONEL BIRKS OF THE 120th
Infantry Regiment launched his GIs
into the attack time and time again.
His 2nd Bn was spread out between La
Houcharderie and the D77, and his 3rd Bn
was positioned diagonally between the D77
and La Houcharderie (excluded).

That Pz.Gren.Rgt. 901 under Oberst Scholze should
resist on these two battalions' front did not surprise Colonel
Birks. But that they should mount a counter-attack threatening his 1st Bn, showed uncommon boldness.

*"Paratroopers from Fallschirmjägerregiment 14 rushed
at C Company under Captain Robert Hogwood who was
just as energetic as the most savage of the paratroopers
that day,"* the 1st Bn history records. Another report gives
more details.

*"When the enemy headed for his lines, the CO ran
from soldier to soldier encouraging them to open fire. He
galvanised them with choice words. At one moment, he
called the artillery which he got to fire 25 yards in front
of his own men. They all remained at their post. Shortly
afterwards, Captain Hogwood was killed. Finally the paratrooper assault broke up when Sergeant Henry Coman-
cho from A Company managed to blow the tracks off a
Panzer with a bazooka. The other tanks turned round.
Without the three tanks' support, the Germans gave up
the attack shortly afterwards."*

In turn, Colonel Birks launched his GIs into the attack
with the support of twenty or so Shermans. He wanted to
finish once and for all with the Green Devils. Having located the paratroopers from 9. and 10./Fallschirmjäger-
regiment 14 dug in in their holes behind the hedges, the
Shermans leapt forward towards the thickets firing with
all their guns.

From the other side of the hedges, the paratroopers
sent over a hail of grenades. The tanks suffered no loss-

Above.
A few weeks after the
landings, a war reporter
took this shot at the HQ
of the Kdr. of the LXXXIV
A.K., General Marcks, in
Saint-Lô. The map spread
out on the wall shows part
of the Normandy coast
occupied by 352.I.D. The
seated Oberst is studying a
bunch of pictures probably
showing the coastal
defences. The officer
standing has been awarded
the Iron Cross 1st Class and
the commemorative insignia
for the capture of the port
of Narvik in Norway. 2,800
of these insignia had been
awarded to the Heer, 2,200
to the Luftwaffe and 3,700
to the Kriegsmarine. This
badge was silver for the
Heer and the Luftwaffe, and
gold for the Kriegsmarine.
(BA 496/3456/24)

17 July 1944...

THE 30th US ID TO THE WEST OF THE RIVER VIRE

Previous page, bottom.

Previous page, bottom.
Wounded are leaving a first aid station on 6x6 trucks. This realistic scene shows how the medical services operated near the front lines. Things had to be done fast, very fast. The ambulances had not landed yet. A body can be seen in the street further back. A stick bearing a Red Cross flag has been fixed to a gutter near the farm door. Equipment has been thrown loose onto the back of the truck and the casualty staring at the camera bears an evacuation tag. These are men from the 82d Airborne Division, probably hit during the fierce fighting on Hill 85, near La Haye du Puits early in July. The division was shipped back to England on July 17.
(National Archives)

es but this was not the case with the infantry. Soon the Kdr. of the 10.Kp., Oberleutnant Herbrechter, was killed by a shell.

Veteran Otto Bernhardt takes up the tale: *"In the afternoon, I was ordered to take command of the 9. and 10. Kps. and the battalion's ordnance officer, Leutnant Witte (III.Bn.) was ordered to take over the 11. and 12.Kps which had lost their company commanders. Leutnant Illgner became Hauptmann Meissner's signals officer. We withdrew to new positions.*

Towards 3 pm, Hauptmann Meissner ordered Leutnant Elsner to get rid of an enemy CP (probably that of the 117th Infantry Regiment) with a handful of Jäger and a Panzer.

At a crossroads a mile to the south of Pont-Hébert, I came across Elsner armed with a Panzerfaust. He told me about his mission. Three minutes later, his group had hardly got going when an enemy tank opened fire on them. Shortly afterwards one of the soldiers in the group returned to tell me that Elsner had been hit by a shell."

Above.
Weather conditions for the Allies in Normandy were bad from the outset. In June, the weather was rainy and in July it became horrendous, literally. As can be seen on this shot, the roads changed into mud. The GIs had to put up with continuous showers, the cold and the fact that their uniforms were continually soaking. Their progress was slow and laborious since the beginning of the campaign.
(National Archives)

Meanwhile, the 2nd and 3rd Bns of the 117th Infantry Regiment under Colonel Kelly tried to reach the bridges spanning La Terrette.

Unfortunately this mission was only completed the following morning because of the bold attack made in the meantime by the indefatigable SS-Obersturmführer Macher, Kdr. of the 16./"Deutschland." Shortly before midday, he had launched what remained of his company to the east of La Terrette, provoking panic in the ranks of the 2/117th Infantry which was forced to retreat. But by the beginning of the afternoon the situation of the SS-Kgp. was getting critical, so Macher had to go back west of the river to face the GIs of the 9th Infantry Division who were more determined than ever to finish with them.

Macher was angry because his attack had started out well. He had an opportunity to reach le Mesnil-Durant and join up with Major Noster's paratroopers which would have plugged the gap between the LXXXIV A.K. and the II. Fallschirmjäger-Korps. Unfortunately events decided otherwise.

It was a miracle that SS-Obersturmbannführer Wilisceny was still alive. Once again the American artillery had chosen his HQ for a target and hundreds of shells fell on it. There were more and more wounded in the tactical group. Many of them thought that they were going to be left to fend for themselves because their comrades had so much to do fighting the Americans. They knew that the front was cracking in places and that they were not strong enough to fight off the enemy. The odds were one battalion against a division. However, SS-Obersturmbannführer Wisliceny did everything possible to evacuate the wounded. He even gave them his own command SPW and the SPW of I.LD even though they were vital for the combatants.

Sheltering in a very narrow trench, a GI is reading the *Stars and Stripes* Army daily and his foxhole companion mail from home. Their Garands are leaning against the parapet. The first man is wearing the issue wool and leather gloves.
(National Archives)

Otto Weidinger, the former Kdr. of the "Der Führer" Regiment and the "Das Reich's" historian, corroborates the fact that SS-Obersturmführer Macher and his sappers in the 16./"D" launched 19 counter-attacks and that they managed to drive off the 9th Infantry Division. During one of these fights, three 19-year-old Waffen-SS jumped onto two Shermans and threw stick grenades inside them, under fire from American riflemen.

At 11pm, the SS-Kgp. was ordered to set up a new line of defence with the handful of Pz.IVs from II./Pz.Rgt. 130 and SS-Obersturmführer Macher was ordered to form the rearguard with his sappers. All Wilisceny's men had

Above.
On 15 July 1944, Lieutenant-Colonel Edward Gill (with a knife sticking out from the top of his boots), commander of the 3/175th Infantry (29th Division), prepares an attack with his officers.
(National Archives)

reached the end of their tether. Fortunately the following day all was calm. This gave Wilisceny time to award medals to the bravest of his soldiers. It was the final day of his attachment to the Panzer-Lehr. Indeed, he had to go back to his original division, 2. SS-Pz.Div. "Das Reich." SS-Hauptsturmführer Brosow replaced him at the head of the tactical group, which remained with the Panzer-Lehr until 23 July 1944.

The Panzer-Lehr was under pressure from all sides and Generalleutnant Bayerlein feared they were going to be pushed back up along the River Vire by the 30th Infantry division, frontally, and the 9th Division which was threatening his left flank.

Fallschirmjägerregiment 14 brought up in support had not been much help and there was not enough fuel. Moreover the 352.I.D., situated to the east of the Vire, broke off towards the south in the Rampan sector, thus thinning out his right flank which was now hanging in the air. He therefore had to move his Kampfgruppen back. The one under Oberst Scholze (Pz.Gren.Rgt. 901) with Fallschirmjägerregiment 14 had to cross the Vire to join up with the 352.I.D. under the protection of Kgp. Welsch (Pz.Gren.Rgt. 902) which was between Rampan and the northwest of Hébécrevon. A large part of Kgp. Scholze crossed the Vire near Rampan using the bridge which was under the waters of the Vire.

This bridge had been built by a company of engineers from Kgp. Kentner, and ever since 24 or 25 June had shortened the supply route for Gren.Rgt. 897 by avoiding Saint-Lô which was impracticable because of the rubble-filled streets. Kampfgruppe Scholze finally took up position on the Hill 83 – Hill 63 line to the east of Rampan.

Seeing that the Panzergrenadiere and the Fallschirmjäger, reorganized under the command of Oberst Scholze had left, Major-General Eddy asked his officers to resume the advance. But a violent counter-attack by Major Brandt made him change his mind. In the end the GIs stayed where they were until the following day.

The "Old Hickory" infantry was luckier than its companions in arms in the 9th Infantry Division because it managed to reach its initial objective: the Saint-Lô – Périers road. From now on, its job was to prevent the enemy using it.

The 29th US ID to the east of the Vire

It was dawn at 04.30 am and wisps of mist pervaded the countryside, covering the 3rd Bn of the 116th Infantry Regiment's columns which advanced silently towards Fallschirmjägerregiment 9's lines.

Major Howie, the new battalion CO, had recommended fixing bayonets because they ran the risk of running into the Germans at any time, given the thickness of the fog.

The soldiers remained on the alert while they advanced rather quickly. Meanwhile, the paras of 13./Fallschirmjägerregiment 9, already set up in observation posts on the heights, were watching the bottom of the valley very carefully. When the fog lifted, they could see several groups of Americans at La Blanche just in front of Martinville.

A runner immediately slipped away to inform the company commander, Oberleutnant Glaser, who immediately ordered his Werfer to get going.

Rudi Frübeisser speaks of these first hours of the day: "As for Oberjäger Kulessa from the regiment's signals platoon, he left with his radio to establish an observation post.

With the help of maps, he would be able to give all the indications needed to bombard the Americans accurately.

Cautiously the GIs moved forward staying in contact with each other with their Walkie-Talkies. Had they not had the support of their courageous snipers, they would have been obliged to remain where they were. Some of them got as close as 200 yards to our positions. They fired and then disappeared back to their initial positions.

Then with shells whistling through the air, the artillery replaced the infantry. The line of defence stretching between La Blanche – Martinville – Le Boulaye was bombarded. Several houses caught fire.

Above.
Some GIs from the 29th Division are marching past an M16 half-track, fitted with quadruple .50 machine guns, which has just been ambushed. Because of the uncertain weather, they have stuffed their raincoats under their belts in case they need them. The M16 was an anti-aircraft gun motor carriage, the four MGs being mounted on a Maxson turret. From the direction the barrels are pointing, it is obviously being used against ground targets. The five-man crew did not have enough time to lower the tailgate which would have widened the field of fire. It is obvious that they were surprised by shots coming from the rear. A GI lies in the middle of the road, probably the victim of a sharpshooter who shot him straight through the head.
(National Archives)

With his Mauser rifle lying on the parapet, this Fallschirmjäger is waiting. He has covered his helmet with a piece of American camouflaged canopy. It is possible that he belonged to FJR6 which had been fighting American paratroopers since 6 June.
(BA 101 I/584/2160/32)

Right.
This extraordinary photo from a series shows two American soldiers discovering a 210-mm heavy gun (*Mörser*). The photo report indicates that a battery of three was on the heights near Saint-Lô. The exact calibre was 210.9 mm. Its shells weighed no less than 242 lb and had a range of 11 miles. The gun weighed 22.7 tons on the move and 16.7 tons in action. It was 19 feet long. Equipped with a special mechanism which enabled it to take up the recoil, it could therefore fire very accurately. These artillery pieces played a very important part in the German defence.
(National Archives via F. Deprun)

Oberjäger Kulessa of the signals platoon was no longer able to carry out his mission: he had been wounded by shrapnel."

An hour and a half later without coming across any opposition, the infantry of the 3rd Bn joined those from the 2nd Bn (Major Bingham) of the 116th Infantry who had not budged a yard for two days. Howie informed Bingham that he, Bingham, had to attack immediately but the latter retorted that his unit had been considerably weakened and that it would be suicidal for his men to comply. Finally the CO of the 116th Infantry, Colonel Dwyer, asked Major Howie to do the job instead.

Meanwhile the fog had lifted and Major Stephani guessed that the Americans were going to come up onto his lines at any moment in the La Madeleine sector. Suddenly the Granatwerfers' 81-mm shells fell upon the 3rd Bn's CP. Major Howie's executive officer, Captain H. Puntenney, recalls:

"The company commanders left Major Howie's CP just at the moment the Fallschirmjägers started a mortar barrage. Before seeking shelter in one of the holes which we usually used, Major Howie turned round to make sure that his men were getting under cover. Suddenly a shell burst near us. Shrapnel hit the Major in the back and apparently his lungs. "God, I've been hit!" he murmured. Blood flowed from the side of his mouth. I caught him as

he lost consciousness, then I called a medic. There was nothing to be done. He died two minutes later. Howie had been in command of the battalion for only four days."

Radio operator John O. Wilson from the regimental signals section was also killed and Staff Sergeant Darrell R. Spicer, the section leader, was seriously wounded by metal shards which cut up his back.

Flashing lights and explosions followed each other. Caught under a deluge of fire, the GIs in the 3rd Bn of the 116th Infantry were pinned down on their departure line. Captain Puntenney had to admit that if he attacked, his battalion would be decimated. The situation of Major Bingham's 2nd Bn was in was just as dire. The German artillery remained master of the field and the Fallschirmjäger held on stubbornly.

At 6 am, elements from I. and II./Fallschirmjägerregiment 9 counter-attacked. Soon they were joined by Leutnant Willi Geck's platoon of runners and rushed the 2nd and 3rd Bns of the 116th Infantry, opening fire with all their weapons.

Major Stephani realised that he was in a position to win the fight. The Americans did not have any support for the moment and in a few moments the Fallschirm.StuG.Abt. 12 assault guns were going to emerge on their flanks.

The first Sturmgeschütz appeared within the defensive perimeter at the moment the XIXth Corps artillery went into action and twenty or so Fallschirmjäger opened a breach in the 3rd Bn's line of defence.

All tensed up, Major Bingham saw a multitude of 155-

Right.
Oberleutnant Kurt Lingsleben of Schnell-Brigade 30 is interrogated by Sergeant Efrain Ackerman. The Signal Corps cameraman, B.J. Caliendo, is getting ready to take this officer's photo; he was probably a company commander. Note the edelweiss, the insignia of the Gebirgsjäger, sewn on his 1943 field cap. Originally Schnell-Brigade 30 was formed from mountain units in February 1944. It was made up of the Schnelle Abteilungen 513, 517 and 518 who were mainly equipped with mortars and heavy machine guns. Only the second Abteilung had artillery: two towed Paks and five 47-mm self-propelled guns. From 6 June 1944 until it was disbanded at the beginning of September 1944, it was attached to 352.I.D.
(Dite/Usis)

mm shells blowing up amidst the Germans who were advancing rapidly towards them. The artillery fire risked turning against his men if the barrage crept any nearer. Major Bingham preferred to stop the bombardment for a moment and get the fighters to intervene. Major-General Gerhardt in person ordered the 506th Fighter-Bomber Squadron to break the German counter-attack at all costs as it was on the point of wiping out the two 116th Infantry battalions.

Forewarned by radio of the coming air force attack, Captain Puntenney and Major Bingham told the company commanders to mark their positions with red panels to make sure they were not massacred by their own pilots.

Just as the assault guns from Fallschirm.Sturmgeschütz-Brigade 12 were crossing the Saint-Lô – Bayeux road, the fighters appeared in the sky. They broke formation to dive on their prey. Unfortunately for the Americans, as they could not make out the infantry's recognition panels, they held back from attacking for the moment.

According to an inquiry carried out by the regimental staff, the units did not display the panels on the front line. According to a report: *"It was suggested we use white underwear and the "Stars and Stripes" which were spotted by the pilots."*

Now caught in the fire from the aircraft, the Fallschirmjägers supporting the tanks scattered. As it was impossible for them to escape from the pilots who had located them on the La Madeleine – Saint-Lô road, the Germans knew that their attack was doomed before it had even got going.

What could Sturmgeschütze do against fighters?

It was 9 pm when the crews reached the rear, pushing the engines to their limits and praying to God they would get away unscathed.

For the 116th Infantry officers, this episode proved that ground to air coordination was vital. As a result, red panels were issued to the platoons so that the fighters would not inflict friendly fire.

The group of twenty or so Fallschirmjägers, who had caused confusion and chaos in the 2nd and 3rd Bn of the 116th lines, now tried to escape from the noose which was beginning to tighten around them. They could only count on themselves and any reinforcements, in whatever form, were out of the question. As a result their offensive capability was reduced to nothing.

The GIs took advantage of the disarray to gun them down and plug the breach. *"Now we have to consolidate the positions because the Germans are still capable of mounting a big attack,"* thundered the 116th's CO to his junior officers. *"To stop them you're going to go and mine no man's land with that stock of Teller mines which we took this morning."*

At nightfall, the 2nd and 3rd Bns of the 116th Infantry Regiment found themselves totally isolated and without resources. Ammunition and food were running low.

The 116th Infantry history stipulates: *"Lieutenants Hallie F. Williams of the anti-tank company and Lewis B. White from the Cannon Company, each with 20 volunteers from their respective companies offered to take vital supplies to the isolated companies. These two patrols left crossing through hedge after hedge in the darkness until they reached their comrades. Unfortunately an accident occurred to Lieutenant Williams who was mistaken for a German. The GIs in the observation posts of the 2nd Bn gunned him down".* These soldiers like the others in the 2nd Bn, could not have known that supplies could be expected because they had been ordered to switch off the only radio they had to save the battery.

The progress made by the infantry regiments of the 29th Infantry Division were limited to less than half a mile. This gain in terrain was obtained by the 115th Infantry. While Major Howie's battalion started off at dawn, the 3/115th attacked on its right flank towards Martinville, via la Planche. Veteran Rudi Frühbeisser noticed this movement. He recalls: *"Major Stephani sent the motorcyclists' platoon, the regiment's elite unit, as reinforcements. Advancing along the Fumichon road, Leutnant Geck's sidecars moved up very quickly to the outskirts of Martinville then sheltered behind the hedges. Shortly afterwards they were engaged in fighting near some houses* (Author's note: at Martinville which only had fifteen dwellings?)

Jäger Bismor was hit in the head. Oberjäger Jörg Werner, Jäger Henkejohann, Obergefreiters Löbner and Fuchs were wounded. Several Panzerschreck teams were wounded. The fighting became even more violent towards midday. The neighbouring company, the 7.Kp. suffered some losses including Obergefreiter and first MG gunner Paul Schwennen who was mortally wounded in the head by mortar bomb splinters.

The 4.Kp., which sent a group as reinforcements, lost Obergefreiter Student who was hit by a shell. During the fighting, Jäger Kalk was killed by a bullet in his head. Feldwebel and platoon leader Neidrich, Oberjäger Anton Saar, Obergefreiters Raszek and Dohn were killed by mortar shrapnel in the chest. Feldwebel Peterka was hit in the throat. Oberjägers Weiss and Bress were both killed. Leutnant Hugo Karger lost his left arm because of a bullet. The Stabsgefreiter Matthias Laufenberg who was always at the head of his company had both hands torn by shrapnel. The fighting went on till nightfall.

The American pressure together with the sustained shooting got heavier. The Americans got closer to our positions, causing more losses on our side. They could not get past our line of defence however. All our wounded were assembled in a house."

Indeed, the 3rd Bn of the 115th Infantry Regiment's progress was halted by German resistance as recorded in the battalion's reports. After capturing two fields, the 1st Bn seemed well under way, but this did not last long. The few dozen soldiers in Schnell-Brigade 30 pulled themselves together when they were reinforced by 15./Fallschirmjägerregiment 9 under Leutnant K.H. Hamann, a veteran of Crete. A counter-attack was immediately organised and it was successful. Having remained in the rear, the 2nd Bn was the 115th's reserve. The CO of this battalion sent a few patrols towards Martinville at the end of the afternoon once the 116th Infantry had left the sector.

These GIs became targets for German snipers hidden in the village. They had infiltrated along the line of advance of the 116th once it had moved on. A long mopping-out session lasted until 11.15 pm at which time the last Fallschirmjäger was killed. Finally the 2nd Bn was ordered by Colonel Ordway, the 115th Infantry's CO, to gather at Martinville towards midnight then get hold of the heights located near La Planche, a hamlet on the road leading directly to Saint-Lô. However the battalion's progress was far from satisfactory for Major-General Gerhardt who asked Colonel Ordway for an explanation. *"Taking this hamlet opens the door wide open to Saint-Lô,"* was Ordway's retort; he knew well enough what was at stake with this operation.

Gerhardt found Colonel Ordway in an advanced state of fatigue. Ord-

way had given the best of himself and he was replaced the following day by Colonel Ednie. The paratroopers from Fallschirmjägerregiment 9 fell back and this enabled the GIs from the 2nd Bn to reach their objective. They dug their holes and set up their defensive positions in the direction of Cauchais, facing another unit of Fallschirmjäger which had held off the 3rd Bn of the 115th Infantry during the day. Moreover the situation of the 175th's first two battalions was dramatic. The 2nd Bn had suffered heavy losses when it had tried to plug the gap with its neighbour on the right, the 2nd of the 116th. It was now only at half its normal strength and the 1st Bn of the 175th had lost its CO, Lieutenant-Colonel William T. Terry.

The day turned into a nightmare for Colonel Paul R. Goode. He called in his 3rd Bn held in reserve to renew the attack. Unfortunately this battalion was not as successful as expected. The 175th had to pull itself together and consolidate its line of defence.

Even if the advances made by the 29th Infantry Division turned out to be slow and costly in manpower, Brigadier-General Cota nevertheless succeeded in getting hold of each of the heights situated to the east of the Vire at the end of seven day's fighting; there had been no other way

Saint-Lô railway station

This is what remained of the railway station at Saint-Lô on 6 June 1944 at 5 pm. Nobody has better described the Mustangs' attack on the station than Mr Henry Bernard, a local eye-witness interviewed by Maurice Lantier, author of *Saint-Lô au bûcher* (St-Lô on the pyre):

"As I was peacefully nibbling at my second biscuit, a swarm of small shiny aircraft appeared suddenly over the town, flying very low. There were fifteen of them and they whirled at roof-top level, looking very busy.

The shape of the bomb under each wing could be seen very clearly. They were machines with square-tipped wings, machine guns along the leading edges of the wings – Mustangs. A few seconds later the three German machine guns nearby woke up with a jump and started clattering, each trying to outdo the other. The air filled with little blue sparks and slight, echoing explosions.

The Mustangs did not heed the fire. When they got back together again, they started whirling around the station like silver moths around a light. The heavy machine guns, their pride hurt by such indifference doubled their efforts, firing frantically. Suddenly one of the planes broke off from the thundering merry-go-round and dived towards the station. Sparks lit up along the wings then went out. The plane left two thin streaks of black smoke behind it which disappeared immediately. At the same time the two bombs dropped and fell diagonally towards the station. The plane then climbed straight up over my house with a tremendous roar which made my windows quake, showing me its belly and lower wing surfaces with their black and white stripes; it banked round then started to fly above its mates.

Then another plane broke off, dived, strafed, dropped its bombs, climbed back up noisily and joined the first one. Then the next, and the next, and so on. You could only hear the rough and metallic sound of the powerful engines, speeding up, slowing down, diving, climbing, the rending noise of machine guns and the heavy, dull explosions of the bombs – all of this accompanied by the clattering obbligato from the German machine guns spraying the air without any visible result. With the last dive over, the merry-go-round made a final round of the town, formed up into a very rough Vee and set off at ease to the north while the thundering faded away. The heavy machine guns fell silent – ashamed – and silent calm returned."

[National Archives]

round these obstacles if they wanted to get hold of the ruined town: Saint-Lô, the XIXth Army Corps's objective.

The next battle waiting for the soldiers of the 29th took place within the town itself. Nothing seemed to be able to stop Task Force C's progress. This was the unit made up specially for the capture of Saint-Lô and it bore the name of its leader: Norman Cota, the division's executive commander.

Task Force C sets off for Saint-Lô

It consisted of the following units: the 29th Cavalry Reconnaissance Troop (minus one platoon), five Shermans from the 747th Tank Battalion, one platoon of the Cannon Company of the 175th Infantry, one platoon of the Anti-Tank Company of the 175th, a detachment from the 29th Military Police Platoon, a platoon from Civil Affairs, a platoon of the 121st Engineer Battalion, the Recce Platoon of the 821st Tank Destroyer Battalion, B Company (12 M10s) of the 803rd Tank Destroyer Battalion, two groups of artillery observers (one from the 227th Field Artillery Battalion, the other from the divisional artillery HQ). Task Force C had to surprise the Germans with its strength and take the last defences before investing the capital of the Manche department.

Below.
Granatwerfers and artillery fired a never-ending deluge of steel onto the GIs at Saint-Lô. They turned out to be formidably accurate. Here a Dodge weapons carrier has been hit by a shell, or even an 81-mm mortar bomb. By some miracle no man has been hit. Most of the time, the mortars were guided by observers hiding in the ruins and the heavy artillery shots came from the heights, to the south of the town.
(Dite/Usis)

18 July 1944...

THE 29th US ID GETS HOLD OF SAINT-LO

At the slightest improvement in the weather, the pilots took off looking for enemy targets. Their missions were made all the more difficult by the abundance of thick hedges in the Saint-Lô region. They could easily mistake their targets. It was only on the main roads, like this one on the photo showing a wrecked Diesel 706 (7 tonnes) Skoda, that they could operate without firing on their own troops. In July, the 7. Armee suffered increasingly heavy losses and supplies became a major problem with all the roads constantly watched over by aircraft. Morale among many German soldiers was very low and they felt, from what they could see, that they were going to suffer even heavier losses.
(National Archives)

WHILE WAITING FOR TASK FORCE C which would only start off at the beginning of the afternoon, the new CO of the 115th Infantry Regiment, Colonel Alfred Ednie, had to pave the way for them.

He asked his 1st Bn to clean up the German defences to the west of the Saint-Lô – Saint-Clair road, and his 2nd Bn to leave Les Planches and the heights there to head south west (les Haras, one of the town's quarters) of Saint-Lô. Major Johns of the 1/115th Infantry engaged his men at dawn. He feared there was going to be strong opposition. The GIs were all the more surprised when the company commanders announced that they had just covered 500 yards without a single shot being fired at them. Five hundred yards may seem derisory but in such bocage country where visibility was extremely limited, this was a real breakthrough!

Johns warned his officers to be cautious nonetheless because the Germans could be waiting for them anywhere. The GIs carried on advancing without pause. They were

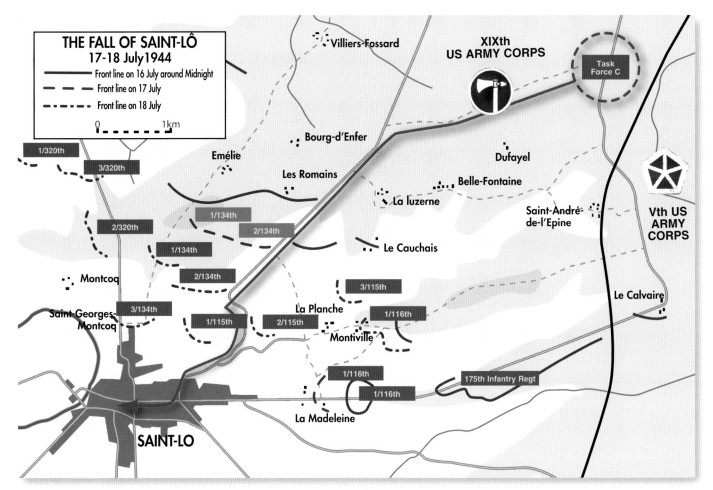

THE FALL OF SAINT-LÔ
17-18 July 1944

Front line on 16 July around Midnight

Front line on 17 July

Front line on 18 July

0 — — — 1km

1/320th
3/320th
2/320th
1/134th
2/134th
1/134th
2/134th
3/134th
1/115th
2/115th
3/115th
1/116th
1/116th
1/116th
175th Infantry Regt

Villiers-Fossard
XIXth US ARMY CORPS
Task Force C
Bourg-d'Enfer
Emélie
Dufayel
Les Romains
Belle-Fontaine
La luzerne
Saint-André-de-l'Epine
Vth US ARMY CORPS
Le Cauchais
Montcoq
La Planche
Le Calvaire
Saint-Georges-Montcoq
Montiville
La Madeleine
SAINT-LO

heavily laden with equipment and weapons. Another hundred yards was crossed without incident so they thought the enemy was dug in further away. In combat formation the first elements crossed the fields, hedges and lanes under the protection of the machine gunners who remained further back, perfectly under cover behind an embankment.

As soon as the scouts reached their objective, they threw themselves to the ground, waited for a few moments then signalled to the rest to come forward and join them. Once the battalion had advanced about 800 yards or so, Colonel Ednie shared the excellent news with General Gerhardt.

This was the moment they had been waiting for so long, for Brigadier-General Cota to get under way and finally snatch Saint-Lô away

from the enemy.

Meanwhile Major Johns' GIs eliminated the last strong points then put themselves on the defensive on heights situated to the west of the Saint-Lô-Isigny road, near Saint-Georges-Montcocq.

They discovered that very few of the town's buildings remained erect. The twin domes of the cathedral were sticking up above the piles of stones which the Germans were going to defend. The battle of the hedgerows was going to give way to street fighting. Why had they fought for a town which was no longer there? They were getting more and more worried. Why had so many of them lost their lives to reach this objective which was so important to the high command?

Waving a white flag, this Grenadier comes up to GIs from Task Force Cota, who has just reached the outskirts of Saint-Lô. He has ditched his equipment, keeping only his bread bag and water bottle Note also that he has placed the chin strap on the visor of his helmet as most German soldiers did during the war. This often saved their lives if a bullet hit the helmet because the helmet strap absorbed the force of the impact and flew off, whereas if the strap was under the chin, the bullet went through the helmet and continued on its lethal trajectory.
(Dite/Usis)

Above.
Each street had to be cleared out and snipers were a major threat. A German sharpshooter equipped with a 98K and telescopic sight could hit a bull's eye at 400 to 600 yards. Obviously with the first shot a man was killed. Locating snipers proved a very difficult task in ruined towns like Saint-Lô. Most of the time the sniper changed places or remained totally immobile. Then a game of cat and mouse started which could last several hours. Once the sniper was spotted, the GIs tried to find the best position to shoot him from. Here two soldiers in the 29th are crawling while two others are rushing towards a small street.
(National Archives)

Right.
One of the twelve TDs from B/803rd Tank Destroyer Battalion in action in the streets of Saint-Lô, near the Café de la Bascule (see also p. 166). This battalion was attached to Task Force Cota from 17 July and fought hard in the town. Its CO, Captain Sydney A. Vincent, Jr., was killed there on 18 July 1944
(Dite/Usis)

While waiting for the decisive push from Cota, the 2nd Bn of the 115th Infantry was ordered to deploy to the east of the Saint-Lô outskirts. This was a measure intended to block all exits for the German entrenched in the town. Positioned on the heights near Saint-Croix de Saint-Lô, they could control everything and ensure that the 3rd Bn of the 116th Infantry was covered while it was heading for the Saint-Lô - Bayeux road.

Leaving a platoon of his battalion to mop up sixty or so Grenadiere who had decided to hold out, Johns was ordered to join up with Task Force C towards 3 pm to take part in the final assault. As his unit was closest to the town and having cleared the road, Major-General Gerhardt

was convinced that Cota was going to need the infantry.

As soon as they spotted the vanguard of Brigadier-General Cota's column, the GIs of the 1st Bn of the 115th Infantry followed them. The Task Force had set off in the following order: A Flail tank (Sherman) which opened up the way by smashing the ground with its chains to set off the mines. Then the scouts, then the tanks followed by the tank destroyers and the riflemen of 1/115th marching in two files on either side of the road. These men had something proud about them; they seemed invincible.

The GIs discovered wrecks of German vehicles shattered by artillery shells in the fields and the ditches along the road. Men and horses alike, horribly torn apart, lay

As soon as the scouts from the 2/115th US Infantry had reconnoitered the area, one of the twelve M10s of the 803rd Tank Destroyer Battalion joined them. Then the infantry arrived and the operation was repeated. Unfortunately it sometimes happened that the tanks could not support the riflemen because of rubble obstructing the roads. This TD is covered with a large number of sandbags for additional protection again armour piercing rounds. A telephone cable reel is stacked on the right side mudguard.
(Dite/Usis)

Officer collar insignia for the 803rd TD Battalion.
(Private collection)

here and there in grotesque poses. The stink was appalling and the sight of the flies swarming over the corpses caused more than one Yank to retch. Hidden between two ruined houses – actually only the front wall were still standing – SP guns opened fire with their Pak when the first Task Force tanks appeared.

They barely had the time to load another round before the armored cars of the 29th Recon. Troop destroyed the anti-tank gun in record time with their 37-mm cannon. The Granatwerfer mortar crews tried to avenge their comrades by bombarding Task Force C which headed for Le Pont de Moulin Bérot which soon came under artillery fire. In spite of this, Brigadier-General Cota urged his men to charge because the enemy artillery fired a salvo of twelve shells every two minutes *"Clearly the Germans are running out of ammunition,"* Cota remarked *"A bit more effort and we'll take Saint-Lô."*

It was 18.00 when the cavalrymen from the 29th Reconnaissance under 1st Lieutenant Edward G. Jones entered the town from the east. Several patrols from the 1st Bn of the 115th Infantry were there to back them up.

Their objective was to reach a square near the town cemetery. This cemetery was miraculously untouched and served as the CP for the future clearing up operations.

The approach was made more difficult by episodic shooting from the artillery and the congested streets. The men were forced to dismount from their jeeps or their half-tracks to move on. They deployed as infantry with their nerves on edge, frightened of snipers. When they came into sight of the square, they were subjected to heavy fire. The Germans were entrenched in the cemetery!

The GIs sought refuge immediately behind the ruins, the houses. The most exposed not having the time to get to cover threw themselves to the ground.

The shattering noise of weapons resounded round the town. Scouts brought up two .50 machine guns, running

and hiding behind the piles of rubble. Once the guns were set up the Grenadiere huddled behind the walls of the cemetery. Then the 75-mm shots from a Sherman could be heard and the scouts were pleasantly surprised to see that one of their tanks had managed to get so far in spite of the many obstacles on the streets.

This German resistance hindered Task Force C's progress. Its vehicles and tanks got in a jam. Leaving behind

Below.
"Hun Hunter," from the 747th Tk Bn. has stopped in Rue Carnot, where Notre-Dame Church is also visible. The GI is the background is Walter E. Hatfield of Princetown, Idaho. According to the Signal Corps caption, he is watching enemy activity with his binoculars...
(National Archives)

156

them a group of machine gunners, the Grenadiere gave up and slipped away by a street leading to the town centre. When the tank slammed one more shell into the cemetery, the machine gunners scarpered and set off after their comrades.

With this first resistance point eliminated, 1st Lieutenant Jones set up his command post in the square, as Major Marr, S-3 of Task Force C, had wished. He had located this strategic spot by reconnaissance plane.

At present, the Engineers started clearing away the streets near the cemetery and enabled the cavalrymen to continue aboard their half-tracks and open the way for the other units of Task Force C.

1st Lieutenant Jones remembers an anecdote: *"I suddenly spotted four German soldiers leaving a house to slip away down an alley. I slowly turned the calibre .50 machine gun in their direction. They looked my way but I do not know why they did not see the armored car. I watched them as I was flipping the safety off. The vibrations that the gun made as it fired tended to lift the barrel of the Browning up a bit and as a result, I sent a burst of bullets along the building without touching a single one of the Germans. But I think I put the fear of God into them!"*

Brigadier-General Cota now knew that he had to take advantage of the Germans' weakness.

They had reached the limits their strength. They were in rags, they were dirty and had not shaved for several days now. They realised that even their determination could not stop Saint-Lô being taken by the Americans.

Brigadier-General Cota issued new orders to his officers. They had to make up three strong points from which they could carry out operations whilst staying in touch one with another. The first point was the general's command post in person; it had to be set up at the intersection of Rue de Bayeux, Rue de Torigny and Rue d'Isigny. The second point had to be established near the bridge over the River Dollée; and the last at the corner of Rue des noyers and Place du Champ de Mars. The three strong points were rapidly reached by one or two tanks or tank destroyers, then joined by GIs from C/115th Infantry, which had been reduced to platoon strength. Their action had not been easy because of sniper fire and shots from an 88 Flak gun located at the beginning of the afternoon.

Lieutenant George E. Wagoner, platoon leader in the 747th Tank Battalion and one of the first to enter the town started a duel with this Jlak gun. Joseph H. Ewing, the eminent 29th Division historian relates: *"Although he had enough shells, Lieutenant Wagoner noticed that his tank could not fire. A shell was stuck inside the barrel. Scorn-*

ing the bullets and shots from the artillery exploding around his tank, he managed to get the faulty shell out! Later while reconnoitering on foot, he was wounded in the hand by a grenade burst. For the courageous leadership he showed with his platoon, Lieutenant Wagoner was awarded the DSC. Captain Sydney A. Vincent Jr., CO of B Company of the 803rd Tank Destroyer Battalion did not have Lieutenant Wagoner's luck. He was killed while coordinating his action with the armor, outside his TD." Lieutenant Grimsehl from A company and Captain Weddle of B company (1st Bn, 115th Infantry) were now ordered to secure the town. A Company headed for the southwest along the banks of the Vire and B Company headed southeast. Captain Leroy Weddle's men had some difficulty moving in this Dantesque backdrop… In order to advance they had to climb up over huge piles of ruins far too often for their liking particularly as they were being watched by Germans waiting for the right moment to shoot them. It was sniper-hunting time. It sometimes took an hour to dislodge them from their hideouts; most of the time they were hiding in high buildings.

Suddenly Weddle heard the rumbling of engines get-

ting closer. All the men were on the alert. They soon saw SPWs transporting Panzergrenadiere. These half-tracks were heading straight for them at high speed. Weddle was worried because the Germans were using the only bridge still intact in the town, the last obstacle before getting to them.

Rather than risk his men's lives by opening fire on a superior opponent, he radioed Colonel Ednie, the regimental commander, who called in the artillery.

In less than five minutes, the German attack was broken. It was the turn of I Company of the 3rd Bn to approach the town. The rest of the battalion followed clearing up the enemy's remaining groups. 80 Germans were captured. Their advance was reasonably easy since the Germans no longer held the heights in the area. When a group of soldiers, led by Lieutenant Clifford Keon from K Company managed to slip into the first houses in Saint-Lô he heard voices coming from a building situated on their right. All their senses were alert.

They could not see any Germans but, as they got closer, they heard that the voices were definitely German. Lieutenant Keon told his men to surround the building then emplace the machine gun less than 200 yards from entrance to the building. In deep discussion the Grenadiere did not notice the Americans. They were totally surprised when they realized they were surrounded; and the subject of their babbling? Whether they should surrender or not! Whilst

K Company continued its dangerous advance, the GIs in L and M Company allowed themselves a break by settling down on the side of the Saint-Lô road. They were so hungry that they swallowed their rations as if they were marvellous meals. Some of them chatted quietly and smoked a cigarette. But this did not last long. They saw a column of forty or so Fallschirmjäger coming their way. Luckily the Germans had not seen the GIs in the road ditches!

In a single move, the Americans jumped to their guns; a calibre .30 Browning machine gun was set up. Technical Sergeant Ambers Glidewell, a platoon leader in M Company and an interpreter ran in the direction of the enemy along the other side of a hedge parallel to the road. It was the only protection the two men had in case the enemy reacted violently. When they were level with the paratroopers, with a firm voice, the interpreter invited them to surrender. Immobile, the paratroopers wondered what to do. One of them, an officer probably, advanced towards the hedge behind which the two GIs were hidden. Holding his MP40 firmly, he shouted to them *"It's you who are going to surrender. You're surrounded."* Then he fired a burst into the hedge at the Americans. Glidewell just had the time to drop to the ground before the 9-mm bullets cut through the air above him. The Browning MG crew was expecting this sort of belligerent reaction and the gunner immediately squeezed the trigger.

The German spun round, his arms stretched out before falling to the ground like a rag doll on the wet road. Other Fallschirmjäger were hit, not only from the machine gun but also from the musketry of the two companies who had a field day. Like a flight of sparrows, the Fallschirmjäger tried to disappear into the hedges on the side of the road. Only a third of the group managed to get away. All the others lay in a blood bath, as much victims of the reaction of their CO as from the GIs' fire.

Finally Brigadier-General Cota had to change the position of his CP because it was too exposed. Artillery salvoes were still falling but much less often than before. A reconnaissance patrol recommended that he move to a distillery with thick walls which looked down on the north of the town. This set up was satisfactory for the general's command post which was now out of harm's way; but this did not take into account the personality Cota who

Left.
The first American soldiers to enter Saint-Lô were led by Lt. Warren Colgan on 17 July 1944. He belonged to the Counter-intelligence detachment of the 35th Infantry Division. Colgan reached the centre of the town then announced the town's imminent liberation to the hundred or so inhabitants and refugees who had stayed in the ruins. But a German patrol put an end to his endeavour and the Americans scarpered. On 18 July, it was Major Dale N. Goodwin's turn to reach the town, with a platoon from the 134th Infantry led by 1st Lieutenant John F. Tracy. This group entered the town from the northeast then advanced to the centre until it was caught under mortar fire. Once they had got the information they wanted, they left unscathed.
(National Archives)

Below.
Clearing up the town started as soon as it had been captured. Some streets were impracticable. This was dangerous work for the Bulldozer drivers because they themselves could cause houses and walls to collapse. This often had to be done deliberately even with the little that remained standing to avoid any risk of accidents. Nothing had been spared this Norman town which paid very dearly for its liberation.
(National Archives)

preferred to be with his men in the heart of he action.

Joseph H. Ewing takes up the tale.

"As Brigadier-General Cota went down a street looking everywhere and giving orders, he was hit in the arm by a piece of shrapnel. He refused categorically to go to the rear for care. Once the medic had tended his wound, he took his cane in his right hand then moved on again. He was evacuated later."

Cautiously the GIs carried on slowly towards the town centre. They were often slowed down by the rubble of the houses or buildings which had been bombed on 6 June. Sometimes they had to go round whole blocks in order to find a way through, or even just a simple passage, which was practicable.

Major Jones walked alongside his men as they went down a road. By his side there was a very nervous medical officer. For ten minutes, everything was very calm, too calm. Suddenly the whistle of a shell drew their attention. The noise was getting closer very quickly. The two officers had just time to fall to the ground before the shell burst a few yards from them. Shrapnel flew off in all directions. Once the steel tempest had subsided, the doctor tried to get up, but he fell down straightaway.

His feet had been torn off by the blast of the explosion. His face grimacing

Above.

A patrol from the 29th looks at two Grenadiere who have been lying there for several days. Both men have been searched as can be seen by the documents scattered over the ground. One of them is still reaching for his 98K rifle and the other carried at least two Panzerfaust antitank weapons.
(National Archives)

Below.

This M5A1 light tank was part of the 747th Tank Bn. operating in Saint-Lô. These light tanks usually carried out reconnaissance missions. The light tank battalions of 1942 were disbanded after North Africa and each company was transferred into Medium Tank Battalions bringing the number of companies up to four, the first three being equipped with M4 Shermans.
(National Archives)

with pain, the doctor, lying on his back, was looking at an invisible spot in the sky. Getting over the shock, the Major, safe and sound, leant over the doctor realising that his condition was serious. He called his men over to help the doctor who then came to. He said to Major Jones, with authority:

Family, right in the heart of the town. The sarcophagus in the crypt was ideal for setting out the staff maps... Brigadier-General Cota was satisfied by the operations carried out by his Task Force and the 1st Bn of the 115th Infantry. But he was still not very at ease.

German resistance in the town started to ebb gradually, but the Germans still had a large body of troops to the south of the town and their artillery was formidable. The perspective of total success was only possible with the cooperation of divisional artillery. The Task Force was not strong enough in case there were counter-attacks during the night. It was now up to the artillery of the 29th Infantry Division to back them up.

Joseph Balkowski writes: *"Liaison officers and observers from the 110th and 227th Field Artillery battalions who had followed the Task Force into the town were in constant radio contact with the operators.*

During the few hours of fighting it had taken to take Saint-Lô, the streets were gradually invaded by their wires. The observers were able very quickly to position themselves in the forefront, at the request of the artillery, to give vital support for the infantry. Several counter-attacks coming from the south were thus broken by our 155-mm howitzers." During the evening, Major-General Gerhardt was certain that Task Force C would hold the town with the help of the artillery. He then contacted Major-General Charles Corlett's HQ to tell him: *"I have the honour to inform the CO of the XIXth Corps that task Force C of the 29th Infantry Division had taken Saint-Lô after 43 days uninterrupted fighting, from the beaches to this town. 29th Let's go!"*.

Suddenly a shower of mortar shells fell on Ednie's CP. Once the storm had passed, the GIs busy chasing snipers ran up fearing for the life of the 115th Infantry CO. Miraculously, he was only lightly wounded. However several men had been killed.

Among the numerous skirmishes which took place here and there, in the middle of the rubble, the following is worth mentioning. A group of GIs was ordered to protect a bridge to the west of the town. They were a bit edgy and chain smoking. Suddenly they found themselves face to face with some Germans in a small street. Nobody knew exactly who fired first. There was deadly firing in the middle of the street. Three Americans were killed and another wounded. On the German side, there were only three survivors.

Darkness fell finally over Saint-Lô. The day had been hard for Brigadier-General Cota who had lost almost a third of his strength, 200 soldiers out of 600. To help him do his job, the 113th Cavalry Group was attached to the 29th Infantry Division and indirectly to Cota's group.

At 2 am, Troop C of the 113th reached the town which was still being bombarded by the enemy artillery. These GIs had been ordered to carry out reconnaissance missions in the southern outskirts, which everybody thought the enemy had abandoned. But this certainly was not the case. Handfuls of Grenadiere from Kampfgruppe Kentner and from the 325.ID. were still hanging on to the ruins and had no intention of surrendering. The brigade's strength had been increased by the remnants of Gren.Rgt. 913 who had been assigned for the defence of Saint-Lô under the name of Kampfgruppe Loges. For a few days now Hauptmann Loges had replaced Oberst Goth who had reached the end of his tether and was now in psychiatric hospital with a nervous collapse. This was far from being a unique case during the Battle of the Hedgerows, both on the German and the American sides.

The American vehicles were stopped in their rush, targeted as they were by the machine gunners. Soon fearsome Granatwerfer bombs fell upon them. Then the German artillery thundered... C Troop found itself in a vice. GIs were killed. The detachment leader, Captain Frank L. Kirby shouted nonstop the same order *"Fall back, fall back!"* but the racket of weapons covered his voice. It took more than an hour for C Troop to rejoin Task Force C despatched further north. Captain Kirby's recce mission was carried out on foot...

A Troop entrusted with the same type of operation on the

"Off you go, go and get them, Major. I'll catch you up later."

Suddenly very angry, Staff Sergeant Gerald Davis walked over to a building with a firm step to plant the divisional flag there. Having reached the windows of the upper floor, he set up the flag with difficulty. Once he had done this, he left the window just as an explosion blasted away just behind him. The flag and part of the wall had disappeared. A Pak gun had just missed him. Davis would have to be a bit more patient before he saw the 29th Infantry Division's Flag floating over the ruins. It was Major-General Gerhardt's Chief-of-Staff, Colonel Edward McDaniel, who had this honour. When he reached the town, he met Major Johns near the Café de la Bascule (or Café Malherbe), just where the CO of the 1/115th had set up his command post. They agreed on the place the flag was to hang from: at one of the windows of the second floor of the Café Malherbe, in full sight of the Germans.

This was provocation. A Signal Corps cameraman filmed the two GIs, Sergeant Davis and Pfc Stein of the 115th infantry hoisting the colours facing south. A few minutes later, an 88 mm Flak gun fired a salvo of shells into the area.

The flag fell down. Stubbornly the two GIs put it back again thus drawing the anger of the German artillery which directed all its cannon onto "Mortar Corner," the new name for the neigbourhood, given to it by Task Force C.

Major Johns did not think that the German artillery had such a big supply of shells. His position had become dangerous so he moved his HQ. If he had not, "Mortar Corner" would have been wiped off the map of the town.

Major Johns set up his HQ in the mausoleum of the Blanchet

Saint-Lô is still alive...

1. Guided by the townspeople, an American patrol advances through the ruins. Finding one's way around was terribly difficult in such conditions.
(Dite/Usis)

2. Only 29 inhabitants of Saint-Lô remained in the town. On 11 July they refused to obey the Feldgendarmerie's evacuation order as they were convinced they were going to be freed soon. Some returned to the town only a few days after it was captured by Task Force Cota and others only returned mid-August. For many, there was a big shock waiting for them: everything had to be started again from scratch. But they had saves their lives; which is not the case in every family in the Manche department. But they all had the same reaction when they met the men from the other side of the Atlantic: they greeted them, welcomed them and drank with them to Freedom.
(Dite/Usis)

3. Corporal Anthony Loanza from New York, Cpl Horace Abrahms from Philadelphia and Private Steve Plavi from Dicksonville help an old woman settle into a lorry which is going to take her to Tessy-sur-Vire. To evacuate evacuees, alternate routes were selected to keep roads open for military traffic.
(National Archives)

4. A jeep from the 29th going through Saint-Lô. A major problem faced the inhabitants when they returned: food. The official ration was 100 grams per day per person. Fortunately, neighbouring farms and the US army were there to make up for it. But for how long?
(National Archives)

break off to Saint-Lô. Oberleutnant von Ausess assigned a sector to the northeast of the town to our Kampfgruppe Loges. It was our last meeting with the CO of Schnell-Brigade 30, this pleasant officer from Franconia, who was killed in the fighting after the taking of Saint-Lô. The later orders came directly from the division. It was said that our CP had been the blockhouse sheltering the former HQ of General Marcks, a place where we were apparently safe. These HQs were in the corner of a big square. I did not like it because there were no firing ports and there was only one door in the direction of the square. But Hauptmann Loges felt safe in the shelter from bombs and shells. We handed out orders to all the groups. With several men I undertook a reconnaissance patrol in front of our positions. We had reached a large building on the square when we heard the sound of tracks. Some Shermans had broken through our neighbours on the right, a parachute division, and who were trying to break further into the town accompanied by their infantry.

From the first floor windows we had a good field of fire and we forced the infantry to get under cover. Soon we managed to get out through the back. The tanks fired on the house at very short range. After 500 yards we reached our blockhouse and informed Loges of the situation. He immediately gave orders to evacuate. The Americans had already started to aim their shots at it. When the firing ceased, we fled from the shelter.

Several streets further on, we made contact with the division. I signalled our position and drew up a report. Then there was the question of "what happened to the blockhouse?" First I did not understand the question until I learnt that Loges, during the briefing, had been ordered to blow up the blockhouse, should it have to be abandoned. We were ordered to take it back again and I insisted that Hauptmann Loges take part in this operation with us. With a few volunteers, we advanced in the direction of the blockhouse but we soon noticed that some tanks with a large number of accompanying infantry had advanced on our right and our left. So as not to get cut off, we returned hastily across the field of ruins. At a crossroads there was a Sherman and a hundred yards away another tank. Having two Panzerfaust, we agreed that I would get rid of the one in front of us while Loges and his men would deal with the second one; my attempt failed because I should have got nearer the tank. Just at the moment when I was kneeling and adjusting the sights, the tank turret swivelled in my direction and fired. I woke up a few moments later and noted that there were cer-

left wing of the 'Blue and Gray' division took note of Captain Kirby's experience because it left its vehicles to the rear. It was a wise decision because German resistance was still just as stubborn.

Mr Claude Paris got hold of this precious eye-witness account from ex-Oberleutnant Hinze, company commander in the Kampfgruppe Loges in his book Les acteurs des premiers jours: "…Under the enemy's nose we managed to

This Stabsfeldwebel of a paratrooper Sturmtrupp poses with his impressive FG42 automatic rifle. The magazine inserted on the side of the breech is loaded with the rifle clips carried in the cloth bandoleer specific to the Fallschirmjäger. This NCO has the third pattern jump smock, whose camouflage pattern of dark green and brown on a light green base blends perfectly with the surroundings. Similar hues have been daubed on his steel helmet. The black strap across his chest is for the special gas mask bag. The paratrooper trousers are blousing on top of the jump boots. While not on at the front, he wears the blue-gray wool *1943 Einheitsfeldmütze*, introduced in September 1943.
(Reconstruction by Militaria Magazine)

tain things which were not working any more. My right arm was hanging from my side and I was bleeding profusely from my back and head. At that particular moment I was unable to get up and while I was there, helpless, a thought flashed through my head: now you'll never be able to play tennis. Since then I have often pondered about that fact: how could I be thinking that in such desperate circumstances? My following reactions were much more practical. I pulled a white hanky with my left hand from my pocket and waved it. To my great surprise, the turret hatch opened and the tank crew made me understand that I could crawl to the side of the road. I crawled a few yards then fainted. Later on I gathered from my comrades that two of them had come to my rescue under the very watchful eyes of the tank crew. I remain grateful to the tank commander and to my comrades for showing me such humanity."

The end of SS-Kgp.
Wisliceny to the west of the Vire

On the 14 July 1944 at midnight, a few Sturmgeschütze and tanks from the Panzer-Lehr started to relieve the 16./"D" which headed for a calmer zone. Nevertheless it was still the reserve for the SS-Kampfgruppe.

SS-Obersturmführer Macher joined the command post of SS-Obersturmbannführer Wisliceny who announced his departure for the following night. He had to return to the SS-Pz. Div. "Das Reich." SS-Hauptsturmführer Brosow would replace him at the head of the staff. The unit was now to be called SS-Kgp. Brosow. As for Macher, he took command of the rest of the tactical group which now comprised only 210 men.

At 11pm, the SS-Kampfgruppe was attached to Pz.Gren.Rgt. 902 of the Panzer-Lehr. The unit placed to the left of the Waffen-SS was the reconnaissance battalion of the Panzer-Lehr and on the right Fallschirmjägerregiment 14 which was now but a shadow of its former self.

SS-Kampfgruppe Brosow continued the fight against the 9th Infantry Division but would no longer take part directly in the fighting for Saint-Lô.

THE 29th DIVISION IN THE RUINS OF SAINT-LO

PLACED AT ALL STRATEGIC POINTS of the town, the GIs under Major Johns (1/115th Infantry) now noticed a powerful concentration of enemy troops advancing towards the southwest of the town.

19 July 1944

There were Sturmgeschütze among them. A counter-attack by Pz.Gren.Rgt.902 was under way. John's battalion was out of radio contact with both divisional HQ and the XIXth army corps. Communications had been cut by the bombardment which had lasted all night. Only the artillery could help them. But the Americans were unable to contact them.

Several linesmen volunteered to try and repair the connection. They slipped between the mountains of rubble and bricks for thirty minutes then succeeded in finding where the cables were severed. They did not know yet with whom they were going to make contact with but in the end, luck was on their side: they reached the fire direction Centre of the 110th Field Artillery Battalion (155-mm)!

The Panzergrenadiere launched their assault in spite of the intensive bombardment which fell shorty after, damaging or destroying the few cannon and assault guns they had. With great accuracy the 155s methodically eliminated the targets which Major Johns indicated to them.

Before succumbing, some Fallschirmjäger (FJR 14) and some Panzergrenadiere tried to get closer to the GIs positions but more shells quickly discouraged them. Many of them disappeared in the explosions. As they were no longer able to advance a single yard, the German soldiers gave

(Continued on page 136)

Previous page, top.
This famous photograph dated 19 July 1944 was reproduced on the front page of many an American paper, upsetting many civilians. Here is the story behind it. Major-General Gerhardt wanted to honour the soldiers of the 29th Division who had fought hard to get hold of Saint-Lô. Symbolically he asked for the body of Major Howie (3/116) to be brought near the cathedral in sight of everyone. At 7.30 a jeep carrying the body of the officer headed for the church. Having taken care to shroud the body in the Star spangled banner, his men placed it onto a pile of rubble. In spite of the danger that still roamed the town, some GIs and a hundred or so civilians gathered at the Ecole Normale and paid tribute to Major Howie by placing bunches of flowers at his feet. Survivors of his battalion still remember the words that their officer liked to repeat to them *"We'll met again at Saint-Lô!"*
(Dite/USIS)

Previous page, bottom.
Among the numerous observation posts used by the American spotters was Notre Dame Church. Captain Gifford wanted an observation post in one of the towers but the stairs had been destroyed. Having some notions of rock climbing, Captain Gifford used ropes to reach his objective. Thanks to his athletic and courageous exploit, he was able to observe enemy troops south of the town, but he needed a radio. In the time it took Captain Gifford to climb down and find one, the Germans had hit both towers.

Right.
Signalmen are repairing a telephone line which had been severed. Note the impacts on the front of the building. German soldiers must have been hiding there behind the windows because the front of the bakery has not been damaged at all.
(Dite/USIS)

BOULANGERIE R. LECOUEY

165

In the Ruins of Saint-Lô

Top.
A Sherman of the 747th Tank Battalion accompanying the GIs from the 115th advancing determinedly in Saint-Lô.

Above.
Another view of the same crossroads, taken shortly afterwards. The divisional colours have been stuck on the wall of café Malherbe at left. The 1/115th CP

was established there at first, and the house took a few hits from an A/T gun. Crewmen of the parked TD lie on the pavement. Two M10s of B/803rd TB Bn. were destroyed in Saint-Lô. Another TD is visible in the background.

Opposite page.
Still the same scene, from a different and closer angle. The café's name and

the flag (blue and red, with a white '29') can be seen. The belt and packs on the curb belonged to soldiers wounded by the shelling, who had been evacuated previously. Fighting has been intense on this spot, many shells cases are visible at right. The second TD in the previous photo has moved.
(National Archives)

Left.
**A deluge has fallen
on this house. Hundreds
of bullets have smashed
against the front wall.
A shell seems
to have exploded inside
the building after blowing
a hole under the upper
windows. Most of the panes
of glass have been broken.
A sniper or some
Grenadiere were hiding
in the building and the three
GIs are simulating a
cleaning out scene.
But in this picture, fiction
merges into reality.
The infantryman on the left
is wearing a shirt with the
divisional insignia. Alas,
the censor has covered it
with a stroke of the brush.**
(Dite/USIS)

up their attack and withdrew, leaving behind them several rearguard groups who tried to cover them as best as possible.

The attack had failed, but Major-General Corlett of the XIXth Army Corps was not satisfied. The enemy troops were entrenched in large numbers on the heights dominating the south of Saint-Lô, half a mile away. Their artillery

Below.
**Preceded by a Sherman
from the 747th Tank
Battalion, some GIs march
cautiously. A large part
of the road is obstructed
by the ruins which make
it difficult if not impossible
for armour to advance.
Often their crews had
dismount and go round
these streets before
going on.**
(National Archives)

continued to harass the GIs who had to go to ground in the devastated city.

Brigadier-General Cota gave the order to mine the approaches to the south of the town in order to forbid access to the enemy. This decision was excellent but it was again easier said than done.

The pioneer platoon of the 115th Infantry anti-tank company dealt with this dangerous mission. Under fire from the Germans, they got close to one of the bridges which was still intact. They tried to cross amidst the burning shrapnel then threw themselves to the ground with their mines.

Alone Private Curtis Williams carried on. The shells were raining down as the artillery fire became more and more accurate. Without noticing the explosions around him, Williams dug in his mines just like during training. It was a miracle he was not hit.

Shortly afterwards his platoon leader, Lieutenant Colin McLeod, joined him. In spite of being seriously wounded, he remained with Williams until the task was over. The artillery bombardment reached its peak between 9.30 and 10.00. Some of the houses still standing collapsed, the town was now in its death throes.

The whole of the 352.ID. front had to be reorganised. During the night of 18-19 July, Generalleutnant Kraiss obtained permission from Generalleutnant Meindl to pull his Grenadiere back to a line situated to the west of Saint-Lô. Two of his regiments were relieved as was Schnell-Brigade 30 which had suffered heavy losses on the town's outskirts. This unit was no longer fit for combat.

Oberstleutnant Ziegelmann gives us accurate information: " *Gren.Rgt. 943* (the Kgp of the 353.ID, assigned to the 352.ID) *was ordered to hold the sector to the east of the Vire with its 650 soldiers. It was reinforced by II./Gren.Rgt. 895 (275.I.D.) which only had 250 men. This battalion positioned itself on the right wing of Gren.Rgt. 943.*

Gren.Rgt. 899 (strength 800 soldiers – 266.ID) *covered the sector to the west of the Vire after leaving the north bend of the Vire. It crossed the river by using the two-tonne bridge built hastily by Oberst Kentner's Pioniere. The bridge was subsequently destroyed. The line of defence was established with scarcely any disturbance from the Americans and moving the regimental artillery batteries and setting*

Above.
"Infantry advancing victoriously in the streets of Saint-Lô" indicates the Signal Corps caption. This photo was taken between 19 and 20 July 1944 because the street has been cleared by bulldozers. Note three German ammunition cases perched on the rubble, on the right. *(Dite/Usis)*

them up went off without any hitches."

Suddenly the GIs' attention was drawn by five aircraft which were heading straight for Saint-Lô. First of all they thought they were fighters which had come to strafe the heights held by their enemy.

A platoon leader in K/115th who entered the town with his men was not alert enough. Advancing single file, they looked up at the sky when the five German planes appeared. They hardly had time to get off the street before

bombs were falling around them with remarkable accuracy.

The platoon would not be able to reinforce A/115th Infantry as planned. Immediately the AA guns from Corlett's army corps came into action, barking furiously, but it was too late, the planes had already disappeared.

Right.
General Marcks' concrete shelter continued to serve as a communications centre in June and July 1944. The blockhouse was then occupied by Hauptmann Loges of Gren.Rgt. 916 during the fighting of 18 and 19 July. But he realised very quickly that it could not be defended. On his own initiative, he abandoned the bunker. Generalleutnant Kraiss, Kdr. of the 352.I.D, chastised him and even ordered him to go back. This blockhouse still exists today at the Place du Champ de Mars. It is there without really being there, because it lies under the new Post Office. *(National Archives/Conseil géral de Basse-Normandie)*

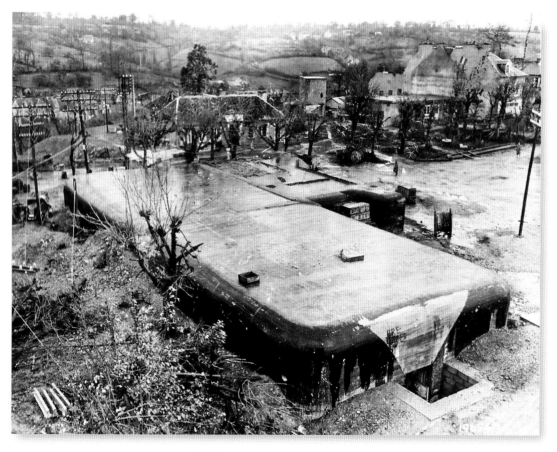

"These GIs are parked near a large German HQ" is the original Signal Corps caption. This could be Generalleutnant von Choltitz's. The scene takes place at the hospital crossroads. Major Friedrich Hayn, Chief of staff of the LXXXIV A.K. says in his book: *"It seemed to me a small miracle that in 1944 the enemy did not know where our HQ was, even though against my advice, it had remained there for some years, in the same building."*

Above.
Ford M8 armored cars of the 29th Reconnaissance Troop under Captain William H. Puntenney gathering at Saint-Lô before leaving the captured town. This unit was the first to enter the town but the rubble had very quickly halted its progress and the scouts had to fight as infantrymen. Designed as a tank destroyer, this vehicle was too weakly-armoured and its M6 37-mm canon was ineffective against the German tanks. It therefore equipped the reconnaissance units. It had a top speed of 55 mph and it weighed 7.35 tonnes, which for an armoured car offered the scouts an excellent means of transport and appreciable firepower with .50 and .30 machine guns.
(National Archives/Conseil général de Basse-Normandie)

THE 29th DIVISION LEAVES SAINT-LO

THE 116th Infantry Regiment was relieved by the 2nd Bn of the 115th Infantry who departed in turn at the end of the afternoon.

The rest of the division was on the point of leaving. The 35th Infantry Division which until then had been fighting to the west of the Vire arrived to carry out the relief.

During the morning it relieved the 175th then the 115th Infantry towards 5 pm. All the infantry battalions of the Blue and Gray gathered near Sainte-Marguerite d'Elle.

Major-General Gerhardt kept his word. The whole 29th Infantry Division was pulled back after Saint-Lô had been taken. He was however forced to leave part of its artillery there an extra week to support the 35th Division. The 29ers however were rather glum. More than 2,000 of their comrades had fallen between Omaha Beach and Saint-Lô. 5,000 others had been wounded. Their average battalion strength was now reduced to single companies. A cemetery had been set up at La Cambe for the 29th Infantry since 11 June 1944. These men had paid with their lives for our freedom.

The soldiers buried there were then transferred to the American cemetery of Saint-Laurent-sur-Mer and La Cambe became a *Soldatenfriedhof* where the several thousand German soldiers killed in Normandy were buried. Today still, as if defying time, the flag of the "Blue and Gray" flaps untiringly above the white marble tombs all beautifully in line and flowered. If you go pass by Saint-Laurent, you will notice that these crosses are facing the future.

You may also call out the names of some of those who lie there to express our gratefulness for their sacrifice... but also, if you go past La Cambe, you may walk about the resting place of those on the wrong side but who went

Above.

After some impressive clearing up work, the 29th Division set off. SHAEF had designated Saint-Lô as an important transport crossroads, and there were no holds barred for taking it. Did the bombings really prevent the Germans moving up to the front or actually disrupt the supply chain? Without sticking one's neck out and being quite objective, it is quite certain that the destruction of the town did not prevent the Panzer-Lehr from coming up and that supplies were still brought up – if only at night – after 6 June 1944. What is certain is that the ruins did complicate troop movements to the front.

(National Archives)

Major-General Corlett, commanding the XIXth US Army Corps, decorating Major-General Gerhardt and thanking him for the proficiency shown by his soldiers.
(National Archives)

After the many events that followed his evacuation from the town, Jacques Petit gave his first impressions of his return to Saint-Lô: *"I tried to identify the skeletons of the houses where my friends used to live and where we spent so many hours at work and play. But often all that was left was just a bit of wall where the rain had already discoloured the shreds of wall paper floating in the wind. My Saint-Lô does not exist any more. A few weeks of madness were enough to wipe out all the landmarks of my youth. How can one find them again, how can one reconstitute one's past in these streets which are nothing more than vague paths leading nowhere?"*
(National Archives/Conseil général de Basse-Normandie

After all the trials endured during the European campaign the joy and happiness of being at home again with his parents is immense. With God's help, this crippled soldier has come home. But how many remained over there, victims of the fate of arms. He was lucky, but he will never forget.
(National Archives)

through the same suffering. Their tombs are both sober and beautiful. The silence shrouding these grounds will help to understand that all these young men are now united, fraternally, having done their duty as soldiers. ❑

173

II. FALLSCHIRMJAGER-KORPS
(Generalleutnant Eugen Meindl)
— **Chef d'état-major**: Oberstleutnant i. G. Ernst Blauensteiner

ARMY CORPS UNITS
— Fallschirm-Nachrichten-Abteilung 12
Oberstleutnant Herbert Flesch
— Fallschirm-Aufklarungs-Abteilung 12
Hauptmann Göttsche
— Fallschirm-Artillerie-Regiment 12
— Fallschirm-Sturmgeschütz-Abteilung 12
Hauptmann Gersteuer
— Fallschirm-Flak-Regiment 12
— Fallschirm-Korps-Naschubeinheiten 12
Oberst Eberhard Hettler

3. FALLSCHIRMJAGERDIVISION
(Generalleutnant Richard Schimpf)
Chief of Staff
Major Lutz Wagner
● **Fallschirmjägerregiment 5**
Kdr.: Major Karl-Heinz Becker
— I. Btl.: Hauptmann Adolf Specht
— II. Btl.: Hauptmann Walter Münter
— III. Btl.: Haupt. Eberhard Boerger
● **Fallschirmjägerregiment 8**
Kdr.: Oberstleutnant Egon Liebach
— I.: Btl.: Major Oskar Wiedemann
— II. Btl.: Hauptmann Karl Voshage
— III. Btl.: Hauptmann Josef Krammling
● **Fallschirmjägerregiment 9**
Kdr.: Major Stephani
— I. Btl.: Major Friedrich Alpers
■1./FJR. 9: Leutnant Waitschader,
Ltn. Armin Stoerz
■2./FJR. 9: Hauptmann Lepzig,
Oberleutnant Frisch
■3./FJR. 9
■4./FJR. 9
— II. Btl.: Hauptmann Kurt Ladwig
■5./FJR. 9
■6./FJR. 9: Hauptmann Ladwig
■7./FJR. 9: Oberleutnant
Axel von de Camp
■8./FJR. 9
III. Btl.: Hauptmann Karl Meyer
■9./FJR. 9
■10./FJR. 9: Leutnant Forscher,
Oberleutnant Hans Grundmann
■11./FJR. 9: Hauptmann Matula
■12./FJR. 9
■13./FJR. 9 (mortars) : Leut. Josef Glaser
■14./FJR. 9 (antitanks)
■15./Fjr. 9 (pioneers)
● **Fallschirmjäger-Art. Abt. 3**
Major Hans-Eberhard von Bauer
● **Fallschirmjäger-Pz. Jg. Abt. 3**
Hauptmann Persch
● **Fallschirmjäger-Pi. Btl. 3**
Hauptmann Karl Beth
● **Fallschirmjäger-Flak-Abt. 3**
Oberleutnant Friedrich, then Major Müller
● **Fallschirmjäger-Nachrichten-Abt. 3**
Hauptmann Hölzner
● **Div. Nachschubführer**
Hauptmann Fölsche

352. INFANTERIE DIVISION
(Generalleutnant Dietrich Kraiss)
● **Gren. Rgt. 914**
Oberstleutnant Ernst Heyna
— I./914
— II./914
● **Gren. Regt 915:**
Oberstleutnant Karl Meyer (KIA
07.06.1944)
— I./915
— II./915
● **Gren. Rgt. 916**
Oberst Ernst Goth
— I./916
— II./916 : Hauptmann Grimme
● **Artillerie-Regiment 352**
Oberst Kurt-Wilhelm Ocker
— I./352 : Major Werner Pluskat
— II./352
— III./352
— IV./352
● **Panzerjäger-Abteilung 352**
Hauptmann Werner Jahn
● **Pionier-Bataillon 352**
Hauptmann Paul Fritz
● **Füsilier-Bataillon 352**
Rittmeister Eitel Gerth
● **Nachrichten-Abteilung 352**
Hauptmann Kurt Ehrhardt
● **Feld-Ersatz-Bataillon 352**
Major Georg Teudesmann
● **Ost-Bataillon 439**
Hauptmann Hans Becker
● **Schnell Brigade 30**
Oberstleutnant von Ausess
● **Flak-Sturm Rgt. 1 (elements)**
Oberst von Kitowski
(06.06 to 19.07.1944)

KAMPFGRUPPE KENTNER
Oberst Kentner
● **Rgt. Stab Gren. Rgt. 897**

■ Stabs-Kp. 897

● I./Gren. Rgt. 897 13./Gren. Rgt. 897
● II./Gren. Rgt. 897 13./Gren. Rgt. 897
● 14./Gren. Rgt. 897
● 1./Pionier-Btl. 266
● III./Art. Rgt. 266
■ Kol. Baumgärtel.
● II./Gren. Rgt. 899
● III./Gren. Rgt. 898 (11.07.1944)

KAMPFGRUPPE BOHM
(tactical group from 353. Inf. Div.)

● I/Gren. Rgt. 941
● Füsilier-Btl. 353
● Art.-Rgt. 353 (elements)

KAMPFGRUPPE HEINTZ
Oberst Heintz
● **Aufkl. Gruppe 984**
● I., II./Gren. Rgt. 984
● 13/Gren. Rgt. 943
● 14/Gren. Rgt. 943
● II. et III./A.-R. 275
● Pionier-Btl. 275
● Füsilier Btl. 275
● Pz.-Jager Kp. 275
● **Fallschirmjägerregiment 14**
Major Noster
— I. Btl.: Hauptmann Schmidt
— II. Btl.: Hauptmann Sauer
— III. Btl.: Hauptmann Meissner
● s. Art.-Abt. 628
Oberst Seidel

LXXXIV. ARMEE KORPS
(Generalleutnant von Choltitz)

PANZER-LEHR DIVISION
(Generalmajor Fritz Bayerlein,
04.02 1944 to 05 02.1945)
Chief of Staff
Oberstleutnant Kauffmann
● **Pz.-Lehr Rgt. 130**
Oberst Gerhardt
Adjutant: Hauptmann Fritzsche then Hptm.
Stcockhammer
— II./Pz.-Rgt. 130:
Major Prinz Schönburg-Waldenburg (killed
on 11.06.1944), Major Helmut Ritgen
Adjutant: Oberleutnant Meyer
■5. Kp.: Hauptmann Trumpa (from
11 June to 12 Dec. 1944)
■6. Kp.: Hauptmann Ritschel
■7. Kp.: Oberleutnant Kues
■8. Kp.: Leutnant Peter
(KIA 11 July 1944)
■Funklenk-Kompanie 316:
Leutnant Adam (21.06.1944)
■Panzerwerkstattkompanie:
Oberleutnant Reinicke
● I./Pz.-Rgt. 6
Major Markowski (to 18.06.1944) Major
Otto (until 09.07.1944)
Adjutant: Oberleutnant Schirp
(until 01.08.1944)
■1. Kp.: Hauptmann von Böttinger
(KIA 11.07.1944)
■2. Kp.: Leutnant Scholz
(KIA 11.07.1944)
■3. Kp.: Hauptmann Schramm
■4. Kp.: hauptmann Jahnke
■5. Kp.: Hauptmann Neubauer
● **Pz. Gren. Rgt. 901**
Oberst Scholze (until 19.07.1944)
Adjutant: Hauptmann Ehricht
— I. Btl.: Hauptmann Philipps (25. 06 to
11.07.1944)
Adjutant: Oberleutnant Gehrke
■1. Kp.: Leutnant Hillermann
(12.06.1944 to 03.1945)
■2. Kp.: Oberleutnant Mersiowski
■3. Kp.: Hauptmann Salzmann
■4. Kp.
— II. Btl.: Major Schöne (01.04 to
11.1944)
Adjutant: Leutnant Genin (10.07.1944)
■5. Kp.: Hauptmann Philipps (until
25.06.1944)
■6. Kp.: Oberleutnant Hagen (from
10.07.1944)
■7. Kp.: Oberleutnant Mahr
■8. Kp.: Hauptmann Pfitzner
■v.: Oberleutnant Knepper
■9. Kp. (s. I.G.) : Hauptmann Hennecke:
Oberleutnant Lankhorst (until Feb. 1945)
■10. Kp. (Pionier) : Hauptmann Klein
■11. Kp. (Flak) : Oberleutnant
Rheinländer
● **Pz. Gren. Rgt. 902**
Oberstleutnant Welsch (08.06 to 29.07.1944,
KIA)
Adjutant: Hauptmann Müller (from
Marck 1944 to 29 July 1944)
Kp. Chef St.: Leutnant Lotz
— I. Btl.: Hauptmann Böhm (28.06. to
28.07.1944)
Adjutant: Leutnant Krahl
■1. Kp.: Hauptmann Böhm
■2. Kp.
■3. Kp.: Oberleutnant Ritter
■4. Kp.: Oberleutnant von Glysczynski
then Oberleutnant Rasmus
■v.: Oberleutnant Rahneberg
— II. Btl.: Hauptmann Böhm (25.06.1944)
Adjutant: Oberleutnant Graas (10.06. to
25.08.1944)
■5. Kp.: Hauptmann H. Neumann,
Oberleutnant Diesslin
■6. Kp.: Oberleutnant Rahneberg, Oberleutnant Grass
■7. Kp.: Oberleutnant Graf
■8. Kp.: Oberleut. Artus, Oberleut. Ebner
■9.Kp. (s. I.G.) : Hauptmann Neumann

■10. Kp. (Pionier) : Leutnant Litt
● **Panzeraufklärungs-Lehr-Abteilung 130:**
Major von Fallois, Hauptmann Hübner
Adjutant: Oberleutnant von
Daniels-Spangenberg
■1. Kp.: Oberleutnant Gollwitzer
■2. Kp.: Oberleutnant Weinstein
■3. Kp.: Oberleutnant Sharein
■4. Kp.: Oberleutnant Exner
(KIA 25 July 1944)
■5. Kp.: Hauptmann Mündelein
■6. Kp.: Oberleutnant Barth
● **Panzerjäger-Lehr-Abteilung 130**
Major Barth
Adjutant: Oberleutnant Wagner
Kp. Chef St. Hauptmann Oventrop then
Oberleutnant Dilg
■1. Kp.: Hauptmann Hermann
(KIA 25 July 1944)
■2. Kp.: Hauptmann Pfendner
■3. Kp.: Hauptmann Oventrop
■4. Kp.: Hauptmann Bethke
● **Panzer-Artillerie-Regiment 130**
Oberst Luxenburger, KIA 08.06.1944 then
Major Zeisler (?)
Adjutant: Hauptmann Graf von
Clary-Aldringen
Bttr. Chef St.: Hauptmann Rothmoser
— I. Gruppe: Oberleutnant Kurtze
■1. Bttr.: Hauptmann Krause
■2. Bttr.: Hauptmann Ziegler?
■3. Bttr.: Hauptmann Theyson?
— II. Gruppe: Major Franke
■4. Bttr.: Hauptmann Kahle?
■5. Bttr.: Oberleutnant Igogeit
■6. Bttr.: Oberleutnant Wicht
— III. Gruppe: Major Zeisler
■7. Bttr.: Hauptmann Wagner
■8. Bttr.: Hauptmann Renftle
■9. Bttr.: Oberleutnant Selbitz
● **Heeres-Flak-Abteilung 311**
Hauptmann Weinkopf
● **Panzer-Pionier-Bataillon 130**
Major Brandt (until 26 July 1944)
Adjutant: Leutnant Cord
■1. Kp.: Oberleutnant Kolbussa
■2. Kp.: Hauptmann Aibenbach
■3. Kp.: Hauptmann Zynda
■s. Pz. Bruko
● **Panzer-Nachrichten-Abteilung 130**
Hauptmann Hauck
■1. Kp.: Hauptmann Hoff
■2. Kp.: Hauptmann Dittmers
— 1. Sanitätskompanie 130
Kp. Chef: Stabsarzt Dr Hepp
— 2. Sanitätskompanie 130
Kp. Chef: Oberstabsartz Dr Bergfried then
Oberstabsarzt Dr Schulz-Merkel
● **Panzerdivisions-Nachschubtruppen 130**
Major Derfflinger
St. Kp.: hauptmann Weigl
■1. Kp.:?
■2. Kp.: Hauptmann Bühler
■3. Kp.:?
■4. Kp.:?
■5. Kp.:?
■6. Kp.: Hauptmann Kaiser
— 3. Werkstattkompanie 130
Major Croce
— Ersatzteilstaffel 130: Leutnant Möller
— Feldersatz-Bataillon 130
Hauptmann Müller

KAMPFGRUPPE WISLICENY
(SS-Obersturmbannführer Wisliceny)

● I./SS-Rgt. « Deutschland »
SS-Sturmbannführer Schuster
● 14./ « D »
SS-Hauptsturmführer Filber
● 16./« D »
SS-Obersturmführer Macher
● SS-Pz. Pi. Btl. « Das Reich »
SS-Hauptsturmführer Brosow.

2nd INFANTRY DIVISION
'Second to None'

Major General Walter M. Robertson
(from 02. 12. 1943)
— Assistant Division Commander
Col. James A. Van Fleet (04. 07 to 01. 08.1944)
● Chief of Staff
Col. John H. Stokes, Jr. (19. 10.1943 to 15.10.1944)

● 9th Infantry Regiment
Col. Chester J. Hirschfelder
● 23d Infantry Regiment
Col. Hurley E. Fuller (19.10.1943 to 11.07.1944) then Lt. Col. Jay B. Loveless (11.07 to 13.09.1944)
— 38th Infantry Regiment
Col. Ralph W. Zwicker (05.07 to 18.11.1944)

— 2nd Reconnaissance Troop (Mechanized)
— 2nd Engineer Combat Battalion
— 2nd Medical Battalion

2nd DIVISION ARTILLERY

Brig. Gen. George P. Hays
(19.10.1943 to 12.11.1944)
— 15th Field Artillery Battalion
(105 mm Howitzer)
— 37th Field Artillery Battalion
(105 mm Howitzer)
— 38th Field Artillery Battalion
(105 mm Howitzer)
— 12th Field Artillery Battalion
(155 mm Howitzer)

SPECIAL TROOPS

— 702nd Ordnance
Light Maintenance Company
— 2nd Quartermaster Company
— 2nd Signal Company
— Military Police Platoon
— Headquarters Company
— Band

9th INFANTRY DIVISION
'The Varsity '

Major General Manton S. Eddy
— Assistant Division Commander
— Chief of Staff
Col. Noah M. Brinson (24.06.944)

● 39th Infantry Regiment
Colonel Harry A. Flint (27.11.1943 to 24. 07.1944)
1st Bn: Lieutenant-colonel Price Tucker
2nd Bn: Lieutenant-colonel Frank D. Gunn
● 47th Infantry Regiment
Col. George W. Smythe (27.11.1943 to 06.03.1945)
1st Bn: Lieutenant-colonel Wendell Chaffin
2nd Bn: Major Woodrow Bailey
3rd Bn: Lieutenant-colonel Donald C. Clayman
● 60th Infantry Regiment
Col. Jesse L. Gibney (02.07 to 04.10.1944)

— 9th Reconnaissance Troop (Mechanized)
— 15th Engineer Combat Battalion
— 9th Medical Battalion

9th DIVISION ARTILLERY

Brig. Gen. Reese M. Howell (27.11.1943)
● 26th Field Artillery Battalion
(105 mm Howitzer)
● 60th Field Artillery Battalion
(105 mm Howitzer)
● 84th Field Artillery Battalion
(105 mm Howitzer)
● 34th Field Artillery Battalion
(155 mm Howitzer)

SPECIAL TROOPS

— 709th Ordnance
Light Maintenance Company
— 9th Quartermaster Company
— 9th Signal Company
— Military Police Platoon
— Headquarters Company
— Band

29th INFANTRY DIVISION
'Blue and Gray'

Major General Charles H. Gerhardt
— Assistant Division Commander
Brig. Gen. Norman D. Cota (13.10.1943 to 31.08.1944)
— Chief of Staff
Lt. Col. William G. Purnell (15.06. to 05.10.1944)

● 115th Infantry Regiment
Col. Godwin Ordway Jr. (13. 06. to 18.07.1944) then Col. Alfred V. Ednie (18 07 to 11.08.1944)
● 116th Infantry Regiment
Col. Philip R. Dwyer (07.07 to 11.10.1944)
● 175th Infantry Regiment
Col. Ollie W. Reed (from 23.06. to 30.07.1944)

— 29th Reconnaissance Troop (Mechanized)
— 121st Engineer Combat Battalion
— 104th Medical Battalion

29th DIVISION ARTILLERY

Brig. Gen. William H. Sands (11.10.1942)
● 110th Field Artillery Battalion
(105 mm Howitzer)
● 111th Field Artillery Battalion
(105 mm Howitzer)
● 224th Field Artillery Battalion
(105 mm Howitzer)
● 227th Field Artillery Battalion
(155 mm Howitzer)

SPECIAL TROOPS

— 729th Ordnance
Light Maintenance Company
— 29th Quartermaster Company
— 29th Signal Company
— Military Police Platoon
— Headquarters Company
— Band

35th INFANTRY DIVISION
'Santa Fe'

Major General Paul W. Baade
— Assistant Division Commander
— Chief of Staff
Brig. Gen. Edmund B. Sebree (26.05. to 27.02.1945)

● 134th Infantry Regiment
Colonel Butler B. Miltonberger
● 137th Infantry Regiment
Colonel Grant Layng, then Brigadier General Sebree
● 320th Infantry Regiment
Colonel Bernard A. Byrne

— 35th Reconnaissance Troop (Mechanized)
— 60th Engineer Combat Battalion
— 110th Medical Battalion

35th DIVISION ARTILLERY

Brig. Gen. Theodore L. Futch
● 161st Field Artillery Battalion
(105 Howitzer)
● 216th Field Artillery Battalion
(105 Howitzer)
● 219th Field Artillery Battalion
(105 Howitzer)
● 127th Field Artillery Battalion
(155 Howitzer)

SPECIAL TROOPS

— 735th Ordnance
Light Maintenance Company
— 35th Quartermaster Company
— 35th Signal Company
— Military Police Platoon
— Headquarters Company
— Band

XIXth Army Corps
(Major General Charles H. Corlett)

3rd US ARMORED DIVISION
Major General Leroy H. Watson
(15.09.1943 to 07.08.1944)

● Combat Command A
Attached to 9th Division 09 to16. 07.1944, Brig. Gen. Doyle O. Hickey
— 32d Armored Regiment
— 3d Bn 36th Armored Infantry
— 83d Armd Rcn Bn
— Co A 23d Armd Engr Bn
— Co C 23d Armd Engr Bn
● Combat Command B
Attached to 30th Division 08 to 16.07.1944). Brig Gen John J Bohn (15.09.1943 to 10.07.1944), then Colonel Dorrance S. Roysden (10.07 to 15.07.944) and Col. Truman Everett Boudinot (from 15.07 to 04 09.1944)
— 33d Armd Regiment
— 36th Armd Infantry (-3d Bn) Regiment
— Co D du 83d Armd Rcn Bn.
— Co B 23d Armd Engineer Bn.
● Combat command R: Col Graeme G. Parks (15.11.1943 to 19.07.1944)

DIVISIONAL UNITS

— 36th Armored Inf Regiment
— 32nd Armored Regiment
— 33nd Armored Regiment
— 23nd Armored Engineer Bn.
— 83d Armored Recon. Bn.
— 143d Armored Signals Co.
3d Armored Division Artillery
Div. Arty Col Frederic G. Brown (15.09.1943)
— 391st Armored Field Artillery Bn.
— 67th Armored Field Artillery Bn.
— 54th Armored Field Artillery Bn.

— 3d Armored Division Trains
— 3d Ordnance Maintenance Bn.
— Supply Battalion
— 45th Armored Medical Bn.
— Military Police Platoon

30th INFANTRY DIVISION « *Old hickory* »

General Leland S. Hobbs
— Chief of Staff
Brig. Gen. William K Harrison

● 117th Infantry Regiment
Colonel Henry E. Kelly
(22.02 to 23. 07. 1944)
1st Bn.: Lt. Col. Robert E. Frankland
2nd Bn.: Lt. Col. Arthur H. Fuller
3rd Bn.: Lt. Col. Samuel T. McDowell
● 119th Infantry Regiment
Colonel Alfred V. Ednie, replaced by Colonel Edwin M. Sutherland on 14 July 1944
1st Bn.: Colonel James W. Cantey, then Major Robert H. Herlong, 13.07.1944.
2nd Bn.: Lieutenant-col. Edwin E. Wallis
3rd Bn.: Lieutenant-Col. Courtney P. Brown
● 120th Infantry Regiment: Col. Hammond Birks
1st Bn.: Lt. Col. Hugh I. Mainord
2nd Bn.: Lt. Col. William S. Bradford, then Lt Col. Eads J. Hardaway, 08.07.1944
3rd Bn.: Lt. Col. McCollum
● 113rd Cavalry Group
Colonel William S. Biddle
● 30th Reconnaissance Troop (Mech)
● 105th Engineer Combat Battalion
● 105th Medical Battalion

30th DIVISION ARTILLERY

Brig. Gen. Raymond S. McLain
(10.05 to 28.07. 1944)
● 118th Field Artillery Battalion
(105 Howitzer)
● 197th Field Artillery Battalion
(105 Howitzer)
● 230th Field Artillery Battalion
(105 Howitzer)
● 113th Field Artillery Battalion
(155 Howitzer)

SPECIAL TROOPS

— 730th Ordnance
Light Maintenance Company
— 30th Quartermaster Company
— 30th Signal Company
— Military Police Platoon
— Headquarters Company
— Band

● 743rd Tank Battalion
Col. John Upham
— Co A. Capt V. Phillips (16 M4 and 8 tankdozers)
— Co B. Captain Charles Ehmka
— Co C. Captain Ned Eldar
● 823d Tank Destroyer Battalion
Major H. K. Lorance

Acknowledgements and thanks

A book does not get written by itself and one like this even less so.
I would like in particular to thank:
Thierry Guilbert who gave me invaluable help and Frederic Deprun, who is keen on the History of armoured units
in Normandy and who contributed his wealth of knowledge of I./Pz.Rgt. 6.
These enthusiasts enabled the iconography of *"Dying for St. Lô"* to be considerably richer.
I should like also to thank Simon Trew, Patrick A. Tillery, from the extraordinary website on American units: *KilroyWasHere.org*
Jean-Luc Leleu and Yves Buffetaut, renowned historians.
Audrey Billaud, Custodian at the Mémorial de Caen who moved mountains to find the unfindable.
A special mention for M. Lemarquand, M. André Letemplier and his family,
Mme Odette Moitier, all witnesses of events during the battle of the hedgerows.
A big thank you for M. and Mrs. Fleury, M. Lenoir, Charles-Edouard de Turquay, Alexis Boban, Phil Logan and Charles Steine, and Jean Erisay at
the Tosny Museum in Normandy.
Finally thanks again to Jean-Marie Mongin for his professional support and to his esteemed colleagues at Histoire & Collections:
Denis Gandilhon, Philippe Charbonnier and Raymond Giuliani who were always ready to help.

Selected bibliography

— *Duel for France*, Martin Blumenson
— *Crusade in Europe*, Dwight D. Eisenhower
— *La bataille des haies*. D. Lodieu article in *Batailles*
— *Bataille de Normandie*, Editions Heimdal
— *The struggle for Europe*, Chester Wilmot
— *D-day paratroopers, the Americans*, Christophe Deschodt & Laurent Rouger, Histoire & Collections 2006
— *Les SS au poing de fer*, Jean Mabire
— *115th Inf. Rgt. in World War Two*, J. Binkowski & A. Plaut
— *History of the 117th Inf. Rgt*, 30th Inf. Div. Association
— *History of the 119th Inf. Rgt*, 30th Inf. Div. Association
— *History of the 120th Inf. Rgt.*, 30th Inf. Div. Association
— *Beyond the beachhead*, Joseph Balkowski, Stackpole Books
— *29th Let's Go!*, Joseph H. Ewing
— *St. Lô*, The Battery Press, Nashville

— *2nd US Inf Div*, The Battery Press, Nashville
— *35th US Inf. Div*, The Battery Press, Nashville
— *Spearhead in the West*
— *La vie à Airel et Saint-Fromond pendant la Seconde Guerre Mondiale*, Bernard Festoc
— *Saint-Lô au bûcher*, Maurice Lantier
— *Victimes civiles dans la Manche*, Michel Boivin et Bernard Garnier
— *KTB der 16./D*
— *KTB der « Deutschland »*
— *SS-Pio.-Btl. 2.*, Kurt Imhoff
— *Der Fallschirmjäger*

Other books by the same author:
– *45 Tiger en Normandie, Histoire et analyse des combats de la s.Pz.Abt. 503 durant la bataille de Normandie*, Ysec Editions.
– *Objectif Chambois, combats de la 90th US Inf. Div.*

pour la fermeture de la poche de Falaise, Ysec Editions
– *D'Argentan à la Seine, combats du bataillon de Panther de la 9. Pz.Div. à la fin août 1944*, Ysec Editions.
– *La Massue, l'odyssée de la 1re division blindée polonaise durant la bataille de Normandie. De l'opération Totalize à la fermeture de la poche de Falaise.* Ysec Editions
– *Combats sur la Seine, tome 1- L'odyssée de la 17. Feld-Div.*, Ysec Editions
– *La Division Meindl. Historique de la première unité de Jäger réalisée avec l'association des vétérans « Der Adler ».* http://didierlodieu.site.voilà.fr
– *The IIIrd Panzer-Korps at Kursk*, Histoire et Collections 2007.

Maps by Antoine Poggioli, Denis Gandilhon and Philippe Charbonnier

Supervised by Denis GANDILHON, Philippe CHARBONNIER, Gil BOURDEAUX, Raymond GIULIANI and Jean-Marie MONGIN
Design and lay-out by Jean-Marie MONGIN et Antoine POGGIOLI
© *Histoire & Collections 2007*

ISBN: 978-2-35250-035-3

Publisher's number: 35250

© *Histoire & Collections 2007*

a book published by
HISTOIRE & COLLECTIONS
SA au capital de 182 938, 82 €
5, avenue de la République
F-75541 Paris Cedex 11 - FRANCE
Fax +33 1 47 00 51 11
www.histoireetcollections.com

This book has been designed, typed, laid-out and processed by *Histoire & Collections* fully on integrated computer equipment.

Pictures integrated by *Studio A&C*

Printed by *Zure*,
Spain, European Union

August 2007